PRAGMATICS OF WORD ORDER FLEXIBILITY

TYPOLOGICAL STUDIES IN LANGUAGE (TSL)

A companion series to the journal "STUDIES IN LANGUAGE"

Volumes in this series will be functionally and typologically oriented, covering specific topics in language by collecting together data from a wide variety of languages and language typologies. The orientation of the volumes will be substantive rather than formal, with the aim of investigating universals of human language via as broadly defined a data base as possible, leaning toward cross-linguistic, diachronic, developmental and live-discourse data. The series is, in spirit as well as in fact, a continuation of the tradition initiated by C. Li *(Word Order and Word Order Change, Subject and Topic, Mechanisms for Syntactic Change)* and continued by T. Givón *(Discourse and Syntax)* and P. Hopper *(Tense-Aspect: Between Semantics and Pragmatics)*.

Volume 22

Doris L. Payne (ed.)

PRAGMATICS OF WORD ORDER FLEXIBILITY

PRAGMATICS OF WORD ORDER FLEXIBILITY

edited by

DORIS L. PAYNE
University of Oregon

JOHN BENJAMINS PUBLISHING COMPANY
Amsterdam/Philadelphia

1992

Library of Congress Cataloging-in-Publication Data

Pragmatics of word order flexibility / edited by Doris L. Payne.
p. cm. -- (Typological studies in language, ISSN 0167-7373; v. 22)
Includes bibliographical references.
1. Grammar, Comparative and general--Word order. 2. Pragmatics. I. Payne, Doris L
1952- . II. Series.
P295.P64 1992
415--dc20 92-53
ISBN 90 272 2905 8 (hb.) / 90 272 2906 6 (pb.) (European; alk. paper) C
ISBN 1-55619-408-0 (hb.) / 1-55619-409-9 (pb.) (U.S.; alk. paper)

John Benjamins Publishing Co. · P.O. Box 75577 · 1070 AN Amsterdam · The Netherlands
John Benjamins North America · 821 Bethlehem Pike · Philadelphia, PA 19118 · USA

Table of Contents

Abbreviations

ABS	absolutive
ACC	accusative
ADJ	adjective
AF	actor focus
AP	antipassive
ALL	allative
ASP	aspect
AUG	augmentative
AUX	auxiliary
BEN	benefactive
CAUS	causative
COMP	comparative
COMPL	complementizer
CONT	continuous
CONTR	contrastive
COP	copula
D	determiner
DAT	dative
DEC	declarative
DEF	definite
DUR	durative
EMPH	emphatic (pronoun)
ERG	ergative
EXCL	exclusive
FEM	feminine
FUT	future
GEN	genitive
GF	goal focus
HAB	habitual
IMP	imperative
IMPERF	imperfect
IMPFV	imperfective
INF	infinitive
INSTR	instrumental
INV	inverted word order
IRR	irrealis
LINK	linking particle
LOC	locative
MASC	masculine
NEG	negative
NOM	nominative
NONFIN	nonfinite
NONPAST	nonpast
NON-TOP	non-topic
OBJ	object
OBL	oblique
PASS	passive
PAST	past
PERF	perfect
PFV	perfective
PL	plural
POSS	possessive
PP	past participle
PR	possessor
PREP	preposition
PRES	present
Q	interrogative
RED	reduplicative
REL	relative
REFL	reflexive
SG	singular
SPEC	specifier
SS	same subject
SUB	subordinate
TOP	topic
UNM	unmarked (case)

Introduction

Doris L. Payne
University of Oregon & Summer Institute of Linguistics

For some time now in linguistics, the assumption has been widely held that for a majority of the world's languages, one can identify a "basic" order of subject and object relative to the verb, and that when combined with other facts of the language, this "basic" order constitutes a useful way of typologizing languages. This tradition began in earnest with the work of Joseph Greenberg (1963), and has been continued by numerous scholars, notably including Lehmann (1973), Vennemann and Harlow (1977), Mallinson and Blake (1981), Hawkins (1983), Nichols (1986), and Dryer (1988).

As debate has continued over varying definitions of "basic", and as an increasing number of investigators encounter languages for which they believe it is not particularly insightful to brand a particular order of grammatical relations as basic, it has seemed of increasing value to some of us to start asking new questions. First, a different twist on the typological question was taken by Thompson (1978) (see also Payne 1990 and **Doris Payne**, this volume), who suggested that the first typological division should be made between those languages in which main clause word order primarily correlates with pragmatic factors, and those in which order primarily correlates with grammatical relations or other syntactic factors. It remains an open research question as to what extent the Greenbergian typology is properly applied to pragmatic order languages. Second, instead of just asking "What is the basic order in Language L (if any)?", attention has been turning to the question of "When there are several possible order patterns in a language, what is the communicative function of one, rather than another, order?" A third crucial research question (which is not explored in this volume) concerns “What historical reanalyses give rise to observed order patterns?”

Explanatory factors behind word order variation are to be found in studies of how the mind grammaticizes forms, processes information, and speech act theory considerations of speakers’ attempts to get their hearers to build one, rather than another, mental representation of incoming information. Thus, three domains must be distinguished: syntactic, cognitive, and pragmatic. In understanding order variation, it is unhelpfully reductionist to seek an explanation in terms of only one domain. In all languages each domain likely makes some contribution to determining the surface order of sentence elements (though the relative contribution from each domain may vary from one language to another). One might think of this as a “modular” approach to the question of word order variation, though from at least a diachronic perspective (if not from a synchronic one as well) it is surely a fiction to suppose that such modules are autonomous from each other. Nevertheless, in terms of research methodology it is helpful, if not crucial, to tease them apart.

A full definition of syntactic, cognitive, and pragmatic domains cannot be developed here. Briefly, however, a description of order phenomena in terms of syntactic categories, particular morphosyntactic constructions, hierarchical structures and head-dependent relations, and grammatical relations would traditionally be termed **syntactic**. (To my mind, however, syntactic categories and grammatical relations are different in essence and it is questionable that they should be termed “syntactic” in the same sense of the word; cf. Payne, this volume).

A **cognitive** account would explore the relationship between order and mental processes or constraints. Among other things, such an account would consider the relevance of limited focal attention, the current status of certain information in the mind of the speaker (e.g. is it in the active focus of attention/memory, or not), and operations concerned with comprehension and integration of information into the already-existing knowledge network or developing mental representation.

A **pragmatic** account would explore the relationship between order and speaker-hearer interactions. Choice of one order rather than another (just as choice of one construction rather than another) can constitute a speech act of “instruction” on the speaker’s part, relative to how the hearer should integrate information into a mental, cognitive representation. In ’O’odham, for instance, placement of nonidentifiable information before the verb essentially constitutes the following speech act: "I as speaker hereby instruct you as hearer to integrate the preverbal NP information into the mental representation you are building as a new major participant about which other incoming information will be relevant." In contrast, placement of nonidentifiable information after the verb essentially constitutes the following speech act: "I as speaker hereby instruct you as hearer to integrate the postverbal NP information into the mental representation you are building as an incidental fact about a major participant or event that you already have in mind." In no way can a pragmatic account be usefully separated from a cognitive one, because the pragmatic acts are centrally concerned with what the speaker assumes is the current cognitive status of information in the mind of the hearer, and with how the speaker wants the hearer to mentally comprehend and integrate the information.

Finally, in some languages the relationship between surface order and cognitive-pragmatic statuses is just as strong and rule governed, as is the relationship in others between order and grammatical relations. If a grammar in the theoretical sense should account for the rule-governed phenomena of language, then there is absolutely no reason to a-priori exclude cognitive-pragmatic phenomena and try to arbitrarily restrict grammar just to "syntactic" phenomena.

So far we have not mentioned any possible connection between semantic status (e.g. agent vs. patient, animate vs. inanimate) and order. The silence here reflects a general silence in the literature on this point (but cf. Tomlin 1986). I would, in fact, venture to guess that there will be no language where an essentially semantic principle governs the majority of order facts for major constituents of the clause. This is because language is ultimately a **pragmatic** tool in the hands of creatures who are nevertheless built to automate or **grammaticize** — "syntacticize", if you will — particularly frequent patterns. Human beings are not primarily interested in describing the semantic facts more or less "as they are" (philosophical issues concerned with the impossibility of objective observation notwithstanding). They are interested in interpreting perceived facts as they fit their own goals vis-a-vis their hearers — a supremely pragmatic task. Thus, if a language should be discovered where some order facts appear to be describable in semantic terms, but in a given context a certain pragmatic principle would predict an alternative order, the pragmatic principle will most surely win out. The overall governing principles would thus be pragmatic, and order would only appear to be semantically based in the norm because of the large majority of cases where semantic and pragmatic principles converge on the same structure. In sum, broadly speaking there appear to be just two types of ordering principles: syntactic and cognitive-pragmatic. Any given language may be primarily sensitive to one type of principle or the other, or may display a more balanced mixture of the two.

The *raison d'être* for this volume is to explore cross-linguistically a range of cognitive and pragmatic factors that correlate with — if not motivate — order variation among major constituents of the clause, above and beyond whatever syntactic constraints there may be. By way of introduction to the problem of teasing out syntactic from cognitive-pragmatic factors, in this volume **Marianne Mithun** and **Kenneth Hale** discuss how in languages where surface order of major constituents may correlate with cognitive-pragmatic factors, certain other facts of the language may, or may not, be dependent on a particular order of grammatical relations. The thesis of Mithun's paper is of such centrality to this volume that, although the paper was previously published, we have requested its inclusion here. Mithun argues that in Cayuga and Coos (North American) and Ngandi (Australian) no order of grammatical relations can be established as basic. Instead, information that is particularly newsworthy is placed first in the clause. Hale describes Warlpiri and Papago (also known as 'O'odham), in which surface order of major constituents is predictable by pragmatic principles similar to that which Mithun proposes. However, Hale's major point is to argue that despite the similar pragmatically-based surface orders, the two languages differ in important ways. In Papago, intonational patterns, determiner allomorphy, and extraction phenomena suggest that a "basic underlying" order of grammatical relations can be argued for; there is no evidence for a similar conclusion for Warlpiri.

What, then, are the cognitive and pragmatic principles that motivate order variation? Given what we currently know, we can provisionally identify four types of factors:

(1) the cognitive status the speaker wishes the hearer to accord the information expressed by a given phrase (e.g. whether the information should be integrated into the current mental representation as an important referential-nonidentifiable entity or not, as relatively more newsworthy/unexpected or not, as the cognitive "foundation" for a discourse unit or not);

(2) whether the speaker assumes something is explicitly contrary to the speaker's current expectations (i.e. various types of "contrastive focus");

(3) whether a clause initiates or ends a discourse chunk; and
(4) whether part of the meaning of a clause is that the information it contains is temporally sequenced relative to information in other clauses.

In their cognitive basis, all of these factors may ultimately be reducible to a single factor having to do with a severely limited amount of **focal attention** (cf. Tomlin and Pu 1991). That is, in a language where order is sensitive to all four sub-factors, the best explanation of the data may be that whatever item is in the speaker's focus of attention at any given time is (probably) placed at the front of the clause. However, it is clear that different languages grammaticize such a cognitive limitation in different ways. For example, in some other language, placing a constituent at the front of the clause before the verb may be possible only when the speaker assumes that certain information is explicitly contrary to the hearer's current expectations (factor two above).

Relative to what cognitive status the speaker wishes the hearer to accord information expressed by a given phrase (factor 1), for a long time the received wisdom was that "theme" preceded "rheme;" in unmarked cases theme expresses given information and rheme expresses new information (cf. Jones 1977: 52ff for a good review). In Firbas' (1964) "Functional Sentence Perspective" terms, information lower in communictive dynamism (theme) preceded information higher in communicative dynamism (rheme). At its outset, the principle was particularly associated with the Prague school and was based on studies of Slavic languages. The dominence of this ordering principle would — at first thought — seem to be upheld by an apparent predominance of SOV/SVO languages in the world, in that (transitive) subjects strongly tend to encode given information, while objects encode given information at something closer to a rate of 50% (Givón 1979).

Morton Gernsbacher and David Hargreaves experimentally substantiate a cognitive theory referred to as the Structure Building Framework that might seem to support aspects of the received wisdom. Gernsbacher and Hargreaves propose that in language-comprehension, a cognitive **foundation** is first laid. From the hearer's perspective, whatever is ordered first will be integrated into a developing mental representation as that foundation. Subsequent information which is coherent with the foundation will then be mapped into the same developing structure of which the foundation is a part. If subsequent information is relatively incoherent with the established foundation, the comprehender will likely begin development of a new mental representation, with its own foundation. In English, at least, perceptually salient, animate, definite, and presupposed concepts are likely to be mentioned first, and appear to constitute particularly good foundations. Such experimental evidence might, then, appear to support the Praguean claims.

A couple of flies appeared in the theme-rheme ointment during the 1970's. Historically, perhaps the first challenge came from **Russell Tomlin and Richard Rhodes'** work on Ojibwa (reprinted here; originally published in 1979). In this paper they claimed that precisely the opposite ordering must be the rule for Ojibwa -- rheme/new information comes before theme/given. Interestingly, Tomlin and Rhodes still deferred to the received wisdom of the day by stating that the Ojibwa rule was reversed from the "language-general tendency". Another challenge came from languages such as Hixkaryana (OVS; Derbyshire 1979), as well as from various VOS languages (cf. Keenan 1978), in which objects occur before subjects.

Throughout the 1980's a number of language-particular studies, by their sheer accumulation, implied that Tomlin and Rhodes were over-cautious in suggesting that Ojibwa was counter to any language-**general** tendency (cf. the articles in Givón (ed.) 1983; Payne 1987a, 1987b; Scancarelli 1987; Givón 1988). Additionally, the studies in this volume by **Mithun**, **Hale**, **Payne**, **Sundberg Meyer, Rude**, **Jacennik and Dryer**, **Cooreman**, and **Givón** although differing in the details of their claims, all show that in no way is it a foregone conclusion that cross-linguistically, information lower in "communicative dynamism" generally comes before information higher in "communicative dynamism".

As noted earlier, in Cayuga, Coos, and Ngandi, particularly "newsworthy" information occurs first in the clause. **Marianne Mithun** argues that "newsworthy" cannot be reduced to new or nonidentifiable (indefinite) information, though "newsworthy" does include shifts in discourse topic and information that is pragmatically marked.

In 'O'odham (Papago), there is a significant correlation between identifiability and order. Pragmatically marked and most nonidentifiable mentions occur before the verb, while some occur after the verb along with all identifiable mentions that are not pragmatically marked. Nonreferential mentions occur on either side of the verb. **Doris Payne**'s paper focuses on placement of nonidentifiable, nonreferential, and quantified noun phrases, and the extent to which pragmatic order principles are grammaticized. One principle is essentially syntactic, in that a certain class of "*h*-words" has a strongly uniform distribution in preverbal position, regardless of the job any particular *h*-word performs. For non-*h* phrases which express nonidentifiable information, preverbal placement strongly correlates with importance of the concept in the discourse, while postverbal placement correlates with unimportance.

Klamath has traditionally been described as "almost completely free" relative to order of grammatical relations. Additionally, both definite and indefinite participants can occur in either preverbal or postverbal position. In a quantified discourse based study, **Karen Sundberg Meyer** shows that a referent is likely introduced before the verb when it is important (as measured by its recurrence in the discourse), or when there is a discontinuity such as a competing referent, a switch in subject, or a break in the hierarchical structure of the discourse. Otherwise, the referent is likely to occur in postverbal position.

In a similar study of Nez Perce, a language also described as having free order of grammatical relations, **Noel Rude** demonstrates a statistically significant correlation between more expected participants and postverbal position, and between less expected participants and preverbal position. Preverbal position is not, however, a reliable index of identifiability, as the majority of nouns in preverbal position are still definite. Unlike 'O'odham and Klamath, there is no apparent correlation between participant importance (as measured by how long a participant persists in the discourse) and order.

Given that languages such as Cayuga, Coos, Ngandi, Ojibwa, 'O'odham (Papago), Klamath, and Nez Perce do not support the Praguean theme-rheme ordering, does it follow that Gernsbacher and Hargreaves' principle of "lay the foundation first" is inapplicable to such languages? Though Gernsbacher and Hargreaves acknowledge that further cross-linguistic experimental evidence is called for, the Structure Building Framework by no means limits "foundations" to concepts that are "low in communicative dynamism" (however communicative dynamism should be translated in explicit cognitive terms). The foundation or "anchor" of a new discourse unit would often, in fact, be previously unexpected and thus commonly be referential-nonidentifiable or high in newsworthiness; and it would surely be a discourse-important concept, likely to persist throughout some portion of the discourse.

Returning to the Slavic question, **Barbara Jacennik and Matthew Dryer** present a multi-factored study of subject placement in Polish. They employ a quantitative methodology to evaluate whether Slavic languages truly have a mirror-image pragmatic ordering principle from the above-mentioned languages, or whether the apparent differences should turn out to be an epiphenomenon of different researchers having applied different methodologies. Jacennik and Dryer's first point is one which all word order scholars should take note of, namely, that it is oversimplistic to simply contrast SV and VS orders. Rather, there are two types of VS clauses with considerably different properties: subject-final and VSX. This study also underscores the importance of examining the discourse function of non-subject phrases in a clause, in order to completely understand the placement of a subject phrase. One of the clearest differences between SV, VSX, and VS clauses is that the subject referent is least predictable in VS clauses, most predictable in VSX clauses, and of intermediate in predictability in SV clauses. They speculate that the critical difference between VSX and VS clauses may be that the former backgrounds the subject and highlights the X element, while in a VS clause the subject is highlighted. That is, the critical variable is "not the order of subject and verb, but rather the contrast between clause-final position and earlier positions in the clause." Jacennik and Dryer conclude that neither the principle of "place the theme first and the rheme last", nor "place unpredictable information before the verb and predictable information later" can be a correct generalization for all Polish subjects.

Several papers in this volume elucidate the correlation between order and hierarchical discourse structure. Barbara Fox's (1985) work on Tagalog was one of the first quantified studies to suggest that the chunking of discourse into units can be a factor motivating word order variation (our factor 3 above). In Tagalog, information occurs before the verb at such points of discontinuity (cf. **T. Givón**'s discussion in this volume). Like Tagalog, Chamorro is a verb-initial Austronesian language. **Ann Cooreman**'s work on Chamorro similarly shows that hierarchical discourse structure motivates preverbal subjects — not their referential continuity (either anaphoric predictability or cataphoric importance of a referent, as measured by the density of mentions of the referent in a given stretch of text). **Sundberg Meyer**'s work also suggests the relevance of hierarchical structure to determining order in Klamath. We note **T. Givón**'s claim here, that discontinuity of any sort may motivate NP preposing, regardless of whether the discontinuity has to do with participants, time, location, action, or thematic structure. In cognitive terms, such order may constitute the laying down of a new foundation; in speech act terms, it may constitute an instruction to the hearer to begin development of a new mental representation or episode.

Finally, we turn to the fourth cognitive-pragmatic factor that is known to affect order in language: temporal sequencing or narrative "main event line." In a very real sense, this is just the opposite side of the discourse chunking coin in that temporal sequencing is a type of coherence that may obtain between predications belonging to the same discourse chunk. In contrast, unsequenced clauses may provide background interpolations about sequenced events or participants, recapitulate a situation at the close of a hierarchical discourse unit, introduce participants, or correct some misunderstanding which the speaker believes the hearer holds. Some of the earliest observations about sequencing and order are found in various articles by Robert Longacre (but see especially Longacre 1990) and in Hopper 1979 (see also 1986). In Old English, for instance, VS and OV orders are found for temporally sequenced clauses with VS initiating a sequence, while SV order is found in clauses that are not temporally sequenced. In this volume, **John Myhill** argues that in a number of languages which, in terms of sheer frequency of clause orders, might be termed "verb initial" but which yet admit some order variation, verb initial patterns correlate with temporal sequencing. Placing some constituent before the verb may correlate with temporally unsequenced clauses. Myhill carefully notes that this does not imply that sequencing alone is what determines order, but only that the correlation is observable.

Like Tagalog and Chamorro, Agutaynen is a supposedly verb initial Austronesian language. **Stephen Quakenbush**'s study simultaneously shows how temporal sequencing can affect order variation, and shows the importance of evaluating one's data base in drawing conclusions about "basic" order. One of Hawkins' criteria for determining "basic" order when there are two competing patterns is frequency (1983: 13; though it is not his only criterion). Quakenbush shows that if discourse genres are not carefully evaluated, one could come up with quite differing claims about order based on sheer frequency: in Agutaynon, verb-initial patterns are most common in narrative; but subject-verb order is most common in non-narrative. Clearly whatever functions correlate with subject-first syntax are occurring more often in non-narrative, and whatever functions correlate with verb-first syntax (presumably, temporal sequencing) are occurring more often in narrative.

Can the correlation between temporal sequencing and order be linked to either the principle of "lay the foundation first," or to the principle of a limited amount of focal attention? A link to the first principle remains an open question, given that Gernsbacher and Hargreaves and other cognitive scientists have primarily investigated the role of nominal elements in building mental representations. Relative to the second principle, Chafe (1987) has noted that in natural discourse, by far the dominant pattern is to have one and only one piece of "new" information per clause. This is likely due to a constraint on the amount of information that can be held in focal attention at any one time. Similarly, it appears that a given clause does only one cognitive-pragmatic job, such as introduce a new participant, correct some supposed misunderstanding of the hearer's, advance the time line, etc. It is extremely rare in natural discourse for a single clause to simultaneously do two jobs: it will not both introduce a new participant and advance the time line; it will not both correct a supposed misunderstanding on the part of the hearer and advance the time line. Speakers normally calibrate the linguistic time line by reporting perceived events; that is, the assertion of an event in a verb advances the time line. If in some language a certain position correlates with "focal attention", whatever constituent of the clause most pertains to the job to be done will be placed in that position. In such a language, we would predict that that position would correlate with verb placement in temporally sequenced clauses.

Finally, it is clear that even if order is grounded in terms of cognitive principles like "lay a foundation first" and a limited amount of focal attention, different languages **grammaticize** such principles to greater and lesser extents. In Yagua, for example, initial position is normally reserved for the verb but a phrase may occur before the verb if it contains pragmatically marked information. Surely this fronted information is in the focus of attention. When the speaker wishes to start a new discourse unit, certain information may also be in the focus of attention — perhaps whatever concept or participant will serve as the new foundation for the unit — but in Yagua this information is not fronted before the verb. It can be presented in an existential-presentative construction with the relevant phrase occurring toward the end of the clause, or it can be presented simply as a post-verbal subject or object.

In contrast to a more "rigid" verb initial language like Yagua, consider the Austronesian languages Agutaynen (**Quakenbush**) and Chamorro (**Cooreman**) which are also traditionally thought of as verb initial. In

Agutaynon and Chamorro, in addition to pragmatically marked information, new foundations for hierarchical discourse units appear to occur before the verb. In fronting such information, the speaker is pragmatically indicating: "You may have thought that up to now X was the foundation/topic of the unit. However, you must now change that expectation and I assert to you that Y is the foundation/topic of the (next) unit". When a clause contains a new foundation, surely this information is in the focus of attention. Compared to Yagua, the range of focal information that can occur before the verb is broader.

If the way in which initial position is grammaticized for expressing information in focal attention is broadened yet further, it will allow initial placement of important nonidentifiable referents, even when such are not particularly functioning as the foundations for larger discourse units. Thus in languages such as Cayuga, Coos, Ngandi, Ojibwa, Walbiri, Papago, Nez Perce, and Klamath, it is likely that whatever information is in the focus of attention in any given predication will occur in initial position — whether it is pragmatically marked, a new foundation for a discourse unit, or simply less expected information.

In sum, we conclude that cognitive-pragmatic factors play a very prominent role in predicting order, and that such factors can be grammaticized. In this context, **T. Givón** reviews several important methodological considerations one should hold in mind when pursuing the distribution of "grammar in text." Givón claims that correlations are often much stronger in the direction of function to structure, than vice versa. This is because it is common for a given structure to have several functions (polysemy), but a given function will ideally be expressed via just a single structure. We might further infer that the direction of strongest predictability also results from the fact that the linguistic code is limited in terms of the number of structural oppositions, while the number of functions to be carried out is less limited (cf. Givón 1981).

A second difficulty reflected in a number of studies is that a strong correlation between a given function and a given form may be uncovered, but some residue of instances remains unaccounted for and appears to be counter to the proposed generalization. Closer inspection of the residual cases may show that the first observed correlation is epiphenomenal, due to the operation of some **other** function which happens to correlate with both the first function and the form in question, and it is this other function which is truly motivating the pattern. One must therefore be careful not to suppose that simply because a statistically valid correlation can be established, that the true function of the form in question has necessarily been uncovered. For further study in this regard, we might raise the case of Nez Perce. Rude notes that although there is a correlation between referential distance (an index of discontinuity) and order, referential distance does not **predict** order in individual Nez Perce clauses. A correlation has been observed, but what other principle or interaction of principles stands behind the observed correlation, which would give closer to a 100% predictive account of order?

We enthusiastically present this collection of papers in the hope that cognitive-pragmatic categories will no longer be a priori banished from "grammar", and as a step toward clarifying what cognitive-pragmatic factors do, and do not, motivate order variation.

References

Chafe, Wallace. 1987. "Cognitive Constraints on Information Flow." *Coherence in Discourse and Grammar* ed. by Russell Tomlin, 21-51. Amsterdam: John Benjamins.

Derbyshire, Desmond. 1979. *Hixkaryana Syntax*. University of London. Doctoral thesis.

Dryer, Matthew. 1988. "Object-Verb Order and Adjective-Noun Order: Dispelling a Myth." *Lingua* 74.77-109.

Firbas, Jan. 1964. "On Defining the Theme in Functional Sentence Analysis." *Travaux Linguistiques de Prague* 1.267-280. Prague: Academia.

Fox, Barbara. 1985. "Word Order Inversion and Discourse Continuity in Tagalog." *Quantified Studies in Discourse* (= a special issue of *Text* 5.1/2) 39-54.

Givón, T. 1979. *On Understanding Grammar*. New York: Academic Press.

Givón, T. 1981. "Typology and Functional Domains." *Studies in Language* 5.163-193.

Givón, T., ed. 1983. *Topic Continuity in Discourse: a Quantitative Cross-Language Study*. Amsterdam: John Benjamins.

Givón, T. 1988. "The Pragmatics of Word-Order: Predictability, Importance and Attention." *Language Typology and Language Universals* ed. by Michael Hammond, Edith Moravcisk, and Jessica Wirth, 243-284. Amsterdam: John Benjamins.

Greenberg, Joseph. 1963. "Some Universals of Grammar with Particular Reference to the Order of Meaningful Elements." *Universals of Language* ed. by Joseph Greenberg, 58-90. Cambridge, Mass: MIT Press.

Hawkins, John. 1983. *Word Order Universals*. New York: Academic Press.

Hopper, Paul. 1979. "Aspect and Foregrounding in Discourse." *Discourse and Syntax* (=*Syntax and Semantics* 12) ed. by T. Givón, 213-241. New York: Academic Press.

Hopper, Paul. 1986. "Discourse Function and Word Order Shift: a Typological Study of the VS/SV Alternation." *Language Typology 1985* ed. by Winfred Lehmann, 123-140. Amsterdam: John Benjamins.

Jones, Linda. 1977. *Theme in English Expository Discourse.* Lake Bluff, Illinois: Jupiter Press.

Keenan, Edward. 1978 "The Syntax of Subject Final Languages." *Syntactic Typology* ed. by Winfred Lehmann, 267-327. Austin: Univ. of Texas Press.

Lehmann, Winfred. 1973. "A Structural Principle of Language and its Implications." *Language* 49.47-66.

Longacre, Robert. 1990. *Storyline Concerns and Word Order Typology in East and West Africa.* (=*Studies in African Linguistics, Supplement 10.*) Los Angeles: UCLA.

Mallinson, Graham & Barry Blake. 1981. *Language Typology.* Amsterdam: North Holland.

Nichols, Johanna. 1986. "Head-Marking and Dependent-Marking Grammar." *Language* 62.56-119.

Payne, Doris. 1987a. "Information Structuring in Papago Narrative Discourse." *Language* 63.783-804.

Payne, Doris. 1987b. "Meaning and Pragmatics of Order in Selected South American Indian Languages." Paper presented at the Wenner-Gren Foundation conference on "The Role of Theory in Language Description", Ocho Ríos, Jamaica.

Payne, Doris. 1990. *The Pragmatics of Word Order: Typological Dimensions of Verb Initial Languages.* Berlin: Mouton de Gruyter.

Scancarelli, Janine. 1987. *Grammatical Relations and Verb Agreement in Cherokee.* UCLA Ph.D. dissertation.

Thompson, Sandra. 1978. "Modern English from a Typological Point of View: Some Implications of the Function of Word Order." *Linguistische Berichte* 54.19-35.

Tomlin, Russell. 1986. *Basic Word Order: Functional Principles.* London: Croom Helm.

Tomlin, Russell & Ming Ming Pu. 1991. "The Management of Reference in Mandarin Discourse." *Cognitive Linguistics* 2.65-95.

Tomlin, Russell & Richard Rhodes. 1979. "An Introduction to Information Distribution in Ojibwa." *Chicago Linguistics Society* 15.307-320.

Vennemann, Theo & Ray Harlow. 1977. "Categorial Grammar and Consistent Basic VX Serialization." *Theoretical Linguistics* 4.227-254.

Is Basic Word Order Universal?[1]

Marianne Mithun
University of California, Santa Barbara

A fundamental assumption underlying much current work in syntactic typology is that all languages have some basic, syntactically defined constituent order. It is usually recognized that this order may be altered somewhat for pragmatic purposes, but the basic order is considered a primary characteristic from which other features of the language can be predicted. It is questionable, however, whether all languages actually have such a basic order. Discourse data from a number of genetically and areally distinct languages indicate that syntactic ordering and pragmatic reordering processes many not in fact be universal. In what follows, it will be shown that forcing such languages into the mold of any basic word order at all is at best descriptively unnecessary, and at worst an obstacle to the discovery of interesting universals.

For many languages, the basic order seems so obvious that criteria for determining it need not be specified. In languages where one order predominates statistically, and any rarer alternative orders are highly marked pragmatically, several reasonable criteria converge to indicate the same choice. For other languages, however, the process is more problematic, since various criteria can lead to conflicting results. Sometimes the decision is based on textual frequency (see Hawkins 1983; Dryer 1983). Sometimes it is whatever order permits the simplest overall syntactic description (McCawley 1970). Sometimes it is the order accompanied by the least morphological marking (Hawkins 1983). Finally, it may be the least pragmatically marked, or neutral order, although identifying pragmatically neutral sentences is itself problematic. In some of these cases, discourse-initial sentences are considered the most neutral because they presuppose no preceding context (Pullum 1977: 266). In other cases, the preferred order for potentially ambiguous clauses has been judged the most neutral (Chomsky 1965: 127). In still others, "simple, declarative, active clauses with no complex verb or noun phrases" are assumed to exhibit neutral order (Chomsky 1957: 107; Greenberg 1966: 74; Pullum 1981). Hawkins, in his ambitious study of word order universals, states that of his three criteria (statistical textual frequency, frequency within the grammatical pattern, and grammatical markedness), simple statistical frequency usually provides a sufficiently sensitive basis for the identification of basic order (1983: 13-14). For many languages, however, grammarians note that nearly all logically possible constituent orders appear with sufficient regularity in main clauses to render identification of even a "preferred order" difficult.

The isolation of pragmatic effects on word order in various languages has also been somewhat problematic, due in part to the well known diversity of terminology and its usage in the analysis of discourse. Linguists associated with the Prague School have traditionally described pragmatic ordering in terms of the concepts "theme" and "rheme". Mathesius (1939) defined the theme as "that which is known or at least obvious in the given situation, and from which the speaker proceeds" in his discourse (cited in Firbas 1964: 268). Firbas (1964, 1972) sought to refine the notion of theme in terms of "communicative dynamism". "By the degree of communicative dynamism carried by a linguistic element, I understand the extent to which the element contributes to the development of the communication, to which, as it were, it 'pushes the communication forward'" (1972: 78). That element carrying the lowest degree of communicative dynamism is called the "theme", that carrying the highest, the "rheme". The Prague School linguists and others (see, for example, Firbas 1964: 270; Greenberg 1966: 100; Lyons 1977: 508; Givón 1979: 296) have remarked that the normal pragmatic ordering of constituents seems to be theme-rheme, or topic-comment. In Firbas' terms, the basic distribution of communicative dynamism is a gradual increase in degree from the beginning of the sentence to the end. Lyons notes that

> Not surprisingly there is a very high correlation, not only in English, but in all languages, between occupying initial position in the utterance and being thematic, rather than rhematic . . . To many scholars it has seemed natural that the cognitive point of departure and the communicative point of departure should coincide. (1977: 507-8)

A number of facts indicate that the interaction between basic word order and pragmatic theme-rheme reordering principles is not constant from one language to the next. Following work initiated by Mathesius (1928), Thompson (1978) pointed out that languages can vary in the relative effects of syntactic, semantic, and pragmatic considerations on surface word order. In languages like English, the syntactic roles of constituents are the primary determinants of word order, while in languages like Russian and Czech, pragmatic considerations have a stronger effect. When pragmatic factors do play a role, furthermore, it is not clear that all languages follow the "natural" progression from theme to rheme. Tomlin and Rhodes (this volume) point out that in Ojibwa, a VOS Algonquian language, the unmarked distribution of thematic information is reversed from the language-general tendency for thematic information to come earlier in a sentence or clause. Givón (1983: 145) reports that Ute, "a mature SOV language with a high degree of pragmatically-controlled word-order flexibility", shows comment-topic order. Similarly, Biblical Hebrew "is rigidly VO but shows a pragmatically-controlled VS/SV variation" (Givón 1983: 28), also with the order comment-topic.

In the sections below, ordering principles will be examined in some of the languages that have posed problems for grammarians and syntactic typologists. It will be shown that for languages of this type, the assumption of any syntactically defined word order can be misleading, as is the assumption of theme-rheme pragmatic reordering. The existence of such languages has important consequences both for the reliability of standard strategies used in detecting basic word order, and for word order typologies.

1. Word order in some perplexing cases

In this section, the ordering of constituents will be examined in three such languages: Cayuga, Ngandi, and Coos. Although unrelated genetically and areally, the three show surprising parallelisms in their surface constituent orders.

1.1 The general character of the languages

Cayuga is an Iroquoian language spoken in Ontario. Each verb contains pronominal prefixes referring esssentially to its agent and/or patient. Thus a verb like *-e-* 'go' appears with an agent pronoun, while a verb like *-nǫhǫk-tani* 'be sick' appears with a patient pronoun. A verb like *-kǫhek-* 'hit' appears with a transitive pronoun referring to a combination of agent and patient. The categories of agent and patient are semantically based in Cayuga, but they are fully grammaticized. Some participants may seem more agentive than others, but they are categorized equivalently by the grammar. Thus one who hits something may seem more agentive than one who sees something or likes something, but all are expressed by agentive pronouns.

Because of the presence of pronominal prefixes, single verbs can stand alone in Cayuga as predications in themselves, and often do.[2]

Cayuga

(1) *Shakó-n̥ǫ̥hwe'-s.*
he/her-like-HAB
'He likes her.'

One or both arguments of the verb may be further identified by a separate nominal. The pronominal prefixes remain unchanged.

Cayuga

(2) *John shakón̥ǫ̥hwe's.*
John he/her-like-HAB
'John likes her.'

(3) *Mary shakón̥ǫ̥hwe's.*
Mary he/her-like-HAB
'He likes Mary.'

Although speakers agree that it is perfectly grammatical to include both a separate agent noun phrase and a patient noun phrase within a single sentence, such full sentences occur relatively rarely in spontaneous discourse. It is easy enough to elicit them from bilingual speakers, however. When asked, speakers agree that all logically possible constituent orders are grammatical: SOV, SVO, VSO, VOS, OSV, and VSO.

Ngandi, an Australian aboriginal language of eastern Arnhem Land, is also polysynthetic with obligatory pronominal prefixes within the verb. As in Cayuga, the prefixes remain in the verb whether separate noun phrases further identify the core participants or not. All Ngandi data here come from texts recorded by Heath (1978).

Ngandi (Heath 1978:192)

(4) *Barma-ma-ŋi.*
3PL/MA-get-PAST.CONT
'They used to get it.'

(5) *Ma-d̑atam-yuŋ barma-ma-ŋi.*
MA-water.lily.fruit-ABS 3PL/MA-get-PAST.CONT
'They used to get water lily fruit.'

(6) *Barma-ma-ŋi ba-d̑inˀ-d̑u-yuŋ.*
3PL/MA-get-PAST.CONT PL-woman-ERG-ABS
'The women used to get it.'

Ngandi nouns are classified into noun classes. The noun referring to the water lily fruit above is of the MA class and accordingly carries a prefix *-ma-*, while the noun referring to the women, of the BA class, carries a prefix *-ba-*. The pronominal prefixes within the verb refer to these classes. In addition, the case role of each noun is marked by a nominal suffix. The noun for 'women' above contains an ergative suffix *-d̑u-*. Absolutive nouns bear no overt case suffixes. (The suffixes glossed as ABS by Heath are not case markers.) Other case suffixes distinguish locative, allative, genitive/dative, originative, ablative, and pergressive nouns. As in Cayuga, clauses containing more than one noun phrase referring to a core argument, here an ergative and absolutive, are possible, but rare. When they do occur, any order is possible.

Coos, an Oregon language, is also polysynthetic with pronominal affixes. Arguments of intransitive verbs are referenced by "loosely prefixed" pronominal clitics on the verb. Arguments of transitive verbs are referenced by combinations of these and transitive verbal suffixes. All data here come from the Hanis Coos texts recorded by Frachtenberg in 1909 and published in 1913 and 1922.

Coos (Frachtenberg (1922: 351, 425)

(7) *e^{E}-ła-ā'mî.*
you-take-I
'I take you along.'

(8) *î'lxa-ts lE ya'bas;*
look.at-TRANS the maggot
'He looked at the maggots.'

(9) *x-ya'bas* *q!m-îts.*
DISCR-maggot eat-TRANS
'Maggots ate him.'

Ergative nouns, like that for "maggots" above, are marked with the prefix *x*-, termed "discriminative" by Frachtenberg. As in Cayuga and Ngandi, clauses containing both a separate agent noun phrase and a separate patient noun phrase are relatively rare, and their word order is variable. As Frachtenberg noted,

> The syntactic structure of the Coos sentence is very simple, and is characterized by the facility with which the different parts of speech may shift their position without changing in the least the meaning of the sentence. (1922: 319)

1.2 Strategies for determining basic word order

Since all word orders occur in all of these languages, the identification of a basic order is not as straightforward as in many other languages. Several strategies are possible.

1.2.1 *Statistical frequency*

A common diagnostic of basic order is statistical frequency (Dryer 1983). Whichever order appears the most often might be considered basic. The crucial constructions, however, clauses containing both separate agent/subject and separate patient/object noun phrases, are relatively rare in spontaneous discourse in all of the languages. Sample counts of clauses in texts indicate that in Cayuga, perhaps 1 - 2 percent of all clauses contain three major constituents; in Ngandi, approximately 2 percent; and in Coos, 2 - 3 percent. Even among these small sets of clauses, all orders are represented. Since such constructions appear so rarely, strong statistical evidence for any order is simply lacking.

1.2.2 *The ambiguity test*

Another frequently cited diagnostic is the word order preferred in potentially ambiguous sentences (Chomsky 1965). A Cayuga speaker was presented with the sentences below, constructed from shorter sentences he had produced in a narrative.

Cayuga

(10) a. *Khyotro:wę̨: Ohswe:kę́' ahǫwati:kwé:ni'.* (SOV/OSV)
Buffalo Six.Nations they.beat.them

b. *Ahǫwati:kwe:ní' Khyotro:wę̨: Ohswé:kę'.* (VSO/VOS)
they.beat.them Buffalo Six.Nations

c. *Khyotro:wę̨: ahǫwati:kwe:ní' Ohswé:kę'.* (SVO/OSV)
Buffalo they.beat.them Six.Nations

He remarked that they were all grammmatical Cayuga sentences, but that in all cases, it was unclear who beat whom. He could not choose a preferred reading. Other similar sentences produced the same reaction. The overall rarity of such full sentences suggests that their very appearance is a marked phenomenon, so that none of them should be considered reliable models of unmarked constituent structure.

1.2.3 *Relative order within pairs*

Predicates do appear frequently in Cayuga with a single nominal constituent. This fact suggests that in order to discover the basic constituent order of Cayuga, one should determine the orders found between pairs of constituents, and then combine the results (i.e. SV and VO, then SVO). This is, of course, analagous to the usual strategy for determining the relative order of morphemes in a language when all of them could not possibly cooccur in a single word. While such a procedure should indicate the relative order of subjects and predicates, and of objects and predicates, it might not show the relative order of subjects and objects if these appear on the same side of the predicate (i.e. SV and OV, then what?) Cayuga has not grammaticized either a subject category or a direct object category (Mithun 1988), but for the sake of comparison, constituents will be labelled according to the roles they would serve if the language were accusative. The single arguments of intransitive clauses will all be labelled S and the patients of transitives O. Since their semantic roles do not enter directly into ordering processes, no distortion results.

Separate subject nominals of any kind are somewhat rare in Cayuga discourse, appearing in approximately 12 percent of the clauses. (All examples cited below were taken from spontaneous narratives or conversation unless otherwise specified.) Sometimes subjects appear before their predicates. The sentence in (11) is from a discussion of how severe the winter is likely to be. Whitemen have predicted a hard winter, but the speaker is not convinced.

Cayuga S V
(11) *Ne:' ki' kwáhs ts'inǫwahe'tá' ahsǫ́ hne:' kaná:kre'.*
it.is just most fishworm still CONTR they.dwell

S V
Tsi't'ęshǫ:'ǫ́ hni' ahsǫ́ thę́' hne:' nę:kyę́ t'eonahtę́:kyǫ:.
birds also still not CONTR this they.have.not.gone
'There are still plenty of fish worms around. The birds haven't left yet either.'

Subjects can also appear after their predicates. The sentence below comes from a description of how to hunt rabbits.

Cayuga V S
(12) ... *thę' thęshatiyę́:ti: wa'ne:' hęnǫ:kwe'tase'shǫ́:'ǫh.*
not they.don't.know today young.men
'The young men of today do not seem to know how to do it.'

Direct object nominals often appear before their predicates.

Cayuga O V
(13) *Ne:' ne' nę:kyę́ ne' kwa'y ǫ́' kę:s akwa:to:wá:s*
it.is the this the rabbit used.to we.hunted
tshike:ksá:'ah.
when.I.was.a.child
'This is how we used to hunt rabbits when I was a kid.'

Objects also appear after their predicates.

Cayuga V O
(14) *Ne:' s'ekę́:s ne' swe'ké:ha henatęhni:nǫ́ kę:s ne' kwa'yǫ'.*
it.is usually the long.ago they.sell usually the rabbit
'A long time ago, they used to sell rabbits.'

Time adverbials can occur on either side of the predicate.

Cayuga T V
(15) *Sǫhé kyę:' nóne:' ka:tǫ́ teyo:nátawenye'.*
night this you.know I.say they.stir.themselves
'As I said, at night, they walk around.'

V T
(16) *O:nę́ kę:s hne:' thó kaya'taní:yǫ:t settsí:ha thó:kyeh.*
then usually CONTR there body.hangs very.early that
'Then usually the body will be hanging there in the morning.'

Locative constituents can appear on both sides of the predicate.

Cayuga L V
(17) *Kḁha:kǫ́: hęhse:'*
in.the.bush there.you will.go
'You will go out into the bush.'

V L
(18) *Teyo:natawenyé' se' ne:' kyotkǫ́:t ohnékakǫ:.*
they.are.stirring just it.is always in.the.water
'They are always moving around in the water.'

Manner adverbs can also precede or follow verbs.

Cayuga Adv V
(19) *Ske:nǫ:'ǫ́ shę nęhse:kwe:ní' tę̥hsátḁhahk.*
slow as so.you.will.be.able you.will.walk
'Walk as slowly as you can.'

V Adv
(20) *Ethsatwata:sé' ske:nǫ́:'ǫh.*
you.will.come.around slow
'You should come around carefully.'

Nearly any word order is possible. As can be seen from the examples above, even the predicates have no constant position.

Ngandi shows the same variation. Separate nominal subjects occur in only about 10 percent of the Ngandi clauses in Heath's texts, but they can occur on either side of their predicates, whether these are transitive or not.

Ngandi (Heath 1978: 206) S V
(21) *Ṇačuweleñ-uŋ gu-jaṛk-yuŋ gu-ja-waḷk, ...*
then-ABS GU-water-ABS GU-now-go.through
'Then water passes through.'

Ngandi (Heath 1978: 206) V S
(22) *Ṇačuweleñ-uŋ gu-ja-geyk-ḓa-ni gu-jaṛk-yuŋ ṇiču?.*
then-ABS GU-now-throw-AUG-PR GU-water-ABS this.way
'Then the water rushes through.'

Objects also appear either before or after their predicates.

Ngandi (Heath 1978: 199)

O V

(23) *Ṇi-ŋaṇa-yuŋ ñaru-ja-bol-kuba-na gamakun?, ...*
NI-honey-ABS 1PLEX/NI-now-go.out-CAUS-PR properly

V O

ñaru-goṛṭa-ŋi ṇi-guŋ-yuŋ, ...
1PLEX/NI-put.in-PAST.CONT NI-honey-ABS
'We take out the honey entirely. (We then put it entirely into the what's-it, the cooliman.) We used to put the honey in.'

Oblique nominals can appear anywhere as well. Instrumentals appear either early or late in the clause.

Ngandi (Heath 1978: 197)

I V

(24) *ma-ḍarpa?-ḍu-yuŋ ñara-ja-ḍerp, ...*
MA-string-INSTR-ABS 1PLEX/A-now-attach
'We attach it (the spearhead) with string.'

Ngandi (Heath 1978: 241)

V I

(25) *barba-ja-poison'em?-ḍu-ŋi maṇga?, ma-mawuya-ṯu,*
3PL/3PL-now-poison-AUG-PCON maybe MA-poison-INST
'Maybe someone poisoned them, with magical poison.'

Datives appear both early and late.

Ngandi (Heath 1978: 212)

Dat V

(26) *ṇi-bot-gu ñaru-bak-waṇ?,*
NI-bee-DAT 1PLEX/NI-BEN-look
'We look for bees.'

Ngandi (Heath 1978: 213)

V Dat

(27) *yanači ñar-ja-ṛuḍu-ni gu-gaḷaŋ-gu,*
longtime 1PLEX-now-go-PRES GU-egg-DAT
'We go for a long time looking for eggs.'

Allative noun phrases, indicating locative goals, can appear early or late.

Ngandi (Heath 1978: 197)

		Allative	V	
(28)	*A-murŋiñ-uŋ*	*ma-gami-gič*	*ñara-yo-ŋana,*	*bulukiˀ*
	A-shovelspear-ABS	MA-spearshaft-ALL	1PLEX/A-put.on-PR	also

		V	Allative
	a-wiḷmur-yuŋ	*ñara-yo-ŋana*	*ma-gami-gič,*
	A-wirespear-ABS	1PLEX/A-put.on-PR	MA-shaft-ALL

'We put the shovel spearhead onto the spear shaft.
We also put the wire spear prongs onto their spear shaft.'

As in Cayuga, all constituent orders appear. Even the predicate can occupy almost any position within the clause.

Constituent ordering in Coos is as variable as it is in Cayuga and Ngandi. Subjects can appear either early or late in their clauses, whether transitive or intransitive.

Coos (Frachtenberg 1922: 426)

	S		L	V	
(29)	*X:ōwā'yas*	*hän*	*djî'letc*	*xal'^{E}mats*	...
	snake	his	at.thighs	it.wraps.around.him	

	L			V		S
	Hän	*we'hel*	*la^{u}*	*he'ṫaq*	*lE*	*x:ōwā'yas.*
	his.to	waist	that	it.arrived	the	snake

'The snake coiled around his thigh. It crawled up to his waist.'

Objects can also appear either early or late.

Coos (Frachtenberg 1913: 7)

	O				V
(30)	*TE*	*kā'wîl*	*hanL*	*îs*	*yō'qat.*
	that	basket	shall	we	two.split.it.in.two

'Let us split this basket in two!'

Coos (Frachtenberg 1913: 6)

		V		O
(31)	*Ûx*	*k:îłō'wît*	*tE*	*L!tā.*
	they	two.saw.it	that	land

'They saw the land.'

The same mobility is characteristic of oblique nominals. Compare the position of the locative nominals in the sentences below.

Coos (Frachtenberg 1913: 7)

	L		V
(32)	*Tsō łtce'îsetc*	*la*[u]	*ûx hî'tō*[u]*ts.*
	now ocean.beach.on	that	they two.put.it.down.

'They put it on the sand beach.'

Coos (Frachtenberg 1913: 18)

	V	L
(33)	*K:îłō'wît*	*łtcîla'aîs.*
	he.saw.it	shore.close.to

'He saw (different kinds of food lying) along the beach.'

Surely speakers would not randomly vary a cue as salient as word order. If order does not signal the syntactic or semantic roles of constituents, perhaps it has a pragmatic function.

1.3 Definiteness

As noted earlier, pragmatic ordering has most often been described as a tendency for thematic information, or topics, to appear before rhematic information, or comments. Unfortunately, themes, or topics, have been defined in a variety of ways. A major characteristic usually associated with themes is givenness, or predictability, while that associated with rhemes is newness, or unpredictability. Recall that Mathesius defined the theme as "that which is known or at least obvious in the given situation, and from which the speaker proceeds" (1939: 234, cited in Firbas 1964: 268). A comparison of the positions of definite and indefinite noun phrases might provide a key to the identification of pragmatic factors in word order, since definite nominals refer to entities that the speaker assumes the hearer can identify, either from general knowledge or specific context. Li and Thompson pointed out, for example, that the tendency in Mandarin and Russian

> to place indefinite nouns after the verb and definite nouns before the verb seems to be a manifestation of a general and widespread tendency among languages to put known information near the beginning of the sentence and new information near the end of the sentence (1976: 172).

None of the three languages described here marks definiteness obligatorily, but definiteness can be specified by means of certain nominalizing particles and demonstratives. Cayuga has a particle *ne'* which can optionally precede definite nominals, including proper and possessed nouns. When this definite particle is inserted into manufactured sentences containing both separate subject and object nominals, a relationship between definiteness and word order can be detected. The particle cannot grammatically precede a nominal early in the sentences below.

Cayuga

(34) a. **Ne' John shakonǫhwé's Mary.* (*ne'S-V-O)
the John he.likes.her Mary

b. **Ne' Mary shakonǫhwé's John.* (*ne'O-V-S)
the Mary he.likes.her John.

c. **John ne' Mary shakónǫhwe's.* (*S-ne'O-V)
John the Mary he.likes.her

d. **Mary ne' John shakónǫhwe's.* (*O-ne'S-V)
Mary ne' John he.likes.her

It can, however, precede a nominal near the end of a sentence, and is often added when full sentences are repeated by speakers. All of the (elicited) sentences below mean 'John loves Mary'.

Cayuga

(35) a. *John shakonǫhwé's ne' Mary.* (S-V-ne'O)
John he.likes.her the Mary

b. *Mary shakonǫhwé's ne' John.* (O-V-ne'S)
Mary he.likes.her the John

c. *Shakonǫhwé's John ne' Mary.* (V-S-ne'O)
he.likes.her John the Mary

d. *Shakonǫhwé's Mary ne' John.* (V-O-ne'S)
he.likes.her Mary the John

e. *Shakonǫhwé's ne' Mary ne' John.* (V-ne'O-ne'S)
he.likes.her the Mary the John

This ordering of indefinite before definite is the reverse of that found in Chinese, Russian, Czech, and many other familiar Indo-European languages for which pragmatic ordering has been described. (It should be emphasized that the sentences cited above were elicited with requests for the specific word orders given, not culled from narratives or conversation.) A survey of spontaneous Cayuga discourse indicates that indefinite nominals do tend to appear near the beginning of their clauses, while definite nominals tend to appear near the end.

Cayuga Indefinite V
(36) *Katsihwá' ki̥hsa:s.*
hammer I.seek
'I am looking for a hammer.' (said in a hardware store)
V Definite
To: ti' nika:nǫ:' nę:kyę katsíhwa'?
how then so.it.costs this hammer
'How much does this hammer cost?'

The indefinite-definite order appears to be characteristic of Ngandi discourse as well. Note the translation of (21) above. When the water is first mentioned, it appears early in the clause and is translated with an indefinite noun. At the second mention, in (22), it appears late, and is translated with a definite noun. In the passage below, the narrator is describing how Aborigines used to get yams and roast and peel them. When the yams are introduced, they are indefinite and appear early. When the skin first appears in the second line, it is identifiable from the preceding context, so it appears late. In the third line, it is identifiable from previous mention, so it appears late again.

Ngandi (Heath 1978: 210-211)
Indefinite V
(37) *bulukiˀ ma-jalma barma-ma-ni, ...*
also MA-yam.sp 3PL/MA-get-PRES

V Definite
ma-ja-bolk-d̪u-ni, ma-guḷaˀ-nut̪ayi-yuŋ,
MA-now-appear-AUG-PRES MA-skin-its-ABS

V Definite
barma-geyk, barma-geyk ma-guḷaˀ-yuŋ guniñ,
3PL/MA-throw 3PL/MA-throw MA-skin-ABS that's.all
'They get round yams (and roast them) ... Their skin comes off. They throw the skin away, and that is that.'

The indefinite-first order is also characteristic of Coos. The identity of the child in the second line below is inferrable from the preceding line; as a definite nominal, it appears late. The person mentioned in the last line is new on the scene, indefinite, and clause initial.

Coos (Frachtenberg 1913: 11)
(38) *Mā la^{u} mîtsī^{i}ltī'ye. Ta la^{u} qanō'tca*
nevertheless that (he).pregnant.became and that outside.to

V Definite V Definite
ł'nuwît lE ā'la. Hats īn qantc la^{u} L!e^{i}tc la ā'la.
(he).pulls the child just not way that go.out his child

Indefinite V
Tsō mä ī^{i}lt.
now person (he).sent.(it)
'Nevertheless he became pregnant. The child was all the time trying to come out, but could not do it. So they sent someone (to the north).'

1.4 Old versus new information

Overt definite marking accounts for a significant proportion of constituent ordering in all three languages, yet it does not account for all of it. A principle must be found that correlates highly with definiteness versus indefiniteness, but explains the remaining cases as well. Consider the following Cayuga passage. A dinner guest was asked whether he liked baked potatoes. He replied that yes, he thought he probably did.

Cayuga
(39) *Ne:' kyę́:'ǫ thréhs i:nǫ́ kyę:'ǫ́ ę́:ke:k. Ne:' tshǫ: ne'*
it.is I.guess too far I.guess I.will.eat it.is only the

Old Definite V
oa'wistá' thę' ní:' t'e:ke:s. Kwiskwís kyę:' hne:' tshǫ:
peeling not I do.I.eat pig just CONTR just

V New Definite
ka:tí:s ne' oá'wista'.
they.eat the peeling
'It's just that I eat them so seldom. I just don't eat the skins. Only pigs eat the skins.'

In the second line, the skins appear before the verb, although they are definite, inferrable and thus identifiable from the previous mention of the potatoes. However, the skins represent newer information than the verb 'eat', which had just appeared in the preceding sentence. In the third line, the skins, now old information, appear late, while the pigs, completely new information, appear first.

The same pattern can be seen in Ngandi. In the passage below, the wood wulčum spears are generic. When first introduced, they appear early. After that, they appear late.

Ngandi (Heath 1978: 187)

	New		V
(40)	*gu-wulčum*	*balaka*	*ñaru-ga-ˀ-yaw-d̪u-ŋi,*
	GU-wood.spear	before	1PLEX/3MASC:SG-SUB-DUR-spear-AUG-P

	V	Old
a-jeñ-uŋ	*bara-ga-yaw-d̪u-ŋi,*	*gu-wulčum-d̪u.*
A-fish-ABS	PL/A-SUB-spear-AUG-P	GU-wood.spear-INSTR

'We used to spear before (with) wulcum spears. They used to spear fish with wulcum spears.'

Coos exhibits the same pattern. New information tends to precede old information, as can be seen in the following passage. Both noun phrases referring to the mat are definite, but the first time the mat occurs, it appears at the beginning of the clause. The second time, it is at the end.

Coos (Frachtenberg 1913: 7)

		New		V
(41)	*TE*	*tc!î'cîl*	*yūL*	*îs yō'qat ...*
	that	matting	if	we.two.split.it

'"Let us split this mat."

(They did so, and went down to examine the earth. The earth was still not solid, even ...)

			V		Old
î	*la*^{u}	*tcī*	*ux hî'tō*^{u}*ts*	*hE*	*tc!î'cîl.*
when	that	there	they.two.put.it.down	the	matting

after they had put down the mat.'

The principle of new information before old predicts the order of constituents in the majority of clauses. It is not surprising that this should correlate so often with the indefinite/definite distinction, since new entities are most often indefinite, and previously established entities are most often definite. There are still some constructions that cannot be explained purely in terms of a preference for new before old, however.

1.5 Newsworthiness

In some cases, both constituents are equally given or equally new. A Cayuga speaker telephoned his friend to announce that he had lost his wallet.

Cayuga				New V		New O
(42)	*Ni:*	*kę:*	*thóne:'*	*ǫkahtǫ́:'*	*ne'*	*akétkw'ęta'.*
	just	here	there	I.lost.it	the	my.wallet

'Mind you, I lost my wallet.'

Both constituents are completely new, neither present nor alluded to in previous discourse (there was none), nor in extralinguistic context (also absent, since this was a telephone conversation). In this case, the new verb precedes the new object. Yet consider the utterance below. A man has just told his friend that he cut his foot with an axe. His friend, horrified, asks if he is badly hurt. He replies no, not really,

Cayuga				New O	New V
(43)	*threhs*	*kyę:'ǫ́*	*to:kę́hs*	*w̥ą̥htahkwatę́:s*	*tewakę́:sǫ:.*
	because	just.suppose	really	thick.shoes	I.wear

'I guess because I had really thick shoes on.'

Again, both the verb 'wear' and the object 'thick shoes' are completely new, neither mentioned in previous discourse, nor referred to subsequently. This time, however, the new object precedes the new verb.

A father, trying to make his daughter hurry in the morning, said,

Cayuga		New V	New S
(44)	*O:nę́*	*kokhwáihse:*	*sanó:ha'.*
	now	she.has.finished.the.food	your.mother

'Your mother has already finished cooking breakfast.'

Both elements are equally new, neither mentioned or alluded to in previous discourse, neither within view of the speaker or hearer, but equally identifiable. Neither is referred to again in subsequent discourse. The new predicate precedes the new subject.

The speaker cited below was describing his misadventures in the woods. No saplings or bushes had been mentioned previously, nor of course any grabbing, or even the coat. The saplings are not totally unexpected, since the setting is the woods; but the grabbing is also not totally unexpected, since the speaker's clothing is torn. Neither is mentioned subsequently. Here the order is new subject before new predicate.

Cayuga

						New S	New V
(45)	*Shę*	*nyǫ́:'*	*n'atǫ:ta:ké:'*	*thó*	*hne:'*	*ohǫ:tá'*	*taka:ye:ná:'*
	so	far	on.the.way	there	CONTR	sapling	it.grabbed.me

akaky'ataw'ithrá'keh.
on.my.coat.
'Along the way, bushes caught on my coat.'

In each of the sentences above, the constituent conveying the principal information of the utterance appears first. The most important part of (42) is the loss, of (43) the thickness of the shoes, of (44) the finished state of the breakfast, and (45), the bushes. Since new information is usually more important than old information, the principle of new before old usually accounts for constituent order.

The importance principle describes Ngandi equally well. In the passage below, the narrator is describing how Aborigines used to fish with a hook and line, in addition to the spears. (The verb root *-woyk-* is translated as 'angling, fishing with line and hook', but contains neither the noun root -jeñ- 'fish' nor the erb root *'ma-* 'get'.)

Ngandi (Heath 1978: 198)

(46)	*buluki?-yuŋ*	*ñar-ga-woyk,*	*ñar-ja-woyk-d̯u-ni*
	also-ABS	1PLEX-SUB-angle	1PLEX-now-angle-AUG-PRES

a-jara-t̯u,	*o-monaŋa-ku-yiñuŋ*	*ñar-ja-bak-woyk*
A-what's.it?-INSTR	A-White-GEN-REL	1PLEX-now-BEN-angle

	Old V	Old O
ñar-ga-woyk-d̯u-ni	*ñara-ga-ma-ni*	*a-jeñ-uŋ,*
1PLEX-SUB-angle-AUG-PR	1PLEX/A-SUB-get-PR	A-fish-ABS

'We also go angling. We go angling with what's it? the thing belonging to Whites, we go angling then. We go angling and catch fish.'

In the last line, both the verb 'get' and the object 'fish' are inferrable old information, in the sense that the entire discussion has been about fishing. (Neither has been mentioned lexically.) Note that here, the old predicate precedes the old object. This is because the point of the discussion is the getting, the fact that when they use a hook and line, they still do catch fish.

The passage below is from a description of plum gathering.

Ngandi (Heath 1978: 195)

(47) *ma-mala-galič-uŋ* *ñarma-ŋu-ni,* *ma-mala-galič-uŋ*
MA-group-other-ABS 1PLEX/MA-eat-PAST.CONT MA-group-other-ABS
New V New Loc
ñarma-gulʔ-d̪u-ŋi *gu-jundu-gi*
1PLEX/MA-pound-AUG-PC GU-stone-LOC
'Some (of the plums) we ate (as they were), others we pounded on a stone (so that they became soft).'

Both the predicate and the locative nominal are completely new. The locative follows the predicate. Compare the passage in (48).

Ngandi (Heath 1978: 211)

New Loc New V
(48) *a-d̪aṇḍiyaʔ-gi* *barma-ja-yo-ŋana,*
A-mat-LOC 3PL/MA-now-put.in-PRES
'We put (that food) on mats.'

Here again, both the locative nominal and the predicate are completely new. No previous mention had been made of mats or putting. In this case, however, the locative precedes the verb. The reason is clear. In (47), the pounding is more important than the rock; while in (48), the mats convey the most important information of the clause.

The same pattern can be seen in the Coos texts. The sentence below is near the beginning of a narrative. There has been no previous mention of any body of water nor of dryness or wetness.

Coos (Frachtenberg 1913: 14)

New V New S
(49) *In tc!le'xEm* *tE* *łā'nik:.*
not.dry that.there river
'There was no low tide.'

Here, the new predicate precedes the new subject. Compare the sentence below, however. Again, both the subject and predicate are new. Yet this time, the new subject precedes the new predicate.

Coos (Frachtenberg 1913: 9)

New S New V
(50) *Haqa'tî* *łaā'ya* *łtce'îsītc* *le'ûx* *nhä'wîs* *L!tā.*
tracks go.to.it beach.on their ready land
'Suddenly they saw tracks on the ocean beach.'

The main point of the clause in (49) is the lack of dryness (because Crow had no chance to get food), while the most important constituent in (50) is the tracks. Sentences like this one suggest a particular way in which constituents may be considered important in discourse.

1.6 Topic shift

The Cayuga passage below comes from the cosmology legend. A woman has fallen from the heavens through a hole in the sky, and as she falls, she wonders what will become of her. Suddenly she notices something.

Cayuga

(51)

Ne'	*nę:kyę*	*ne'*	*nę*	*eya'tǫkyé'*	*nękwá'*
the	this	the	then	her.body.is.flying.along	and.then

a'ǫn̥i̥hna:tó:k	*tho:kyeh*	*ne:'*	*nǫ̀he:'*	*ne:'*	*tsi't'ęshǫ́:'ǫh,*
she.noticed.it	there	it.is	you.know	it.is	birds

ha'tekatiy'atá:ke:	*tho*	*katikyęnǫ:kyę́'s*
many.bodies	there	they.are.flying.around

teyakotíkḁhne:'	*shęnhǫ́:*	*nę:kyę*	*eyá'tǫkye'.*
they.are.looking.at.her	where	this	her.body.is.flying
		S	V

Ne:'	*ne'*	*o:nę́*	*nę:kyę*	*tsi't'ęshǫ́:'ǫ*	*teyotiya'towéhtǫ*
it.is	the	now	this	birds	they.are.thinking

atkatiya'to:wéht	*ne'*	*nǫ́ne:'*	*nę:kyę́*	*a:kenat'enyę́:te'* ...
they.thought	the	you.know	this	they.should.try

'And then, as she was falling, she noticed birds, all different kinds of them, flying around there, looking at her, as she fell. Now at this time, these birds were thinking that they should really try (to lessen her misfortune).'

Note the early position of the underlined *tsi't'ęshǫ́:'ǫ* 'birds' in the second sentence. This noun is neither new information, since the birds were just mentioned in the previous clause, nor necessary for disambiguation, since the zoic plural pronoun in the verb 'they are thinking' clearly refers to the birds and not to the woman. It is prominent for another reason. It represents a new topic, a new point of view. The text continues to describe the birds' decisions and their resulting attempts to save the poor woman. A shift in topic can thus be considered sufficiently important to appear early in a sentence.

Not all new subjects appear clause-initially. A man and his wife had left a tape recorder running for a long time as they conversed about a wide range of different things, including what was scheduled at the longhouse that evening, who might be putting on a supper and how it would be done, a neighbor who was to get her fortune told, and when the husband was planning to return from his weekend trip. At that point a car was heard outside. The wife said:

Cayuga
(52) *Kwé: sakáeyǫ', thó:kyeh.*
well they.(FEM).arrived.again that
'Well, they're back.'

The husband answered:

Cayuga
(53) *O:nę́ ki' kyę:' sakáeyǫ', kashehawáhkshǫ'.*
now just then they.returned your.daughters
'Yes, your daughters have returned.'

The daughters had not been mentioned at all up to this point, but the significant part of the message here was the return rather than the daughters, because it meant that the conversation was over. The daughters were not introduced as new topics.

The same importance of new topics can be seen in the Ngandi texts. The passage below is part of the narrator's reminiscences about his experiences as a police tracker. He and two others had captured a criminal and taken him to the government office, where they sat waiting. Finally,

Ngandi (Heath 1978: 250)
New Topic S V
(54) *ṇi-Ted Ervin-yuŋ ṇi-yimi-ñ-ʔ* '...'
MASC:SG-Ted Ervin-ABS 3MASC:SG-say-PPUNC-0
'Ted Ervin (a high-ranking government official) said, '...'

Ted Ervin, a new topic, appears at the beginning of the clause.

The function of topics within narratives can often be seen by comparing the contexts of different constructions. The first sentence below is part of a description of the various kinds of foods the Aborigines used to collect. The narrator has just mentioned that they used to roast and eat euros and antelopine kangaroos.

Ngandi (Heath 1978: 192)

New Topic O V S
(55) *ma-d̪atam-yuŋ, barma-ga-ma-ŋi ba-d̪inʔ-d̪u-yuŋ,*
MA-water.lily.fruit-ABS 3PL/MA-SUB-get-PC PL-woman-ERG-ABS
'The women used to get water lily fruits (seed pods).'

Both the water lily fruit and the women are new information here, neither previously mentioned nor inferrable. This discussion is about types of food, however, so the water lily fruit appears first. The narrator continues discussing the food: 'We ate that food, we ate vegetable food'.

In a different narrative, the same speaker mentioned the same custom. This time, he had said, 'Then we get up and leave. We are going now for vegetable food instead of meat, for water lily root corms, fruits, and stems — we eat that.'

Ngandi (Heath 1978: 210)

New Topic S V
(56) *ba-d̪iŋʔ yanači ba-ja-wuḷup, ba-ja-d̪iŋʔ-gu*
PL-woman all.along 3PL-now-bathe 3PL-now-woman-DAT

maṇgaʔ ma-guyk barma-ma-ni, ...
maybe MA-water.lily.species 3PL/MASC-get-PRES
'The women go into the water, (that work) is for women. Maybe they get guyk, ...'

Both the women and going into the water are completely new here, as before, but this time the women appear first in the clause instead of last. This passage is about women and women's work. The women remain the topic of the next several clauses.

The same prominence of new topics can be seen in the Coos texts. The narrative cited below begins with a description of Crow and his habits. Then a new character is introduced.

Coos (Frachtenberg 1913: 15)

New Topic S V
(57) *Xyî'xē^{i} dä'mîl la^{u} ha'lqait. La^{u}*
one man (to).that.one (he).came.to.him that.one

xwändj ī^{i}lt ...
that.way (he).told.it.to.him
'Once a man came to Crow, and said, ...

The narrative continues with the man's suggestions.

1.7 Contrast

Important contrasts are not limited to new topics. Any constituent representing a focus of contrast is generally considered sufficiently important to occur early in the clause, whether it is indefinite or definite, new or old, a topic or not. These constituents represent a focus of contrast.

The following (elicited) Cayuga sentences illustrate the positions of contrasting constituents.

Cayuga					V	S
(60)	*Thę'*	*t'a:ke:ká's*	*ohya',*		*kę̥hswahéhs*	*ní:'.*
	not	do.I.like.it	fruit		I.hate.it	I
	'I don't like fruit, I hate it.'					

Cayuga					S		V
(59)	*Thę'*	*ní:'*	*t'a:ke:ká's*	*ohya',*	*Péte*	*hne:'*	*hó:ka's.*
	not	I	do.I.like.it	fruit	Pete	CONTR	he.likes.it
	'I don't like fruit, Pete does.'						

The use of the separate pronoun *ni:'* 'I, myself' in the last sentence above is interesting. Languages with pronominal affixes usually contain separate pronouns as well, although they appear much less frequently in discourse than free pronouns in languages without the affixes. Grammarians of such languages often note that the separate pronouns seem to appear near the beginning of clauses unusually often. This is no accident. In polysynthetic languages, separate pronouns have a special function; they generally indicate special emphasis or contrast. The contrastive force of the independent pronouns can be seen in the Cayuga sentence below. The speaker was provided with a context and asked to translate the English sentence 'I'm the one who broke it.'

Cayuga		
(60)	*I:'*	*atkriht.*
	I	I.broke.it
	'I'm the one who broke it.'	

Pronominal contrasts are not automatically the most important elements of their clauses, as can be seen in (58) above. They may also be used to set up a double contrast. Offered a platter of chicken, the dinner guest said:

Cayuga

(61) ***Ohsi:ná'*** *ki'* ***ní:'*** *ę:ke:k.*
leg just I I.will.eat.it
'I'll have a leg, myself.'

This reply contrasts two entities: the drumstick as opposed to other pieces, and the speaker as opposed to the other diners. Here the drumstick contrast took precedence over the diner.

The other languages exhibit similar ordering of contrastive information. In each Ngandi clause below, the initial constituent represents the focus of some contrast.

Ngandi (Heath 1978: 201)

(62) ***gu-d̪awal-ˀñirayi-gi-yuŋ*** *ma-gami-bugiˀ* *ñar-ga-jaḷ-d̪u-ŋi,*
GU-country-our-LOC-ABS MA-spear-only 1PLEX-SUB-hunt.kangaroo

gu-ni-ˀ-yuŋ *gu-d̪awal-yuŋ* *ba-wan-gu,* ***ñer-yuŋ***
GU-this-Ø-ABS GU-country-ABS PL-PRO-GEN we-ABS

gu-na-ˀ *ŋuri,*
GU-that-Ø north
'In our country we used to hunt kangaroos with spears only. This country belongs to someone else. As for us, (we were) there to the north.'

Before the Coos sentence below, the narrator described a bargain suggested by Crow. Crow wants to exchange his lightning for the evening low tide. The bargain is accepted, and Crow obtains the tide,

Coos (Frachtenberg 1913: 18)

(63) ***Halt!*** *xä'ka* ***hE*** ***lō'wak***^{u} *L!ā*^{a}.
now he the lightning has.as.booty
'while the other man came into possession of the lightning'

The contrastive pronoun *xä'ka* 'he' occurs near the beginning of the clause. The second focus of contrast, the lightning, follows.

Any kind of constituent, pronominal, nominal, or verbal, can be the focus of a contrast. In all cases the ordering is the same. If the contrast is the main point of the predication, and thus the most important, the focus of the contrast will appear initially.

1.8 The determination of word order in Cayuga, Ngandi, and Coos

1.8.1 *The newsworthiness principle*

Word order in these languages is thus based on pragmatic considerations, on the relative newsworthiness of the constituents to the discourse. An element may be newsworthy because it represents significant new information, because it introduces a new topic, or because it points out a significant contrast.

A test for the "most newsworthy first" principle is provided by questions and answers. Presumably in normal conversation, the most important constituent of an answer is that which corresponds to the interrogative word of the question. In Cayuga, this word appears initially, whether it functions as an agent, patient, time, location, or anything else.

Cayuga S-V

(64) Q. *Sǫ: ęsne:'?*
who you.two.will.go
'Who are you going with?'

A. *Sam ęyá:khne:'.*
Sam we.two will.go
'I'm going with Sam.'

O-V

(65) Q. *Tę' ho'tę' a:yę:' ihse: a:shni:nǫ'?*
what it.seems you.think you.would.buy
'What do you think you'd like to buy?'

A. *O:, akya'tawi'thrá' ki' a:yę́:' ki̥hsa:s a:khní:nǫ'.*
Oh dress just seems I.seek I.would.buy
'Well, I am just looking for a dress.'

T-V

(66) Q. *To: ti' n'aonishé' tho hekae's?*
how then so.it.lasted there they.two.were.there
'So how long were they there?'

A. *Tekhní: akyaǫtatokęhthé' konáhtękyǫ:.*
two weeks they.two.were.away
'They were away for two weeks.'

L-V

(67) Q. *Kaę ti' hęswe:'?*
where then you.all.will.go.there
'Where are you all going then?'

A. *O:, othow'eké hęyá:kwe:'.*
Oh at.the.cold we.will.go.there
'Oh, we'll go up north.'

Q-V

(68) Q. *To: ti' nika:nǫ:'?*
How then so.it.costs
'So how much does it cost then?'

A. *Kéi n'ate'wę̄nya:w'é: sikwa:ti:há nika:nǫ́:'.*
four so.hundreds a.bit.beyond so.it.costs
'It costs a little more than four hundred dollars.'

Answers to alternative questions yield the same evidence. The constituent that provides the most important information, the one whose information answers the question, appears first.

Cayuga S-V

(69) Q. *Atisn̥i̥hthaę' kę́h, John, Mary k'ishęh?*
you.two.talked ? John Mary or
'Did you talk to John or Mary?'

A. *Mary ki' akyakhn̥i̥htháę'*
Mary just we.two.talked
'I talked to Mary.'

OV

(70) Q. *Otí:, kę́h, kha:fí nikę́'ǫ ęhsnekęha'?*
tea ? coffee either you.will.drink
'Will you have tea or coffee?'

A. *Otí: ękhnékęha'.*
tea I.will.drink
'I'll have tea.'

Answers to yes-no questions provide the same evidence again.

Cayuga L-V

(71) Q. *Kahǫwakǫ́: kęh ha'káęhtahk?*
in.boat ? they.went.there
'Did they go by boat?'

A. *Thę'. Tekatęhné ha'káęhtahk.*
no in.it.flies they.went.there
'No. They went by airplane.'

Poss-V

(72) Q. *I:s kęh satshe:nę́' thó:kyę so:wa:s?*
you ? your.pet that dog
'Is that your dog?'

A. *Ęhę́ ', í:' ake:tshé:nę'.*
yes I my.pet
'Yes, it's mine.'

The same ordering characterizes Ngandi answers. The constituent that answers the question appears first.

Ngandi (Heath 1978: 250)

(73) Q. *ṇi-ñja miriʔ ṇi-ni-ʔ-yuŋ?*
MASC:SG-who Q MASC:SG-this-0-ABS
'Who is this?'

A. *Ṇi-wačinbuy ṇi-na-ri-yuŋ*
MASC:SG-Wacinbuy MASC:SG-that-IMM-ABS
'That is Wacinbuy.'

Coos questions and answers show the same pattern.

Coos (Frachtenberg 1913: 10)

(74) Q. *Eᵋxtcī'tcū mä?*
thou.what.sort person.(are)
'Who are you?'

A. *Ŋîloxqai'nîs mä îl.*
I.medicine person.(am) surely
'I am a medicine man.'

This newsworthy-first principle appears to be the same as that first described by Firbas in terms of communicative dynamism ('the degree to which a sentence element contributes to the development of the communication'), but in reverse. Do Cayuga, Ngandi, and Coos exhibit essentially the same type of ordering as a language like Czech, but backwards? If they do, and if it is assumed that a progression from theme to rheme is inherently more natural cognitively, are Cayuga, Ngandi, and Coos somehow less natural or logical?

1.8.2 *The naturalness issue*

Themes, or topics, as noted earlier, have been variously defined as the elements carrying the lowest degree of communicative dynamism or oldest information, as the starting point of an utterance (Mathesius 1939), and as the focus of the speaker's empathy (Kuno 1976). Themes establish an orientation and a perspective, so they typically appear first in a sentence (Halliday 1967). If themes do indeed provide such a point of departure, how can Cayuga, Ngandi, and Coos speakers leave them until the end?

An examination of discourse shows that these speakers do not save orienting material until the end any more than English speakers do. Narratives typically open with an establishment of the general topic of discussion. This is usually sufficiently significant to fill an entire sentence or intonation unit. (See Chafe 1980.) Other orienting devices, such as time and perhaps location, are set early as well. The following passages open narratives.

Cayuga

(75) *Ta: ahi:' ne:' a:kathro:wí' shę niyohtǫhné:' ne'*
now I.thought this I.would.tell how it.used.to.be the

swé:'keh.
long.ago
'Now I thought I would talk about how things used to be a long time ago.'

Ngandi (Heath 1978: 229)

(76) *waḷkundu-yuŋ ṇaki? waḷkundu baru-ga-maka-na,*
Walkundu-ABS there Walkundu 3PL/BU-SUB-call-PRES

ṇi-ṛuḓu-ŋi ṇi-yul-yu:::ŋ
3MASC:SG-go-PAST.CONT MASC:SG-man-ABS
'There at Walkundu (a place south of the Roper River), they call that place Walkundu, a man was going along there.'

Coos (Frachtenberg 1922: 419)

(77) *Ûx sla'tcînī.*
they.two.cousins.(were).mutually
'Once upon a time there were two cousins.'

If new themes appear early, what of the most common themes, those already established and present in the mind of the speaker? Speakers typically establish a topic and stay with it for a certain length of time. In the absence of counterindications, hearers normally expect the topic to remain constant. Since it is expected, a continuing topic need not occupy a prominent position in the clause. Reference to it within the pronominal prefixes on the verb confirms its continuation without unduly distracting the hearer. The hearer is not actually waiting in suspense until the verb appears with its pronominal markers, since a topic shift would normally be signalled early in the clause.

Word order in Cayuga, Ngandi, and Coos, is thus not simply a mirror image of that in a language like Czech. The overall principle is somewhat similar, in that items are arranged according to their newsworthiness, but the mirror image model is inappropriate in two ways. For one, elements that establish a significant orientation for the first time, whether it be the point of view of the topic, the time, the location, or the reliability of the statement, occur early, just as they do in Czech. For another, items that signal the continuation of such orientation, such as an unchanged topic, time, or location, often do not appear as separate constituents at all, but rather as bound affixes.

1.8.3 *The markedness of pragmatic ordering*

These are not the only differences between languages like Cayuga, Ngandi, and Coos, and those like Czech. As mentioned above, members of the Prague School and, more recently, Thompson (1978), have noted that languages can vary considerably in the extent to which surface word order is controlled by syntactic or pragmatic considerations. In languages like English, order is determined primarily by the syntactic functions of constituents. In languages like Czech, their pragmatic functions play a greater role. Cayuga, Ngandi, and Coos, would appear more similar to Czech in this respect.

They are not the same, however. Recall that when presented with sentences containing alternative word orders, Cayuga speakers will not even choose a preferred order out of context. Marta Roth informs me that Czech speakers, on the other hand, are very conscious of "normal" word order. Alternate orders apparently do occur more frequently in Czech than in English. Yet when presented with these orders out of context, speakers are strongly aware of their marked status.

Asked to translate transitive sentences like 'Daniel quickly drank the milk' out of context, this Czech speaker consistently supplied SVO versions like that below.

Czech	S		V	O
(78)	*Daniel*	*rychle*	*vypil*	*mléko.*
	Daniel	quickly	drank	milk

'Daniel quickly drank the milk.'

(Vanessa Flashner informs me that among her spoken Polish texts, approximately 87 percent of the clauses show SVO or VO order.)

Asked for an appropriate full answer to subject questions like 'Who drank the milk?', the Czech speaker simply added heavy stress to the subject, rather than altering word order. (As in English, one-word answers like 'Daniel' are perfectly appropriate. Transitive sentences with full subject and object noun phrases are probably no more frequent in natural Czech discourse than in English.) Verb-initial orders were interpreted as questions, and object-initial orders as fragments of relative clauses. When presented with the alternative order SOV, the speaker agreed that this was grammatical, but would require some obvious reason for the added emphasis on the verb and adverb, such as the added clause below.

Czech	S	O		V		V
(79)	*Daniel*	*mléko*	*rychle*	*vypil*	*a*	*odešel.*
	Daniel	milk	quickly	drank	and	left

'Daniel quickly drank up the milk and left.'

These responses do not contradict the work of the Prague School linguists. Firbas states, for example, "Even in Czech, of course, the possibility of freely changing the order of words is limited" (1964: 278 note 17). Pragmatic considerations apparently do in fact enter into surface word ordering in Czech more freely than in English, perhaps due in part to the case suffixes on nouns. It is still a very different process from that operating in languages like Cayuga, Ngandi, and Coos, however. Pragmatic reordering in Czech results in relatively marked structures sometimes described as "archaic" or "overly literary", whereas Cayuga speakers seem less inclined to find any order more marked than the others.

Does this mean that languages like Cayuga, Ngandi, and Coos have no mechanisms for highlighting unusual pragmatic situations? Not surprisingly, they all do have constructions exactly for this purpose, and these constructions are used somewhat more frequently than devices such as clefting and pseudo clefting or topicalization in English.

In Ngandi, such constructions involve the prefix *-ga-*, which sometimes functions as a weak subordinator, although it occurs freely on main verbs. Heath (1978: 122-3) describes the construction as follows.

> The usual way to focus a constituent is to put it at the beginning of the clause, followed by a subordinated verb [with] *-ga-*. There appear to be no significant restrictions on the type of constituent which may be focused in this way, and examples are attested of NPs in virtually all surface cases (except perhaps the genitive) and of various kinds of adverbs occurring in focused position. Ngandi focus constructions may be literally translated with English topicalised or cleft sentences, but it should be emphasised that the Ngandi constructions are much more common than these English types.

He then provides examples of focused constituents of all types. Here are a few.

Ngandi (Heath 1978: 123)

(80) *ṇi-Conklin, ŋaya, ṇi-jambuḷaŋa, ñar-**ga**-ṛiḓ-i.*
MASC:SG-Conklin I MASC:SG-Wallace 1PLEX-SUB-go-PPUN
'Conklin, I, and Wallace were the ones who went.'

(81) *jipaʔ guṇukuwič ñar-**ga**-ñawk-ḓu-ŋ.*
later tomorrow 1PLEX-SUB-speak-AUG-FUT
'Tomorrow is when we will talk.'

Coos shows similar constructions.

Coos (Frachtenberg 1913: 17)

(82) *Tsäyä'na^{u}tc wîx:ī'lîs lᴇla^{u}*
small.(PL).in.the.manner.of food that.is.the.one

qaʟ!āxex:ī'we.
it.begins.to.flop.back.and.forth.
'All kinds of food (fishes) began to flop around.'

Cayuga also makes frequent use of such devices.

Cayuga

(83) *Ha'te:yǫ́: **ki'** ase'shǫ́:'ǫh, **né:'** thó:kye teyéhsnye'.*
all.kinds just new.ones it.is that one.cares.for.it
'All kinds of vegetables, that is what they're growing.'

Cayuga, Ngandi, and Coos, have devices for accomplishing the same grammatical and pragmatic functions as languages like English and Czech, but these devices are distributed differently over various areas of the grammar. One result of this is a radical difference in the degree of markedness of alternative word orders.

2. Standard strategies for detecting basic order and pragmatically based languages

As noted earlier, the usual criteria for establishing the basic word order of a language include statistical frequency, descriptive simplicity, and pragmatic neutrality. What do these criteria indicate when there is no arbitrarily defined basic order, that is, when all ordering is the result of pragmatic considerations?

2.1 Statistical frequency

Does the fact that word order is pragmatically based mean that all possible orders appear with equal frequency? In fact it does not. On the relatively rare occasions when a single clause contains both a separate subject nominal and an object nominal, the order OVS appears slightly more often than the other logical possibilities. Does this mean that OVS should be considered the basic order after all? Establishing a fundamental order on the basis of a slight statistical advantage in a comparatively rare construction seems unnecessary, unless it can provide some significant descriptive or typological advantage. In fact, the assumption of an arbitrary basis could cut off fruitful exploration prematurely. The inequalities in occurring orders in languages like Cayuga, Ngandi, and Coos, reflect interesting facts about the actual workings of language. The fact that subjects appear near the end of clauses more often than at the beginning in a pragmatically based system indicates that subjects are typically the least newsworthy. This finding is not unrelated to Givón's statistical studies of definiteness. As he notes, "in human language in context, the subject is overwhelmingly definite" (1979: 51). The fact that separate objects appear more often near the beginning of clauses indicates that objects are more often used to convey newsworthy information. Although Givón found that in general, direct objects are roughly 50 percent indefinite and 50 percent definite in English texts, "the

50 percent indefinites are the bulk of the indefinite nouns in the text . . . The accusative or direct object position is thus the major avenue for introducing new referential arguments into discourse, at least in English." (1979: 52).

2.2 Descriptive simplicity

A major justification for assuming the existence of an arbitrary, syntactically determined constituent order in the description of a language would be its power as a descriptive device. For languages with relatively rigid, syntactically defined surface word order, the establishment of this order at the outset has obvious utility. The description of rarer, morphologically and pragmatically marked alternative orders as the result of the movement of constituents out of their normal position is mechanically simple. For languages like Cayuga, Ngandi, and Coos, however, it is not at all clear that arbitrarily selecting one order as basic, then scrambling this order a large proportion of the time, is simple, revealing, or realistic. Since alternative orders are unaccompanied by additional morphological material, there is also no formal motivation for one choice over another.

2.3 Pragmatic neutrality

A third criterion for determining the basic constituent order of a language is the selection of the least pragmatically marked order, that order which presupposes the least. As noted earlier, it has been suggested that the most pragmatically neutral sentences of all must be discourse-initial, since there is no preceding linguistic context to establish information. Pullum (1977: 266) remarks, "where a discourse environment could not be present, i.e. discourse-initially, . . . the basic order would be expected." In fact, as mentioned above, the beginnings of narratives generally represent an especially highly marked situation. Topics must be established before anything else can be attended to. Confining a study of word order to initial utterances would limit the investigation to a highly specialized corpus of utterances with a relatively unusual function, that of establishing referents and point of view.

Most discourse does not even open with "main, declarative, affirmative, active clauses". Conversations often begin with questions. In fact, of 30 recorded Cayuga conversations, 21 began with questions. (Greetings were not counted as initial sentences.) Another 2 opened with commands.

The relatively rare declarative conversation openers provide little indication of a basic constituent order, since they consist almost solely of verbs and particles.

Cayuga

(84) *Akǫ:kę́’ sǫ:té’ syęthwáhsǫh.*
I.saw.you last.night you.were.planting
‘I saw you planting last night.’

(85) *Kwé:, tętwa’ęnáę’ akę́’ ęyó:hę’.*
Well, we’re.playing.snowsnake it.seems tomorrow
‘Well, it seems we’re playing snowsnake tomorrow.’

(86) *A:yę́:’ s’atrehtḁhétk’ęse:’.*
it.seems your.car.got.bad.on.you
‘You seem to be having car trouble.’

Narrative openers present the same problem. The two sentences below open long narratives, the first highly formal, the second more informal.

Cayuga

(87) *Ęke:ka:tǫ́:’ shę nikyḁǫ̥hwętsḁhkyǫ́ ne:’ tshiḫwa’hé*
I.will.tell.it how so.the.earth.originated it.is when.first

tsha’ǫhwętsá:tęh.
when.the.earth.began
‘I will tell how the earth originated; when the earth first began.’

(88) *Né:’ ki’ kyę: thó:kyę ne’ a:sanits’ǫta:tó:wa:t*
it.is just this that the you.would.hunt.fish
‘This is how you hunt fish.’

All of these opening sentences are characterized by their small number of major constituents. This is due in part to the high productivity of noun incorporation in Cayuga. (See Mithun 1984). Most of the verbs in the examples above contain an incorporated noun stem (‘pole’, ‘car’, ‘earth’, ‘fish’). These nouns are incorporated for a reason. Cayuga speakers normally introduce one new concept at a time, not unlike speakers of other languages. The single verb represents a single, complex, but unified concept.

As can be seen in (76) and (77) above, narrative openings in Ngandi and Coos generally illustrate the same characteristic of few major constituents, because their function is to introduce one new idea at a time.

The one-idea-at-a-time tendency is also reflected in the so-called "afterthought constructions" which appear frequently throughout texts in all of these languages. Often when a full nominal appears, it is not an integral part of the intonation unit containing its predicate. During the description of how to hunt rabbits, for example, the Cayuga speaker said:

Cayuga

(89) *Onatate:nyǫ́'* *s'ekyę:',* *ne'* *kwa'yǫ'.*
they.have.roads you.know the rabbit
'They have roads, you know, rabbits.'

The intonation break between *s'ekyę:'* 'you know' and *ne' kwa'yǫ'* 'the rabbit(s)' is more a change in pitch than a pause. Final nominals like the rabbits above are pronounced with significantly lower pitch and often somewhat softer volume than the preceding constituents. Such nominals are not literally "afterthoughts", in the sense that the speaker simply forgot to mention them earlier. They are provided as insurance that the hearer will be able to keep reference straight. Often they repeat a referent which has not been mentioned for a while, like the rabbits in (89). In other cases, they are used to clarify the identify of a referent, as below. The verb 'to fish' in (90) does not contain any overt mention of 'fish', so when the speaker said 'that is what we will live on', he felt it necessary to clarify what 'that' referred to.

Cayuga

(90) *Ęyǫkwatahnyǫ:k.* *Ne:'* *ki'* *tshǫ:* *kwáhs*
we.will.put.hook.in.water it.is just only all

ęyakyonhéhkǫhǫ:k, *otsǫ'tá'* *kanyo'shǫ́:'ǫ* *ne'* *kyę:'ǫ́* *hni'*
we.will.live.on.it *fish* *wild.animals* *the* *I.guess* *too*

tę́' ho'tę́' *ęyakwatshę́:i'.*
what we.will.find
'We will fish. That is mainly what we will live on, fish, game, too, I guess, whatever we find.'

Such constructions are not equivalent to regular subject or object noun phrases in languages like English, in that they are not as tightly bound to their predicates intonationally. Because of the pronominal prefixes, they are never necessary for grammaticality. Their lower and softer pronunciation mirrors their function as backgrounded appositives.

Ngandi and Coos also frequently exhibit such constructions. Heath (1978: 53) mentions "the "afterthought" construction so common to languages in this area, where a core nuclear clause is pronounced and then one or more constituents giving more precise specification of arguments in the clause are added after a pause." During his description of life in the old days, a Ngandi speaker was discussing various tools. He said:

Ngandi (Heath 1978: 190)
(91) *a-jeler bara-ma-ŋi, ba-jawuʔ-jawulpa-d̯u-yuŋ,*
A-stone.axe 3PL/A-get-PCONT PL-RDP-old man-ERG-ABS
'The old people used to get stone axes.'

The final noun phrase serves simply to remind us of the continuing topic.

The Coos narrator cited in (92) had just mentioned that all kinds of food began to flop around. Hearing the noise, Crow decided to open his eyes, but someone yelled at him. After a while, Crow was permitted to open his eyes.

Coos (Frachtenberg 1913: 18)
(92) *Tsō k:îlō'wît hᴇ wîx:ī'lîs,*
now (he).saw.it the food
'He saw the different kinds of food.'

The final noun phrase serves to ensure that we remember what was there to be seen.

Such constructions also provide a device for keeping heavy information from blocking the flow of discourse. When a constituent is so heavy that its early appearance would interfere with the presentation of information, it may be represented early in the clause by a deictic particle, then filled in later by the "afterthought."

Coos (Frachtenberg 1913: 16)
(93) *Mīʟ halt! eᴱne xle'îtc eᴱʟ!äts ten̥*
please now thou with.it.with thou.speak this.my

xʟ!ē'yîs.
with.language
'Now try my language.'

The usual devices for discovering basic constituent order thus provide little clear evidence for any underlying order in these languages. The statistically more frequent orders are no more pragmatically neutral than any others. Discourse-initial sentences do not provide good models of neutral order, since their pragmatic function is to establish the initial theme of the discourse. They are, furthermore, frequently non-declarative, and in any case rarely contain enough constituents to shed any light on basic order at all.

3. Word order typology and pragmatically based ordering

Another justification for assuming the existence of an arbitrary, syntactically defined constituent order underlying every language would be its utility as a basis from which to predict other structural features. Discovering correlations among different constituent orders has been a major goal of word order typologists since the pioneering work of Greenberg (1966). Greenberg and many others, such as Lehmann (1973, 1974), Venneman (1974, 1975), and Hawkins (1979, 1980, 1983), have uncovered strong patterns among the types of word orders that occur within languages. At the same time, their work has revealed the complexity of ordering relations. Many statements must include provisos like "with overwhelmingly greater than chance frequency" or "usually", etc. The formulation of such principles as tendencies rather than absolute universals does not render them invalid, but, rather points up the number of factors involved. Hawkins has carefully excluded from his work those languages in which the determination of underlying order is problematic, so that the strength of his conclusions is not compromised by inaccurate starting points. This exclusion has of course been both appropriate and necessary in initial investigations. It would now seem, however, that an understanding of the applicability of word order universals to languages exhibiting little evidence of basic word order should be a useful part of the formulation of such unversals.

Greenberg's first universal involves the relative order of subjects and objects:

> 1. In declarative sentences with nominal subject and object, the dominant order is almost always one in which the subject precedes the object. (1966: 110)

If the dominant order is assumed to be the most frequent, then Cayuga, Ngandi, and Coos are clearly exceptions to this first principle, since the order OVS shows a small statistical advantage. Greenberg included the word "almost" for a reason explained in a note:

> 5. Siuslaw and Coos, which are Penutian languages of Oregon, and Coeur d'Alene, a Salishan language, are exceptions. (1966: 105)

(The sources of Greenberg's Coos information were Frachtenberg 1913 and 1922, those used here.)

Other universals posited by Greenberg involve ordering relations between verbs and their auxiliaries, adpositions and their objects, and between nouns and modifiers such as adjectives, relative clauses, numbers, and demonstratives. As noted earlier, a salient characteristic of languages like Cayuga, Ngandi, and Coos, is their high polysynthesis. What other languages express in several words, these languages often express in one. This fact has a significant effect on questions of ordering.

In some cases, there is no basic word order simply because a concept is expressed in a single word. The relative positions of verbs and auxiliaries in Cayuga and Ngandi are such a case. Like a number of the languages in Greenberg's original survey, these languages have no separate auxiliaries. Tense, aspect, and mode are expressed by combinations of verbal prefixes and suffixes. (Coos has several separate particles with temporal meanings such as 'about to', 'shall/will', 'intend', and 'usually/frequently/ habitually'. Each of these can either precede or follow the verb (Frachtenberg 1922: 383-4).)

In Cayuga, Ngandi and Coos, the functions performed by prepositions or postpositions in other languages are often accomplished by affixes on nouns.

Cayuga

(94) *Kanyata:'-**ke*** *ha'he'.*
lake-**LOC** there.he.went
'He went to the lake.'

Ngandi (Heath 1978: 189)

(95) *ba-ga-ṛuḓu-ŋi gu-ḓawal-**gič**-uŋ,*
3PL-SUB-go-PCONT GU-country-**ALL**-ABS
'They went to (their) country.'

Coos (Frachtenberg 1922: 323)

(96) ***x**-kwîle'L-**ē̆ⁱtc*** *n̥-djī*
from-sweathouse-**in** I-came
'I came from the sweat-house.'

Mixing discussions of the relative orders of roots and affixes with those of the orders of words would seriously interfere with an understanding of universal syntactic principles.

Some locations are expressed by separate words in these languages. A Cayuga speaker was asked to translate the English sentences given here as glosses. The sentences were thus not spontaneous responses to actual situations; so, although technically grammatical, they may be somewhat unnatural pragmatically. In the first sentence, *ohna'ke:* 'behind' might appear to function like a preposition.

(97) a. *Ohna'ké: shę kanǫhsó:t ha'étakse:'*
behind where house.stands there.she.ran
'She ran behind the house.'

A few moments later, the sentence below was given. This time, *ohná'ke:* might appear to function like a postposition.

(97) b. *Shę kanǫhsó:t ohna'ké: ha'étakse:'.*
where house.stands behind there.she.ran
'She ran behind the house.'

According to the speaker, both are equally grammatical. In fact, an examination of the use of *ohná'ke:* in spontaneous discourse indicates that it is not an adposition at all, but, rather, a deictic particle, used appositionally in the sentences above. Hawkins (1983: 16) has suggested that prepositions and postpositions are better and more general type indicators than constituent orders VSO and SOV. Languages like Cayuga, Ngandi, and Coos, do not provide counterexamples to this hypothesis, but neither does the hypothesis provide a motivation for chosing an arbitrary constituent order.

Other ordering relations first investigated by Greenberg involve nouns and their modifiers, such as adjectives, relative clauses, and genitives. In languages like Cayuga, Ngandi, and Coos, adjectival words tend to be predications. Heath notes:

> Noun-phrases which have more than one constituent are typically formed by apposition ... By using the term 'apposition' I am trying to indicate that the various constituents are often formally independent of each other; they often each have a complete set of affixes and may be separated from each other by pauses and even by other constituents such as a verb. (1978: 52)

This of course reflects the one-idea-at-a-time tendency. It is extremely difficult to find single noun phrases containing both an adjectival constituent and a separate noun in spontaneous discourse. Instead, the modifier is normally a separate predication, as in the Cayuga, Ngandi, and Coos passages below.

Cayuga

(98) *Ne:' ki' he' hne:' wakyes'aké ne' a:sató:wa:t.*
it.is just also CONTR it.is.easy the you.would.hunt
'Also, it's an easy way to hunt, as well.'

Ngandi (Heath 1978: 268)

(99) *ṇi-wolo ṇi-yul-yuŋ, ṇi-warjak,*
MASC:SG-that MASC:SG-man-ABS MASC:SG-bad
'That man is a bad man.'

Coos (Frachtenberg 1922: 424)

(100) *L!a'nēx ye$^{\varepsilon}$ne^{u} kwä'sîs.*
new.is thy ball
'Your ball is new.'

Since these are predicate adjectives rather than attributive adjectives, the prediction does not apply.

In Cayuga and Ngandi, adjectival verbs may incorporate the nouns they modify to form a single constituent. The resulting complex verb can then function either as a predication or as a nominal.

Cayuga

(101) *akya'tawi'thr-í:yo:*
(it-)-dress-nice
'a/the dress is nice' or 'a/the nice dress'

Ngandi (Heath 1978: 262)

(102) *ŋi-yuŋ buluki? gu-d̪awal-wiṛipu-gi ŋa-ga-ṇ-i:, ...*
I-ABS also GU-country-other-LOC 1SG-SUB-sit-PC
'I was staying in a different country, ...'

Again, since such expressions consist of single words, the relative orders of their constituent morphemes cannot be compared to the relative orders of nouns and adjectives in languages like English or French.

Because words corresponding to adjectives in languages like English are full predications in Cayuga, Ngandi, and Coos, the distinction between adjectives and relative clauses is not a sharp one. As in the case of adjectives, material translated into English relative clauses may simply be a separate sentence, as in the Coos example below.

Coos (Frachtenberg 1913: 6)

(103) *Ûx kwîna'ē̈ⁱwat hE hemkwî'tîs. Hats*
they two.look.at.it.frequently the heavy.waves just

yî'qa xwändj wēL!L!ä'nī lE xāᵃp.
continually in.this.manner goes.over.back.and.forth the water
'They looked frequently at the waves, that rolled back and forth continually.'

Alternatively, material corresponding to English relative clauses and their heads may be incorporated into single words, as in the Cayuga example below.

Cayuga

(104) *A'aw̥ę̥hthé' ne' aket'ithrǫ:ni'.*
it.got.strong the I.made.tea
'The tea I made really got strong.'

On the extremely rare occasions when separate constituents appear comparable to adjectives or relative clauses in other languages, the modifiers and heads can appear in either order. Example (105) was elicited as a translation.

Cayuga Modifier N

(105) *Kę:kę́: nikay'ato'tę́:' aketshe:nę́' takú:s oká:nyas.*
it.is.white such.is.its.body my.pet. cat it.is.lousy
'My white cat has fleas.'

N Modifier

(106) *Thó ti' ni:yóht nę:kyę́ ne:' akǫ:kwé kowíyaętatre'.*
there so so.it.is this it.is she.person she.is.getting.a.child
'That's the way it is with this woman who is expecting a child.'

Ngandi (Heath 1978: 230) Modifier N

(107) *a-ja-bolk-d̪-i a-d̪arpal a-jara a-ñalk,*
A-now-appear-AUG-PP A-big A-what's.it A-rain
'A big rain appeared then.'

N Modifier

(108) *ba-wanʔ-d̪u-ni gu-jaṛk gu-wanar*
3PL-look-AUG-PR GU-water GU-huge
'They see a huge body of water.'

Coos (Frachtenberg 1913: 14) Modifier N

(109) *Hēkwa'īn lE'γī xkwî'na^{u}tc le'ûx hä'wîs L!tā.*
very good appearance their ready land
'The appearance of the world which they had created was very good.'

Coos (Frachtenberg 1913: 13) N Modifier

(110) *Tsō ā'yu ûx kwîna'ē^{i}wat le'ûx*
now surely they.two.look.at.them.frequently their.two
mî'l̄aq sī^{i}L'nē^{i}.
arrows joined.together
'They shook the joined arrows.'

Nominal-genitive orders show the same variation. A noun identifying a possessor may appear on either side of the possessed noun. Both of the genitive constructions below were taken from the Cayuga cosmology legend.

Cayuga

(111) *ne' tho nę:kyę aethwé' nę:kyę k'anów'ake*
the there this we.would.put.it this on.its.back
Genitive N
shęnhǫ́: niyakota:tę́ǫ, kanyahtęko:wá k'anów'ake.
where so.she.remains great.turtle on.its.back
'We would put this (dirt) there on his back where she is sitting, on the big turtle's back.'

Cayuga N Genitive

(112) *akoti'skhwáę' nę:kyę k'anów'ake nę:kyę kanyahtękó:wa*
they.set.her this on.its.back this great.turtle
'they set her on the back of this great turtle'

Compare the two Coos genitive constructions below.

Coos (Frachtenberg 1913: 8) Genitive N

(113) *... ûx lemī'yat lE mexä'ye û kwä'x^{u}.*
they.two.to.stand.up.caused.it the eagle his feathers
'Then they stuck into the ground the feathers of an eagle.'

(Frachtenberg 1913: 15) N Genitive

(114) *Halt! xä lä û L!ē'yîs hE tsn̥'na.*
now he his his language the thunder
'The other man received Thunder's language.'

Finally, several constructions do exist in which the order of constituents is constant. Numbers tend to precede the nominals they quantify, but this is of course consistent with the newsworthiness principle. The relative order of determiners and nominals is generally invariable. Definiteness is not obligatorily marked in Cayuga, and no indefinite article is used. As noted earlier, an optional particle *ne'* may precede definite nominals, including proper and possessed nouns. When it appears, it precedes the nominal it modifies. This position is, of course, functional. In Cayuga, morphological verbs, like any clauses, can function as syntactic nominals. They need carry no overt markers of nominalization. The result is that normal discourse can consist largely of verbs. The particle *ne'* is most often used to indicate that what follows is functioning syntactically as a nominal.

Cayuga
(115) *akaǫnihnató:k* ***ne'*** *nóne:'* *nę:kyę* *ne'* *kowiyáę̨tatre'*.
they.noticed the you.know this the she.is.getting.a.baby
' ... they noticed that she was expecting.'

The Coos article *lE/hE* is similar. Frachtenberg notes, "the article has a general nominalizing function, and when prefixed to adverbs, adjectives, etc., gives them the force of nouns." (1922: 320)

Coos (Frachtenberg 1913: 50)
(116) *N̥'ne* *ītE* *lE* *e*^{E}*dōwāyExtā'îs* *qa*^{u}*'wa*
I.(am) EMPH **the** you.wanted night
'I am the one (whom) you wanted last night.'

If these particles floated throughout sentences, their function as cues to the roles of following constituents would be compromised.

Except for Greenberg's first syntactic universal, Cayuga, Ngandi, and Coos provide strong evidence neither for nor against the most discussed word order universals. Most of the universals simply do not apply, because they are defined over rigid word orders. Positing a basic, syntactically defined constituent order for such languages provides little predictive power. The recognition of pragmatically based languages is crucial to serious work on syntactic topology, however, not only because they represent a significant proportion of the world's languages, but also because of the obvious danger of misclassifying them. As many of the elicited examples cited earlier demonstrate, it is only too easy to force a language into an inappropriate syntactic model on the basis of data elicited or analyzed out of context.

4. The pragmatically based type

Against a backdrop of Indo-European languages, the Cayuga, Ngandi, and Coos pragmatic ordering of constituents from highest to lowest communicative dynamism seems unusual. Yet this phenomenon is actually not as rare as might be assumed. It is especially common among languages that also share another morphological characteristic: a full set of substantive bound pronouns referring to all core arguments. Many languages contain bound pronouns for only first and second persons, like Lakhota or Parengi (Aze and Aze 1973), or for only first, second, and some third persons, like Caddo. Such languages more often exhibit a basic syntactically defined constituent order; Lakhota, Parengi, and Caddo are basically verb-final.

A crucial feature of purely pragmatically ordering languages may be the nature of the grammatical relationships between the verb and associated constituents. In languages like Cayuga, Ngandi, and Coos, the pronouns bear the primary case relations to the verb. The associated noun phrases function grammatically more as appositives to the pronominal affixes, rather than directly as verbal arguments themselves.

5. Conclusion

An assumption upon which much current descriptive and typological theory is based, namely, that all languages have some basic, syntactically defined, word order, is thus not universally valid. In a number of languages, the order of constituents does not reflect their syntactic functions at all, but rather their pragmatic functions: their relative newsworthiness within the discourse at hand. Constituents may be newsworthy because they introduce pertinent, new information, present new topics, or indicate a contrast.

These pragmatically based languages differ in several important ways from some of the more familiar, syntactically based languages that exhibit "pragmatic reordering" such as right and left dislocation. First, in syntactically based languages, pragmatic reordering is highly marked. Deviation from the basic, syntactically defined word order indicates an unusual situation. In pragmatically based languages, on the other hand, all ordering reflects pragmatic considerations. Unusual situations are marked by other means. Second, in syntactically based languages, pragmatic reordering is usually assumed to result in a theme-rheme order, with elements of lower communicative dynamism at the beginning of clauses, followed by increasingly more important or newsworthy elements. In the pragmatically based languages examined here, the order is nearly the reverse. Constituents appear in descending order of newsworthiness. This does not result in a simple rheme-theme order, however. New themes, newsworthy in their own right, appear early, as do other orienting elements like time and location. Continuing themes, as well as continuing times and locations, usually do not appear as separate constituents at all. Since pragmatically based languages are typically highly polysynthetic, such information is often referenced morphologically within the verb.

Languages of this type often share another structural feature: full sets of obligatory bound pronouns. It is actually these pronouns that bear the primary grammatical relations to their verbs. In pragmatically ordered languages, separate noun phrases can function somewhat differently than in languages without bound pronouns. They typically serve more as appositives to the bound pronouns than as primary arguments themselves.

Pragmatically based languages do not provide strong evidence against most word order typologies. Most of the implicational universals that come out of such typologies are simply inapplicable. It is only too easy, however, to misclassify languages of this type on the basis of the criteria usually employed to determine basic order; such misclassification could have serious consequences for any typology purporting to be exhaustive.

Notes

1. This paper was originally written in 1983 and presented at the conference on Coherence and Grounding in Discourse held at the University of Oregon in the spring of 1984. The Proceedings of the conference did not appear until 1987.

2. I am very grateful to Cayuga speakers Marge Henry, Reg Henry, and Jim Skye, who generously contributed their expertise. I especially appreciate the many long hours of patience contributed by Mr. Henry, as well as his insight and keen sensitivity to the intricacies of his language. I am also very grateful to Marta Roth for sharing her expertise on Czech, to Sandra Thompson for many helpful suggestions, and to Wallace Chafe for fruitful discussions about discourse in general.

References

Anderson, J. M. & C. Jones, eds 1974. *Historical Linguistics 1.* Amsterdam: North Holland.

Aze, F. Richard & Trish Aze. 1973. "Parengi Texts." In: *Trail*, 213-362.

Boas, Franz, ed. 1922. *Handbook of American Indian Languages.* (= Bureau of American Ethnology Bulletin 40.2.) Washington: Government Printing Office.

Chafe, Wallace. 1980. "The Deployment of Consciousness in the Production of a Narrative." In: Chafe, ed., 9-50.

Chafe, Wallace. ed. 1980. *The Pear Stories: Cognitive, Cultural, and Linguistic Aspects of Narrative Production*. Norwood, N. J.: Ablex Publishing Corp.

Chomsky, Noam. 1957. *Syntactic Structures*. The Hague: Mouton.

Chomsky, Noam. 1965. *Aspects of the Theory of Syntax*. Cambridge, Mass.: MIT Press.

Clyne, P. et al., eds. 1979. *Papers from the Fifteenth Regional Meeting of the Chicago Linguistics Society*. Chicago: University of Chicago.

Cole, Peter & Jerrold Sadock, eds. 1977. *Grammatical Relations.* (= Syntax and Semantics Vol. 8.) New York: Academic Press.

Dryer, Matthew. 1983. "Coos Word Order." Paper presented at the Western Conference on Linguistics, University of Oregon, Eugene.

Firbas, Jan. 1964. "On Defining the Theme in Functional Sentence Analysis." *Travaux Linguistiques de Prague* 1.267-280.

Firbas, Jan. 1972. "On the Interplay of Prosodic and Non-Prosodic Means of Functional Sentence Perspective." In: Fried, 77-94.

Frachtenberg, Leo J. 1913. *Coos Texts.* (= Columbia University Contributions to Anthropology Vol 1.) New York: Columbia University Press.

Frachtenberg, Leo J. 1922. "Coos". In: Boas, 297-430.

Fried, V., ed. 1972. *The Prague School of Linguistics and Language Teaching*. London: Oxford University Press.

Givón, T. 1979. *On Understanding Grammar*. New York: Academic Press.

Givón, T. 1983. "Topic Continuity in Discourse: an Introduction." In: Givón, 1-43.

Givón, T. 1983. *Topic Continuity in Discourse.* Amsterdam: John Benjamins.

Greenberg, J.H. 1966. "Some Universals of Grammar with Particular Reference to the Order of Meaningful Elements." In: Greenberg, ed., 73-113.

Greenberg, J.H. ed. 1966. *Universals of Language*, 2nd ed. Cambridge, Mass.: MIT Press.

Halliday, M.A.K. 1967. "Notes on Transitivity and Theme in English." *Journal of Linguistics* 3.37-81, 199-244.

Hawkins, John A. 1979. "Implicational Universals as Predictors of Word Order Change." *Language* 55.618-648.

Hawkins, John A. 1980. "On Implicational and Distributional Universals of Word Order." *Journal of Linguistics* 16(2).193-235.

Hawkins, John A. 1983. *Word Order Universals*. New York: Academic Press.

Heath, Jeffrey. 1978. *Ngandi Grammar, Texts, and Dictionary*. Canberra: Australian Institute of Aboriginal Studies.

Kuno, Susumo. 1976. "Subject, Theme and Speaker's Empathy: a Re-examination of Relativization Phenomena." In: Li, 417-444.

Lehmann, W.P. 1973. "A Structural Principle of Language and its Implications." *Language* 49.47-66.
Lehmann, W.P. 1974. *Proto-Indo-European Syntax*. Austin: University of Texas Press.
Li, Charles N., ed. 1975. *Word Order and Word Order Change*. Austin: University of Texas Press.
Li, Charles N., ed. 1976. *Subject and Topic*. New York: Academic Press.
Li, Charles N. & Sandra Thompson. 1976. "On the Issue of Word Order in a Synchronic Grammar: a Case Against 'Movement Transformations'." *Lingua* 39.169-181.
Lyons, John. 1977. *Semantics*. Cambridge: Cambridge University Press.
Mathesius, Vilem. 1928. "On the Linguistic Characterology of Modern English." *Actes du Premier congres international de linguistes à la Haye*.
Mathesius, Vilem. 1939. "O tak zvanem aktualnim cleneni vetnem." (On the so-called functional sentence perspective). SaS 5.171-174. (Reprinted in *Cestina a obecny jazykozpyt* (The Czech language and general linguistics). Prague 1947, 234-242).
McCawley, James D. 1970. "English as a VSO Language." *Language* 46.286 299.
Mithun, Marianne. 1984. "The Evolution of Noun Incorporation." *Language* 60.847-894.
Mithun, Marianne. 1988. When Grammaticization is Superfluous. Paper presented at the Symposium on Grammaticization, University of Oregon, Eugene. To appear as "The Role of Motivation in the Emergence of Grammatical Categories: the Grammaticization of Subjects. In: Traugott and Heine.
Pullum, Geoffrey K. 1977. "Word Order Universals and Grammatical Relations. In: Cole and Sadock, 249-77.
Pullum, Geoffrey K. 1981. "Object-Initial Languages." *International Journal of American Linguistics* 47.192-214.
Thompson, Sandra A. 1978. "Modern English from a Typological Point of View: Some Implications of the Function of Word Order." *Linguistische Berichte* 54.19-35.
Tomlin, Russ & Richard Rhodes. 1979. "An Introduction to Information Distribution in Ojibwa." In: Clyne et al., 302-320. Reprinted in this volume.
Trail, R. ed. 1973. *Patterns in Clause, Sentence, and Discourse in Selected Languages of India and Nepal. Part III, Texts.* Norman, Oklahoma: Summer Institute of Linguistics.
Traugott, Elizabeth C. & Bernd Heine eds. 1991. *Approaches to Grammaticalization*, 2 Volumes. Amsterdam: Benjamins.
Vennemann, Theo. 1974. "Topics, Subjects and Word Order: from SXV to SVX via TVX." In: Anderson and Jones, 339-376.
Vennemann, Theo. 1975. "An Explanation of Drift." In: Li, 269-305.

Basic Word Order in Two "Free Word Order" Languages[1]

Ken Hale
Massachusetts Institute of Technology, Cambridge MA

0. Introduction

Mithun (1987; see also this volume) has recently questioned the notion that all languages have a "basic word order", where this is taken to be a strictly grammatical notion, governed by strictly grammatical principles. In an excellent study of three languages belonging to the type commonly said to have "free word order", she shows that certain generally accepted tests for determining basic word order do not identify such a word order for any of these languages. Instead, observed word order there is governed by a pragmatic consideration, to wit, the "relative newsworthiness of constituents to the discourse" (p. 304), and not by narrowly grammatical considerations which are relevant to "basic" constituent order. The present paper attempts to elaborate somewhat on Mithun's observations by examining another pair of so-called "free word order languages" — Papago (Uto-Aztecan, American Southwest) and Warlpiri (Pama-Nyungan, Central Australia) — in an effort to develop a conception of grammar and language which distinguishes clearly between word order as a grammatical phenomenon and word order as an aspect of language use and discourse, a distinction also made by Thompson (1978) and Dryer (1989), among others. The two languages I have chosen to discuss are appropriate to this discussion because, while both exhibit a surface ordering of constituents which qualifies as Mithun's "pragmatically based type" (cf. Payne 1984, 1987, for relevant data on Papago; and Swartz 1985, 1987, for relevant data on Warlpiri), they differ markedly in respect to the question of "basic word order".

On the basis of certain facts of Papago grammar, it is possible to argue that that language retains the head-final (SOV, etc.) basic constituent ordering of its Tepiman and Uto-Aztecan ancestors, despite the fact that this ordering, in root clauses at least, is textually infrequent in narratives. Verb-final ordering for Papago, it should be noted, is not in line with the assumption of knowledgeable investigators that Papago is verb-initial (cf. Saxton 1982; and Saxton and Saxton 1969), like its modern Tepiman relative Northern Tepehuan (Bascom 1982). Nor is it in line with Dryer's observation, based on Payne (1987), that the orders VS (verb-subject) and VO (verb-object) dominate in textual frequency (Dryer 1989: 73). The head-final "basic" order emerges as likely only through a consideration of principles of grammar.

By contrast, Warlpiri belongs to the type studied by Mithun, i.e., the type for which it makes little sense to speak of any particular basic order.

In the course of the discussion to follow, I will present evidence for this difference in free word order typology, primarily through an examination of the role of grammatical **government** as it is reflected in the surface syntax of Papago. The status of Warlpiri in this regard will emerge primarily by contrast with Papago.

1. Some elementary observations on word order and use

Warlpiri shares with the majority of Australian languages the characteristic of free word order, a fact which has been noted in a variety of published and unpublished works on the language (e.g., Nash 1985; Laughren 1987). This characteristic is exemplified, for example, by the fact that the subject, object, and verb of a transitive sentence may appear in any relative order in relation to one another, as in (1) below:

(1) a. *Karnta-ngku ka yarla karla-mi.*
woman-ERG PRES yam dig-NONPAST
'The/a woman is digging yams.'

b. *Yarla ka karla-mi karnta-ngku.*

c. *Karla-mi ka karnta-ngku yarla.*

d. *Yarla ka karnta-ngku karla-mi.*

e. *Karla-mi ka yarla karnta-ngku.*

f. *Karnta-ngku ka karla-mi yarla.*

The sole requirement is that the "auxiliary" — the element *ka* (PRES) 'present (tense)' in this instance — must appear in a fixed position within the sentence; this is the second position, i.e., "Wackernagel's position", if the base of the auxiliary is monosyllabic (as here) or if it is phonologically null.

Free word order is also a property of certain Uto-Aztecan languages, including Papago, for which it has likewise been reported in the literature (see, e.g., Zepeda 1983). Although some of the orders are, to be sure, textually infrequent, Papago exhibits the same range of relative orderings, within simple transitive sentences, as does Warlpiri. Thus:

(2) a. *Wakial 'o g wipsilo ha-cecposid.*
cowboy AUX3 D calves them-brand:PL
'The cowboy is branding the calves.'

b. *Wipsilo 'o ha-cecposid g wakial.*
c. *Ha-cecposid 'o g wakial g wipsilo.*
d. *Wipsilo 'o g wakial ha-cecposid.*
e. *Ha-cecposid 'o g wipsilo g wakial.*
f. *Wakial 'o ha-cecposid g wipsilo.*

Here again, the auxiliary (AUX) appears in second position within the sentence. Otherwise the order of arguments, in relation to the verb and to each other, is "free" in Papago, as in Warlpiri.[2]

To say that Warlpiri and Papago have "free word order" is to say simply that constituent orderings of the type illustrated above are **grammatically** well-formed. The evidence presented in the form of word order variants, as in (1) and (2) above, relates to grammar, narrowly defined, and not to aspects of language use, where notions like **acceptable, appropriate, marked/unmarked, usual/unusual**, or the like are relevant. In actual Warlpiri or Papago usage, certain of the orderings in (1) and (2) are extremely rare — though this depends on the type of discourse in which the sentences are used. In fact, with both arguments overtly expressed, any one of those sentences would be textually infrequent, since in the typical situation one or the other, or even both of the arguments (subject, object) would be "thematic" within the discourse and, accordingly, elided in these languages, which freely permit so-called "pro-drop" or "null anaphora".

The foregoing merely reiterates the well-known fact that word order, and elision as well, as matters of **grammar**, belong to a different sphere from word order, and elision, as matters of **usage** and **discourse**. Thus, the

"BASIC word order" of a language, where this is taken to be a grammatical notion, cannot be determined by studying principles of discourse. On the other hand, the facts of the actual use of word order and elision can **primarily** be understood through the study of principles of discourse.

The latter concern has been examined in detail for Warlpiri and Papago in the excellent studies of Swartz (1985, 1987) and Payne (1984, 1987). At the risk of oversimplifying matters and possibly misrepresenting the findings of these researchers, I will attempt to express, jointly, the fundamental principles which they have discovered — the two languages, it seems to me, employ the same discourse principles. I will use the term "expression in focus" (EIF) to refer to a constituent (argument, direct or oblique, etc.) which is, relatively speaking, "in focus". This is the expression whose referent is taken by the speaker to be "new" to the audience, or "new" in relation to the discourse — "newsworthy", in the terminology of Mithun (1987). It includes what Swartz (1985: *passim*) calls the "sentence topic" and what Payne (1987: 786) refers to as "non-identifiable information", for which "the hearer is instructed to open a new active discourse file", as well as "pragmatically marked" information (e.g., content-question words). The notion "in focus" here is a relative one. An argument, the object, for example, is **relatively** more, or less, "in discourse focus" by comparison with some other argument, the subject, say. If an expression is not an EIF, then it can be said to be an "expression out of focus" (EOF), again, in a relative sense. Given this terminology, the discourse principles governing word order and elision in the two "free word order" languages under consideration here can be expressed in preliminary fashion as follows:

(3) *Ordering Principles in Discourse*:
    a. EIF precedes the predicator (e.g., the V).
    b. EOF follows the predicator, or it is elided.

These principles must, of course, interact properly with principles of grammar — thus, for example, elision is subject to the principle of the recoverability of deletions; and the precedence relations here hold among clause-mates (i.e., "precede" and "follow" are **local** relations); etc.

The discourse principles set out in (3) will, among other things, account for the ordering and elision pattern of question-answer dialogues of the sort represented in (4) and (5) below:

(4) Warlpiri:
Q: *Nyiya ka karla-mi karnta-ngku?*
what PRES dig-NONPAST woman-ERG
'What is the woman digging?'

A: *Yarla ka karla-mi.*
yam PRES dig-NONPAST
'She is digging yams.'

(5) Papago:
Q: *Ṣa:cu 'o ceposid g wakial?*
what AUX3 brand art cowboy
'What is the cowboy branding?'

A: *Wisilo 'o ceposid.*
calf AUX3 brand
'He is branding the/a calf.'

In the question, the **question word** is the EIF, and consequently precedes the verb.[3] The subject, being relatively "out of focus", follows the verb. In the answer, the **answer** to the question, i.e., the object, is the EIF and, accordingly, precedes the verb. By contrast, the subject is the EOF and, in this case, it is elided.

The principles given in (3) also account for the relative textual rarity of the order SOV in narratives and dialogues — e.g., just 3 out of 128 Warlpiri transitive clauses (Swartz 1987: 23), and just 1 out of 236 Papago transitive clauses (Payne 1987, calculating from tables 3 and 4, p. 793). In those styles, the arguments within a clause are normally, from the point of view of the discourse, in an asymmetrical relation one to the other and, consequently, at least one is post-verbal or elided. It should not be surprising, however, to encounter head-final order in the relatively neutral, "laboratory-like", context of a grammatical discussion, such as that found in Alvarez (1972), where Papago sentences are cited in isolation with the express purpose of exemplifying just the argument structures of predicators. In such a context, the sentences are not being "used" in the generally understood sense of "discourse use"; rather, they are serving merely to illustrate grammar. The usual situation of discourse asymmetry of arguments is not motivated in this context, and since both arguments are "new", in an intuitively clear sense, given that each such illustrative sentence is out of context, their appearance in preverbal position is not surprising, and it is consistent with the principles set out in (3).

The ordering statements in (3) are a composite formulation, possibly over-simplified, of the basic principles of word order in certain types of discourse (ordinary narrative and dialogue), as reported by Payne and Swartz in their careful studies of the two languages at issue here. Certain marked constructions (e.g., clefting for focus, dislocation for topic) are only partially accommodated by (3), to be sure, and those preliminary principles do not, by any means, pretend to account for the full range of discourse types and styles of delivery. They have been formulated here simply to reemphasize the fact that word order as a discourse matter is distinct from word order as a matter of grammar. The terminology used in (3) — "expression (relatively) in focus (within the discourse)" (EIF), and so on — is appropriate to the formulation of principles of discourse, inasmuch as it makes reference to discourse notions.

On the other hand, principles of **grammar** relevant to word order are formulated in strictly **grammatical** terms, making reference to grammatical notions — e.g., such notions as "head of construction", "grammatical function", "government", and the like. The sections following will be concerned with the relationship between word order and grammar, and the question of "basic word order", in Papago and Warlpiri, which will be taken up in that order.

2. Grammar and basic word order in Papago

The findings of Payne (1984, 1987) show that, from the point of view of discourse, there are word order asymmetries in Papago; not all orderings have the same value in discourse. Among other things, for example, it is relevant to Papago usage and discourse what precedes the verb and what follows it. But discourse is not the only thing that gives rise to asymmetries in relation to Papago word order. Some asymmetries, at least, are explained most convincingly in terms of grammatical considerations. In Papago surface structures, these asymmetries are realized at least in the following aspects of grammar: (1) intonation, or tonal phrasing (cf. Hale and Selkirk 1987); (2) allomorphy within the class of determiners; and (3) certain extraction, or movement, operations in syntax. There is reason to believe that all of these point to a "basic" word order in Papago, in the sense of a unique word order in the initial syntactic projection from the lexicon. That is to say, they give evidence of a d-structure for Papago in which a specific ordering relation holds (within a phrasal category) between the lexical head and its complements. The three phenomena just mentioned will be discussed individually in the following subsections, and their putative relevance to the question of basic word order will be discussed in a fourth subsection.

2.1 Tonal phrasing in Papago

In Papago, normal intonation contours are assigned in an entirely mechanical manner (cf. Hale and Selkirk 1987). Within the intonational domain, or "tonal phrase", a LHL (low-high-low) contour is assigned as follows:

(6) *LHL Tonal Association (left to right)*:
  a. Assign L to unstressed vowel(s), otherwise delete L;
  b. Assign H to stressed vowel(s) and all intervening vowel(s);
  c. Assign L to unstressed vowel(s), otherwise to stressed vowel.

This tonal association is illustrated by the following Papago sentence:

(7)	(L L		HH H	HL)
	Nap	*g*	*siikĭ*	*ñeid?*
	Q:AUX:2SG	art	deer	see:IMPERF

'Do you see the deer?'

This sentence constitutes a single intonational domain — i.e., a single tonal phrase. (The second L, it should be noted, is associated with the automatic epenthetic schwa vowel inserted between /p/ and /g/, not indicated in the orthography.)

As can be seen, the LHL contour is assigned just once to the string in (7) — and this is expected if (7) is just one tonal phrase. This phrasing is observed regularly when the complement of a verb (the object in this case) directly precedes it. That is to say, in the ordering OV (object-verb), the object and the verb always belong to the same tonal phrase. But the relation between tonal phrasing and constituent ordering is not symmetyrical. If the object follows the verb, the two constituents belong to distinct tonal phrases:

(8)	(L L	HL L)	(	HL L)
	Nap	*ñeid*	*g*	*siikĭ?*
	Q:AUX:2SG	see	art	deer

'Do you see the deer?'

This pattern applies generally, with explicable, and irrelevant, exceptions (discussed in detail in Hale and Selkirk 1987) — thus, (9) below is observationally true cross-categorially in Papago:

(9) *Tonal Phrasing*:
Where a category XP is the complement of a lexical head H:
a. XP and H belong to the same tonal phrase if they appear in the order XP W H;
b. XP and H belong to distinct tonal phrases if they appear in the order H W XP.
(Where W is null, another complement, or a modifier of H.)

That is to say, a complement forms a tonal phrase with the head of the construction to which it belongs if it precedes the head, but not if it follows. From the point of view of intonation, then, the arrangement XP H evidently corresponds to a single structural unit, while H XP evidently does not.

2.2 Determiner allomorphy in Papago

The class of determiners in Papago includes the category commonly called "pronouns". In the singular, these exhibit two forms in most varieties of Papago, a long form, and a short form. The long form is regularly used in construction with nominals, as in expressions such as *hegai 'o'odham* 'that person', *'iida 'ali* 'this child'. The long-short alternation is observed primarily when they function alone as arguments (e.g., as subject or object), and the distribution of the alternants correlates with word order, according to a pattern precisely analogous to the asymmetrical tonal phrasing observed above (cf. Hale and Selkirk 1987, and Pranka 1983 for more detailed discussion):

(10) *Determiner Allomorphy*:
If a determiner phrase DP (appearing without an associated nominal head) is the complement of a lexical head H, then:
a. DP takes the short form (e.g., *heg*) in the order DP W H;
b. DP takes the long form (e.g., *hegai*) in the order H W DP.

This is exemplified in (11) below:

(11) a. (L H HL)
Nap heg ñeid?
Q:AUX:2SG that see:IMPERF
'Do you see that?'

b. (L HL) (H LL)
Nap ñeid hegai?
Q:AUX:2SG see:IMPERF that
'Do you see that?'

We have indicated the tonal phrasing, as well as the allomorphy, to illustrate the parallelism.[4]

It should perhaps be mentioned that the distribution of the determiner allomorphs does not have to do simply with their gross positioning in the sentence, e.g., final versus non-final. What matters is the ordering relative to the head of the construction to which the DP is related — thus, a non-final DP will assume the long form if it follows the verb (or other head category) of which it is a complement:

(12) (L HL) (H LL)(L H L L)
Nt o hikc hegai g ñ-nawas-kaj
AUX:1SG:T FUT cut:PERF that art my-knife-INSTR
'I will cut that with my (pocket-)knife.'

Here, even though it is not final in the sentence, the DP *hegai* constitutes its own tonal phrase and appears in the long form, as expected given its position relative to the verb.

2.3 Extraction rules and word order

In the formation of relative clauses in Papago, the "relative" argument is represented by a gap, or empty category, within the embedded clause. We assume that this gap arises through movement and is therefore a "trace". When the complement of a verb is extracted, it is not possible to "see" the trace and, thereby, to determine its location. If it *were* possible to see a trace, then its location might be expected to exhibit an ordering asymmetry in relation to the verb. While a trace itself cannot be seen, it is nonetheless possible to say something about extraction and ordering. It is possible to extract from a postpositional phrase (PP) in Papago, leaving behind the (perfectly visible) "stranded" PP superstructure, consisting of the postposition (PP) and a preceding specifier (SPEC). But this extraction is subject to the following condition:

(13) *Extraction from PP*:
If PP is a complement to a verb V, then:
a. a NP object of PP may be extracted if PP appears in the order PP W V;
b. a NP object of PP may not be extracted if PP appears in the order V W PP.

This condition is formulated in more absolute terms than it should be, perhaps, inasmuch as sentences which I have constructed in violation of (13) — precisely for the purpose of testing its general validity — have sometimes been accepted by speakers. I cannot account for this fact, at present, but I have found no exceptions to (13) in "natural" speech, volunteered texts, or the like. Moreover, the example of "oblique object" relativization cited by Saxton (1982: 251) conforms to (13), as expected, despite the fact that Saxton's general view of Papago word order would have the oblique expression in post-verbal position basically.

Assuming that (13) is essentially correct, we observe again that there is something special about the relative ordering of constituents in relation to the head of a construction. The following sentences illustrate pre- and post-head orderings of a postpositional complement (tonal phrasing is included as well):

(14) a. (L L HH H H H H L)
Nap 'am miisa weco cicwi?
Q:AUX:2SG SPEC table under play:IMPERF
'Are you playing under the table?'

b. (L H L) (L HH H H L)
Nap cicwi 'am miisa weco?
Q:AUX:2SG play:IMPERF SPEC table under
'Are you playing under the table?'

Extraction of the object of PP, in the formation of relative clauses, is possible only where the PP is ordered before the verb, as in (15a) below (in which *t*, trace, indicates the extraction site):

(15) a. *hegai miisa [map 'am t weco cicwi]*
that table COMP:AUX:2SG SPEC under play:IMPERF
'that table that you are playing under'
b. **hegai miisa [map cicwi 'am t weco]*

Another extraction operation involving PP structures is illustrated in (16) below:

(16) (L L H L) (HH H H L)
Nap 'am t cicwi miisa weco?
Q:AUX:2SG SPEC play table under
'Are you playing under the table?'

Here the sub-maximal projection of the PP-category (i.e., the P'-projection, containing the postposition and its object) has been separated from the SPEC (leaving a trace, presumably, as indicated). This stranding of specifiers exhibits the expected asymmetrical patterning — a specifier may be stranded in pre-head position only. Like the specifier associated with postpositional phrases, that associated with nominal expressions may also be stranded, as in (17) below, where the determiner (in the short form, as expected) is stranded in preverbal position:

(17) (L H HL) (H L L)
Nap heg t s-maac 'o'odham?
Q:AUX:2SG that POS-know person
'Do you know that man?'

Extraction operations, like tonal phrasing and determiner allomorphy, show that head-complement ordering is relevant to a descriptively adequate account of Papago grammar. It is appropriate now to consider what general grammatical relation, if any, is involved in all of this and how such a relation might be implicated in deciding the issue of basic word order for this language. In the following subsection, I will suggest that the relevant grammatical relation is **government** (cf. Chomsky 1981).

2.4 Government and word order in Papago

The fact that a complement (XP), say the object of a verb, forms a tonal phrase with the head (H) to which it is grammatically related when the two elements appear in the order XP H suggests that there is a correlation between this ordering and the grammatical relation which holds between XP and H. Thus, it is not surprising, for example, that a verb and its object should form a unit, since, at some level of syntactic representation, namely d-structure, the verb must govern its object. For a head to govern its complement, it must appropriately and locally command it — briefly, the complement must be dominated by the phrase-level projection of the the head, and no barrier which excludes the head may dominate the complement (cf. Chomsky 1986).

If we assume that a head governs its complement and that tonal phrasing is sensitive to government (as suggested in Hale and Selkirk 1987), then the principles regulating tonal phrasing might be required to conform to the following generalization:

(18) *Tonal Phrasing and Government*:
A phrasal category XP belongs to the same tonal phrase as its governor H.

If this is correct, it will account for the observed intonation on constructions in the head-final form XP W H. But by the same token, an XP which follows H must not be governed by H, since it does not belong to the same tonal phrase as the latter, even where XP is an **argument** of H.

All of this makes sense, of course, if we assume that the head-final ordering is basic and that the alternative ordering is derived by extraposition, removing XP to an adjoined position outside the governing domain of H, as illustrated below for extraction from VP:

(19) *Extraposition from VP*:

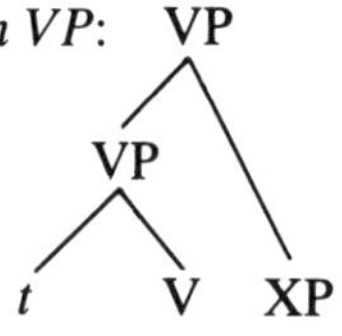

In (19), the extraposed XP is adjoined to the right of the host VP, placing it outside the domain governed by V. This follows, since (technically at least) the extraposed XP is no longer dominated by VP (but only by a segment of that projection). The trace remaining within the VP, however, is properly governed, as required. If this is correct, then it is not unexpected that the postposed XP would constitute its own tonal phrase, given (18) above.

On the assumption that it is indeed true that government and tonal phrasing correlate in the manner suggested above, then the ordering statement embodied in (20) below must also be true for Papago:

(20) *Basic Word Order in Papago*:
In a given construction projected from a lexical H, the head-final order XP W H is **basic**, in the sense that it is the ordering projected from the lexicon to define the d-structure level os syntactic representation.

This follows, given the requirement that the government relation holds between H and XP at d-structure. The alternative ordering, under our assumptions, cannot be basic, since XP is not governed by H in the order H W XP. Thus, we are forced to the conclusion, given these assumptions, that Papago has a particular basic word order — to wit, that in which the lexical head is final within the category it projects.

The asymmetries associated with determiner allomorphy and extraction can be understood in the same way.

The short form of a singular determiner must, evidently, be governed. If a DP (unaccompanied by the lexical projection NP) follows the head of a construction with which it is associated (e.g., a VP of which DP is the object), then it will be ungoverned and, therefore, must assume the long form. But if it precedes the head, then it will be governed, and the short form will be possible. Again, if this is correct, this argues that the basic word order in Papago is XP W H, as formulated in (20) above.

It has been argued often that extraction from adjuncts, if possible at all, is severely restricted (cf. Huang 1982). Assuming that extraction is impossible from an adjunct of the type represented by XP in (19) above, then the asymmetry associated with extraction in Papago can be explained in terms of government. Extraction is possible from a governed (e.g., preverbal) position, but not from an ungoverned position. Thus, it is the prehead position, not the post-head position, which is basic in Papago, given our assumptions.

Papago is a language with extremely free word order, in the sense that the variety of grammatical surface constituent orderings available as realizations of the projections into syntax of a given verb and its arguments, say, approximates the theoretically possible linear arrangements (e.g., six permutations for a verb and two arguments, two for a noun and its possessor complement, and so on). It is nonetheless possible, I have argued, to show that Papago has a **basic** word order — to wit, that in which the lexical head of a construction is final. Deviations from this basic ordering must be derived by movement.

In the following section, I will briefly discuss Warlpiri from this point of view.

3. Grammar and basic word order in Warlpiri

Considerations of the sort used above in arguing for a basic word order in Papago fail to yield any comparable result for Warlpiri. In fact, with one possible exception, the relationship between grammar and ordering suggests a conclusion similar to that reached by Mithun in her study of Coos and Cayuga (of North America) and Ngandi (of northern Australia) — namely, that they are languages with "purely pragmatic ordering" (Mithun 1987). In his detailed study of Warlpiri, Swartz, comparing Warlpiri with those languages which Mithun examined, concluded that:

(21) *Warlpiri Word Order* (Swartz 1987: 42-43):

> ... Warlpiri too is a pragmatically ordered language. By that is meant that there is not a basic word order in Warlpiri from which all other orderings are variations. Rather, given that the primary case relations are between the verb and the pronominal affixes, and given that the major constituent noun phrases serving as subject, object, and indirect object are relatively rare, every occurence, and the subsequent positioning, of such noun phrases represents a marked phenomenon determined by the pragmatic requirements of the surrounding discourse.

In general, I concur with this characterization of Warlpiri word order, though I do not agree with the implication that a so-called "pragmatically ordered language" necessarily lacks a **basic** word order. Papago, I maintain, shows that the correlation implied here cannot be correct; Papago **has** a basic word order yet it seems to qualify as a "pragmatically ordered language". And, of course, there is no **necessary** correlation between pragmatic ordering and the lack of a basic word order.

Before discussing the implications of the possibility that Warlpiri lacks a basic word order, I would like to mention one possible qualification, having to do with the position of a morphologically unmarked object relative to its governor in infinitival constructions, as illustrated by the bracketted clause of (22) below:

(22) *Ngarrka ka-rna nya-nyi [karli jarnti-rninja-kurra].*
man PRES-1SS see-NONPAST boomerang trim-INF-OBJCOMPL
'I see the man [trimming a boomerang].'

The object of the infinitival (i.e., *karli* 'boomerang'), in this unmarked form, must appear in immediate pre-verbal position (cf. Laughren 1987: 23). This is, of course, not true in **general** of objects, only of phonologically unmarked objects of infinitivals.

This might, of course, be taken as evidence that Warlpiri does, after all, have a basic word order — specifically, that according to which a complement precedes its governor, i.e., the head-final order, as in Papago. However, the only real evidence for this comes from the infinitival constructions, and there is some reason to believe that the principle involved in these constructions has to do not with word order itself but with a general requirement that the righthand margin of a construction, nominal or verbal, bear the functional signature (complementizer, case) appropriate to it. In the case of (22), the infinitival verb must bear the complementizer *-kurra* (OBJCOMPL) 'objective complementizer'. This is a fact of Warlpiri morphology. The object NP must, therefore, precede the verb in order to satisfy the righthand-signature requirement (cf. Laughren 1987 for a fully elaborated conception of the principles involved here). The object could, it happens, also bear the complementizer, thereby acquiring its own signature — thus, *karli-kirra* (boomerang-OBJCOMPL). In that case, it could be reordered in relation to the infinitival verb; or it could even be separated from the dependent clause altogether:

(23) a. *Ngarrka ka-rna nya-nyi [jarnti-rninja-kurra karli-kirra].*
b. *[Karli-kirra] ka-rna ngarrka nya-nyi [jarnti-rninja-kurra].*

These data do not force us to conclude that the apparent "fixed word order" in (22) is anything other than a special case of the general Warlpiri principle according to which the overt morphological marking of a phrase appears (minimally) on its righthand periphery. If this is indeed all that is involved, then (22), and the constructions it represents, do not provide conclusive evidence for a basic word order.

What does it mean, precisely, to say that a language lacks a basic word order? There are a number of possibilities, all of which have been discussed in the literature. Two, rather disparate, views on this question seem to me to have promise.

According to one conception of the matter — represented, e.g., by the work of Farmer (1980, 1984) — the syntactic projections which define the d-structure representations of sentences permit complements to be freely ordered in relation to one another, the ordering relative to the head being determined by government. If government is unidirectional, then the position of the head will be fixed in relation to its immediate complement (e.g., final, as in Japanese; or initial, as in English). But, if government is not directional, the position of the head will also be free (as in Warlpiri, supposedly).

According to another view — mentioned by Mithun (1987) and Swartz (1987), and fully elaborated by Jelinek (1984) — overt nominal expressions are not, strictly speaking, the **arguments** of a predication. Rather, the office of argument (subject, object, etc.) is filled by the pronominal (i.e., person-marking) morphology in the verb and/or auxiliary system. Overt nominal expressions are adjuncts, not arguments. They are, however, **construed** with the "actual" arguments (the pronominal morphology) in some manner akin, perhaps, to that in which a postposed phrase (in English, French, or Italian, say) is construed with a pleonastic pronoun (e.g., overt *it, il*, or non-overt *pro*), or to that in which a dislocated nominal is linked to a resumptive pronominal (overt or non-overt).

I would like to consider briefly a third alternative which combines features of these two proposals. It makes crucial reference to the fact that Warlpiri possesses a rich system of case and complementizers and assumes that case and agreement, both rich in Warlpiri, are expressions of a single system related to the "visibility" requirement for the assignment of thematic roles. In Warlpiri, according to this view, a NP argument of a verb, for example, is not directly governed by the verb itself but by the case category associated with it. The case, in turn, serves to render the NP "visible" for the assignment of theta-roles by the verb — for this, the verb must appropriately command the case-marked NP, and vice versa. Since the command relations are not inherently directional, and since an argument need not be directly governed by the verb, no ordering relation (between a verb and its object, for example) is required by the grammar. The only structural requirements which must be satisfied have to do with "visibility". A case-marked NP, for example, must be within the local domain of the head (e.g., the verb) with which it is interpreted, i.e., from which it receives its theta-role.

In developing this notion, we might assume that the grammar of a verb or other predicator involves two distinct but related projections, (1) the theta-projection, an unambiguous projection of the lexical category, say V, introducing its arguments in an asymmetrical arrangement of specifier and complement (cf. Hale and Keyser 1989); and (2) the case-projection (or case-and-agreement projection), with parallel organization of argument positions, each identified with the corresponding position in the theta-projection (see Lebeaux 1988 for the origins of certain aspects of this conception of grammatical organization). The two projections might be opposed as "lexical" and "functional", the second comprising elements belonging primarily to the category of inflectional morphology. In any event, the two go hand in hand as essential components in the grammatical realization of linguistic expressions.

Speculating in this vein, we might suppose that in languages of the highly configurational type, like English, arguments are expressed overtly within the theta-projection. There, the basic (s-structure) ordering of arguments must, let us assume, respect the c-command relations inherent in the lexical projection, in the following sense: if an element c-commands another element E, it may not be linearly separated from E by a third element E' unless it also c-commands E' (i.e., there is no "line crossing" in the theta-projection in the syntactic representation at s-structure). Observed variations in word order are necessarily by movement, as assumed for Papago, as well as for English and other well-known grammatical systems.

By contrast, we might assume, in certain less configurational languages like Warlpiri, nominal arguments are realized overtly only in the case-projection. Let us speculate that in this projection there is no correlation between c-command and linear ordering (i.e., line crossing is allowed at s-structure). If this is true, then there are no constraints on word order within the clause. Thus, Warlpiri has free word order in the sense that no **particular** order is necessarily projected in syntax (cf. Vergnaud and Zubizarreta 1982 for a related proposal).[5]

This view of Warlpiri syntactic projections is consistent with the fact that no convincing evidence (e.g., from cross-over, binding, reconstruction, or government) has been forthcoming in support of a movement analysis of surface word order in the language (cf. Farmer, Hale and Tsujimura 1986 for a remark concerning weak cross-over in Warlpiri; and see Webelhuth 1989 for detailed discussion of movement and free word order in Germanic and other languages). Pre-auxiliary positioning of phrasal constituents, which may involve a leftward movement, is evidently always "short" (cf. Pranka 1983 for relevant discussion of this process in Papago); accordingly, even if this does indeed involve movement, it has no observable effects, apart from the local reordering. Lack of evidence for standard movement operations does not, of course, support the view suggested here — it is merely consistent with it.

4. Concluding remarks

Warlpiri and Papago share the characteristic of extremely free word order. While some evidence can be marshalled to support the notion that Papago has a basic word order, no corresponding demonstration can be made for Warlpiri, as yet.

However, in their fundamental grammatical organization, Warlpiri and Papago, like all languages, give evidence of an identical structural projection from lexical categories. That is to say, the two languages are in accord with all languages so far documented in, among other things, placing the subject in a maximally prominent, asymmetrical c-command relation over the object, a circumstance which is reflected in the systems of anaphoric binding and argument obviation. Thus, in both Warlpiri and Papago, an anaphoric object can only be bound by an immediately superordinate subject, and an anaphoric subject can only be bound by an immediately superordinate matrix argument (cf., Hale 1983; and Simpson and Bresnan 1983 for discussions of this in relation to Warlpiri).

Therefore, Warlpiri and Papago are fundamentally the same. The difference must be minimal. We cannot say as yet that we have a theory which correctly determines both the identities and differences between Warlpiri and Papago, or between any like pair of languages. But the recognition of a dual projection of syntactic structure — a functional projection and a lexical projection — brings with it the natural question of where, i.e., at which projection, overt nominal arguments are expressed. If languages can differ in this regard, then this may be the source of the difference between the two types of "free word order".

Notes

1. I am grateful to the Department of Linguistics, University of Oregon, for making it possible for me to present an earlier version of this paper at a colloquium in 1987 and, in that context, to receive many valuable comments. I wish also to indicate my appreciation for the work of Doris Payne and Stephen Swartz — it is an essential component in any attempt to understand fully the nature of free word order in Papago and Warlpiri.

2. Nominal arguments are always accompanied by a determiner, represented here by the neutral article *g*; this happens to be deleted sentence-initially in the Papago speech illustrated here, but not in the closely related Pima.

3. The initial position of question words might be, and probably is, determined by grammatical factors as well — factors having to do with the projection of logical form from s-structure.

4. For some speakers, both long and short forms may appear in pre-head position. So far as I know, however, all speakers agree in restricting the short form to that position alone.

5. The fixed OV ordering in Warlpiri infinitivals, if not due to the morphological requirement mentioned above, might be due to theta-projection of the object, rather than the case-projection assumed for that argument in finite clauses.

References

Alvarez, Albert. 1972. "Appendix" (to Hale). *New Perspectives on the Pueblos*, ed. by A. Ortiz, 111-133. University of New Mexico Press.

Bascom, Burt. 1982. "Northern Tepehuan." *Studies in Uto-Aztecan Grammar, Volume 3: Uto-Aztecan Grammatical Sketches*, ed. by R. Langecker, 267-293. Dallas: Summer Institute of Linguistics.

Chomsky, Noam. 1981. *Lectures on Government and Binding*. Dordrecht: Foris.

Chomsky, Noam. 1986. *Barriers*. Cambridge, Mass: MIT Press.

Dryer, Matthew S. 1989. "Discourse-Governed Word Order and Word Order Typology." *Universals of Language*, ed. by M. Kefer and J. van der Auwera. *Belgian Journal of Linguistics* 4: 69-90.

Farmer, Ann K. 1980. *On the Interaction of Morphology and Syntax*. MIT Doctoral Dissertation, Cambridge, Mass.

Farmer, Ann K. 1984. *Modularity in Syntax*. Cambridge, Mass: MIT Press.

Farmer, Ann K., Ken Hale, and Natsuko Tsujimura. 1986. "A Note on Weak Crossover in Japanese." *Natural Language & Linguistic Theory* 4: 33-42.

Greenberg, Joseph H. 1963. "Some Universals of Grammar with Particular Reference to the Order of Meaningful Elements." *Universals of Language*, ed. by J. Greenberg, 73-113. Cambridge, Mass: MIT Press.

Hale, Ken. 1983. "Warlpiri and the Grammar of Non-Configurational Languages," *Natural Language & Linguistic Theory* 1: 3-47.

Hale, Ken, and Samuel J. Keyser. 1989. "On the Syntactic Character of Thematic Structure," MIT ms. (to appear).

Hale, Ken, and Lisa Selkirk. 1987. "Government and Tonal Phrasing in Papago." *Phonology Yearbook* 4: 151-183, ed. by C. Ewen and J. Anderson. Cambridge: Cambridge University Press.

Huang, C.-T. James. 1982. *Logical Relations in Chinese and the Theory of Grammar*. MIT Doctoral Dissertation, Cambridge, Mass.

Jelinek, Eloise. 1984. "Empty categories, case, and configurationality", *Natural Language and Linguistic Theory* 2.39-76.

Laughren, Mary. 1987. "The Configurationality Parameter and Warlpiri", Northern Territory of Australia Department of Education (ms). To appear in *Configurationality*, ed. by L. Maracz and P. Muysken. Dordrecht: Foris.

Lebeaux, David. 1988. *Language Acquisition and the Form of Grammar*. University of Massachusetts, Amherst, Doctoral Dissertation.

Mithun, Marianne. 1987. "Is Basic Word Order Universal?' *Coherence and Grounding in Discourse*, ed. by Russell S. Tomlin, 281-328. Amsterdam: John Benjamins.

Nash, David. 1985. *Topics in Warlpiri Grammar*. Garland.

Payne, Doris. 1984. "Information structuring in Papago", Paper read at the *Conference of Friends of Uto-Aztecan*, UCSD, La Jolla, June 1984.

Payne, Doris. 1987. "Information Structuring in Papago Narrative Discourse," *Language* 63: 783-804.

Pranka, Paula. 1983. *Syntax and Word Formation*. Doctoral Dissertation, MIT, Cambridge, Mass.

Saxton, Dean. 1982. "Papago." *Uto-Aztecan Grammar, Vol 3: Uto-Aztecan Grammatical Sketches*, ed. by R. Langacker, 93-266. Dallas: Summer Institute of Linguistics.

Saxton, Dean, and Lucille Saxton. 1969. *Papago & Pima Dictionary*. Tucson: University of Arizona Press.

Simpson, Jane, and Joan Bresnan. 1983. "Control and Obviation in Warlpiri," *Natural Language & Linguistic Theory* 1: 49-64.

Swartz, Stephen. 1985. "Pragmatic structure and word order in Warlpiri." Summer Institute of Linguistics, Australia. MS.

Swartz, Stephen. 1987. *Measuring Naturalness in Translation by Means of a Statistical Analysis of Warlpiri Narrative Texts with Special Emphasis on Word Order Principles*. Thesis manuscript, Pacific College of Graduate Studies.

Thompson, Sandra. 1978. "Modern English from a Typological Point of View: Some Implications of the Function of Word Order." *Linguistische Berichte* 54: 19-35.

Vergnaud, Jean-Roger, and Maria-Luisa Zubizarreta. 1982. "On Virtual Categories." *MIT Working Papers, No. 4*.

Webelhuth, Gert. 1989. *Syntactic Saturation Phenomena and the Modern Germanic Languages*. University of Massachusetts, Amherst, Doctoral Dissertation.

Zepeda, Ofelia. 1983. *A Papago Grammar*. Tucson: The University of Arizona Press.

The Privilege of Primacy
Experimental Data and Cognitive Explanations[1]

Morton Ann Gernsbacher & David Hargreaves
Department of Psychology
University of Oregon
Department of Linguistics
University of Oregon

Many things are arranged sequentially: the order in which children are born into a family; the order in which words occur in a sentence; and the order in which utterances occur in a discourse. Sequential order requires that some things come first. Items, events, or stimuli that occur in initial position often gain a unique psychological status. Indeed, some of the earliest experiments in contemporary American psychology document the psychological privilege of primacy.

For instance, the qualities of a person that we learn about first, figure most prominently in the impression we form of that person (Asch 1946). Consider the traits listed in (1) versus (2) below.

(1) smart, artistic, sentimental, cool, awkward, faultfinding
(2) faultfinding, awkward, cool, sentimental, artistic, and smart

If subjects are given a list of traits and are asked to imagine a person with such traits, they form a more favorable impression if they are given the traits arranged in order (1), and they form a less favorable impression if they are given the very same traits but arranged in order (2) (Anderson and Barrios 1961). The more favorable traits are primary in order (1); the less favorable traits are primary in order (2).

Consider the hand-written character in Figure 1. If that character is preceded by the letter **A**, subjects perceive it as the letter **B**. If the same character is preceded by the number **12**, subjects perceive it as the number **13** (Bruner and Minturn 1955). Perception depends on what character comes first.

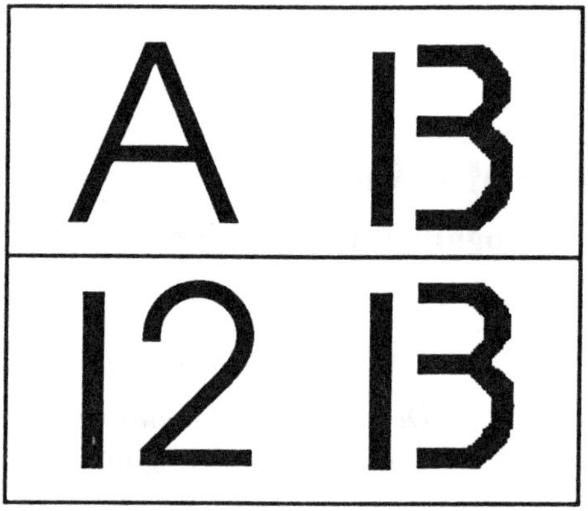

Figure 1

Forming impressions of people and recognizing hand-written characters demonstrate the privilege of primacy. Primacy effects also occur during language comprehension. In the next section, we review a large array of primacy effects that occur during sentence and discourse comprehension. These effects have been documented in a myriad of laboratories using a variety of experimental tasks. Consistently, a particular advantage is observed: The information that occurs first in a phrase, clause, sentence, or passage gains a privileged status in the comprehenders' minds.

Primacy effects in sentence and discourse comprehension

In some experiments, researchers measure how long it takes comprehenders to read each word of a sentence. In these experiments, subjects typically sit before a computer monitor; each word of a sentence appears in the center of the monitor. Subjects press a button to signal when they have finished reading each word. After each word disappears, another one appears. In this way, researchers can measure how long subjects need to read each word.

A consistent finding in these word-by-word reading time experiments is that the first word of a sentence takes longer to read than later-occurring words (Aaronson and Ferres 1983; Aaronson and Scarborough 1976;

Chang 1980). In fact, the same word is read more slowly when it occurs at the beginning of a sentence or phrase than when it occurs later. For example, the word *bears* occurs at the beginning of a clause in sentence (3) below.

(3) *Even though Ron hasn't seen many,* ***bears*** *are apparently his favorite animal.*

But *bears* occurs at the end of a clause in sentence (4) below.

(4) *Even though Ron hasn't seen many* ***bears****, they are apparently his favorite animal.*

Subjects read the word *bears* more slowly when it occurs at the beginning of a clause than when it occurs at the end (Aaronson and Scarborough 1976).

In some experiments, researchers measure how long it takes comprehenders to read each sentence of a passage. In these experiments, each sentence of the passage appears in the center of a computer monitor. Subjects press a button to signal when they have finished reading each sentence; the sentence then disappears, and another one appears. In this way, researchers can measure how long subjects need to read each sentence.

A consistent finding in these sentence-by-sentence reading time experiments is that initial sentences take longer to read than subsequent sentences (Cirilo 1981; Cirilo and Foss 1980; Glanzer, Fischer and Dorfman 1984; Graesser 1975; Haberlandt 1980, 1984; Haberlandt and Bingham 1978; Haberlandt and Graesser 1985; Olson, Duffy and Mack 1984).

In fact, initial sentences take longer to read than later-occurring sentences, even when the initial sentences are not the topic sentences of the paragraphs (Greeno and Noreen 1974; Kieras 1978, 1981). In addition, comprehenders take longer to read the beginning sentence of each episode within a story than other sentences in that episode (Haberlandt 1980, 1984; Haberlandt, Berian and Sandson 1980; Mandler and Goodman 1982). Similar phenomena occur when comprehenders encounter nonverbal materials, such as picture stories "told" without any text. For instance, researchers can set up a situation where subjects view each picture of a nonverbal picture story, one picture at a time. Although they can take as long as they want to view each picture, subjects spend more time viewing the beginning picture of each story and the beginning picture of each episode within a story than they spend viewing later-occurring pictures (Gernsbacher 1983).

To examine how comprehenders understand spoken language, some researchers play previously recorded sentences to subjects. The subjects' major task is to comprehend the sentences as well as they can. But often they have the additional task of monitoring for a specific word or a specific phoneme. When they hear the target word or phoneme, they press a button, and their reaction times are recorded.

A consistent finding in these monitoring studies is that reaction times are longer when the target phonemes or target words occur at the beginning of the sentences or clauses than when they occur later (Cairns and Kamerman 1975; Cutler and Foss 1977; Foss 1969, 1982; Hakes 1971; Marslen-Wilson, Tyler and Seidenberg 1978; Shields, McHugh and Martin 1974).

For example, when listening for the word *bears* in sentences like (3) and (4) above, subjects identify it more slowly in sentence (3) than in sentence (4). This is because *bears* occurs at the beginning of its clause in sentence (3), but it occurs at the end of its clause in sentence (4). At the beginnings of clauses, comprehenders are laying foundations.

Another tool for studying comprehension involves measuring the brain's electrical activity (or brain waves). These event-related brain waves can be recorded from the subjects' scalps while they are listening to or reading sentences. A particular brain wave is elicited by the first content word of a sentence (as opposed to words that occur later in the sentence). First content words elicit larger than average N400 brain waves. N400 brain waves are the negative component of the event-related brain waves that occur about 400 milliseconds after the stimulus. N400 brain waves are associated with difficulty in processing; for instance, less familiar words and words that are unexpected (from the context) also elicit large N400s (Kutas, van Petten and Besson 1988).

So, the sentence-by-sentence reading time data, the word-by-word reading time data, the phoneme-monitoring data, the word-monitoring data, and the event-related brain wave data all display the same pattern: Comprehenders spend more cognitive capacity processing initial words and initial sentences than later-occurring words and sentences. The picture-by-picture viewing time data demonstrate the same pattern. That similarity suggests that the pattern is not specific to language comprehension, but is a general phenomenon that occurs during comprehension of both linguistic and nonlinguistic information. But rather importantly, this pattern does not occur when the stimuli are less comprehensible — for example, when the sentences, paragraphs, or picture stories are self-embedded or extensively right branching (Foss and Lynch 1969; Gernsbacher 1983; Greeno & Noreen 1974; Hakes and Foss 1970; Kieras 1978, 1981).

Memory phenomena also demonstrate the privilege of primacy. For instance, the first content words or pictures of those first content words provide the best recall cues for their sentences (Bock and Irwin 1980; Prentice 1967; Turner and Rommetveit 1968). Similarly, the beginnings of story episodes provide the best cues for recalling those story episodes (Mandler and Goodman 1982). Indeed, when asked to recall the main idea of a paragraph, comprehenders are most likely to select the initial sentence — even when the actual theme is a later-occurring sentence (Kieras 1980).

Why do these primacy effects occur in language comprehension? In our research, we take the view that language comprehension draws on general cognitive processes (as well as language-specific processes). The general cognitive processes underlie non-language tasks as well. This commonality might arise because, as Lieberman (1984) and others have suggested, language comprehension evolved from other nonlinguistic skills. Or the commonality might arise simply because the mind is best understood by reference to a common architecture.

The Structure Building Framework

In our effort to understand the general cognitive processes that underlie language comprehension, we have proposed a simple framework we call the Structure Building Framework (Gernsbacher 1990; Gernsbacher in press). According to the Structure Building Framework, comprehension involves building coherent, mental representations or **structures**. These structures represent phrases, clauses, sentences, passages, and so forth. Building mental structures involves several cognitive processes. The first cognitive process is laying a foundation for their mental structures. The next cognitive process is mapping: Incoming information that coheres or relates to previous information is mapped onto the developing structure. However, if the incoming information is less coherent or less related, a different cognitive process is engaged: Comprehenders automatically shift and a new substructure is developed. Therefore, most mental representations of discourse comprise several branching substructures.

It is the process of laying a foundation that we propose underlies the primacy effects we described earlier. Comprehenders take more time to read words when they occur at the beginnings of sentences, clauses, or phrases because during the beginnings of sentences, clauses, and phrases, mental foundations are being laid. Similarly, comprehenders take more time to read sentences when those sentences occur at the beginnings of passages or episodes, because during the beginnings of passages or episodes, mental foundations are being laid. Similarly, comprehenders need more time to respond to target phonemes or words when those target phonemes or words occur during the the beginnings of sentences and phrases, because during the beginnings of sentences and phrases, mental foundations are being laid. Laying the foundation for a mental structure requires some mental effort; therefore, less mental effort is available to read words or sentences or to respond to target phonemes or target words.

Comprehenders recall sentences better when cued by initial words because the initial words form the foundations for the sentence-level mental structures. Similarly, comprehenders recall episodes better when cued by initial sentences because the initial sentences form the foundations for the episode-level mental structures. So, according to the Structure Building Framework, primacy effects occur in sentence and discourse comprehension because of the general cognitive process of laying a foundation.

The Advantage of First Mention in sentences

Another primacy effect that could result from the process of laying a foundation is what we refer to as the Advantage of First Mention. The advantage is this: After comprehending a sentence involving two participants, it is easier to remember the participant mentioned first in the sentence than the participant mentioned second. For example, after reading the sentence,

(5) *Tina beat Lisa in the state tennis match.*

if subjects are asked whether the name *Tina* occurred in the sentence, they respond considerably faster if *Tina* was the first person mentioned in the sentence, as she was in sentence (5), than if *Tina* was the second person mentioned in the sentence, as she is in,

(6) *Lisa beat Tina in the state tennis match.*

So the first-mentioned participant is more accessible from comprehenders' mental representations, which is what we mean by the Advantage of First Mention.

The Advantage of First Mention has been observed by several researchers (Chang 1980; Corbett and Chang 1983; Gernsbacher 1989; Stevenson

1986; von Eckardt and Potter 1985). One explanation draws on the Structure Building Framework's proposal that comprehension involves laying a foundation: First-mentioned participants are more accessible both because they form the foundations for their sentence-level structures, and because it is through this foundation that subsequent information is mapped onto the developing mental structure.

Because foundations can be based only on the information that comprehenders initially receive, first-mentioned participants must serve as the foundation for their sentence-level structures. Then, after a foundation is laid, subsequent information must be mapped onto that foundation; therefore, first-mentioned participants achieve even more accessibility because it is through them that subsequent information — including information about later-mentioned participants — is attached to the developing structure.

To summarize, we suggest that the Advantage of First Mention is a function of structure building: First-mentioned participants form the foundation of their sentence-level structures, and, therefore, the remainders of the sentences are represented *vis à vis* those initial participants.

Our proposal resembles the following idea advanced by MacWhinney (1977) in a paper aptly titled, "Starting Points":

> The speaker uses the first element in the English sentence as a starting point for the organization of the sentence as a whole. Similarly, the listener uses the first element in a sentence as a starting point in comprehension. Both the speaker and the listener seem to use special techniques for attaching the body of the sentence to the starting point. (p. 152).

MacWhinney's notions of "using a starting point" and "attaching the body of the sentence to the starting point" are captured in the Structure Building Framework's processes of laying a foundation and mapping subsequent information onto that foundation.

However, there are other explanations of the Advantage of First Mention. For instance, first-mentioned participants might be more accessible because of the structure of English: In English declarative sentences, first-mentioned participants are typically the syntactic relation called "subject," and they typically fill the semantic role considered "agent."

In a series of experiments, we investigated whether the Advantage of First Mention was due to these other factors (Gernsbacher and Hargreaves 1988). These experiments used the following laboratory task: Subjects read sentences that were presented word-by-word in the center of a video monitor. Each sentence was about two participants. After the last word of each sentence disappeared, a test name appeared. The subjects' task was to verify as rapidly and accurately as possible whether that test name had occurred in the sentence they just finished reading.

Is the Advantage of First Mention due to semantic agency?

In previous experiments, the first-mentioned participants were always semantic agents. Perhaps the Advantage of First Mention is actually an advantage of agency. Agents might gain a privileged place in comprehenders' mental representations for several linguistic and psycholinguistic reasons.

Semantic agents tend to be more animate (Clark 1965; Johnson 1967), more active (Osgood 1971), more positively evaluated (Johnson 1967), and more imageable (James 1972; James, Thompson and Baldwin 1973). Because of these characteristics, several theorists have suggested that agents are more likely to attract attention (Zubin 1979), stimulate empathy (Kuno and Kaburaki 1977), and match the speaker or listener's perspective (MacWhinney 1977). Semantic agents are also more likely to be their sentences' syntactic subjects (Greenberg 1963), topics (Givón 1983), and themes (Tomlin 1983). So, along many dimensions, semantic agents hold an advantage over semantic patients. Perhaps that is the basis of the Advantage of First Mention.

We empirically investigated this possibility in the following way: We constructed 32 sentence sets; an example appears in Table 1. Each sentence set comprised four versions of a prototype sentence. In two of the four ver-

Table 1

Agent
Tina *beat Lisa in the state tennis match.*
Lisa beat ***Tina*** *in the state tennis match.*
Patient
Tina *was beaten by Lisa in the state tennis match.*
Lisa was beaten by ***Tina*** *in the state tennis match.*

sions, the test names were the agents and either the first- or second-mentioned participants. In the other two versions, the test names were the patients and either the first- or second-mentioned participants.

In other words, we manipulated whether the test names were the first- versus second-mentioned participants, and whether the test names were the semantic agents versus patients. We also constructed 32 lure sentences whose test names had not occurred in their respective sentences (so the correct response to the test names following these sentences was "no"). The lure sentences resembled the experimental sentences in syntactic form: Half were in the active voice, and half were in the passive voice.[2]

We tested 96 subjects, whose average reaction times to the test names appear in Figure 2. As Figure 2 illustrates, we observed only an Advantage of First Mention. That is, first-mentioned participants were more accessible than second-mentioned participants, regardless of semantic agency. We replicated these results when we tested another 120 subjects using the same materials and procedures. We again observed only an Advantage of First Mention. So, comprehenders must represent sentences in such a way that first-mentioned participants are more accessible. But semantic role is not the factor underlying this greater accessibility.

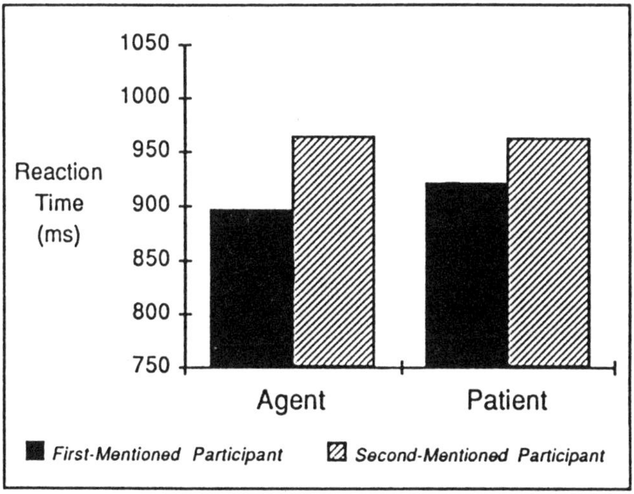

Figure 2. (*From Gernsbacher and Hargreaves 1988*)

Is the Advantage of First Mention due to syntactic subjecthood?

In previous experiments, the first-mentioned participants were always their sentences' syntactic subjects. However, in two other experiments we attempted to tease apart the Advantage of First Mention from an advantage for syntactic subject. We did this in one experiment by having both participants be subjects, as opposed to only the first-mentioned participants being subjects. Our sentences used joined-subject constructions, as in sentence (7), and single-subject constructions, as in sentence (8).

(7) *Tina and Lisa argued during the meeting.*
(8) *Tina argued with Lisa during the meeting.*

Our stimuli comprised three types of sentences. The first type was built around what we called lexical reciprocal verbs. These verbs described actions in which the two participants engaged in mutually complementary actions, and both participants were agents. For example, *argue*, *debate*, and *converse* are lexical reciprocal verbs. In the joined-subject condition, as in sentence (7) above, both participants were subjects. In the single-subject construction, as in (8) above, the first-mentioned participants were subjects, and the second-mentioned participants were objects of the preposition *with*.

The second type of sentences in our stimuli involved reciprocal anaphors. These sentences contained transitive verbs that could occur with reciprocal anaphoric expressions such as *each other* or *one another*. When used this way, both participants were subjects, as in

(9) *Tina and Lisa annoyed one another at the conference.*

However, when used without the reciprocal anaphoric expression, the first-mentioned participants were agents/subjects while the second-mentioned participants were patients/direct objects, as in

(10) *Tina annoyed Lisa at the conference.*

The third type of sentences in our stimuli were comitatives. These sentences contained simple intransitive verbs that did not involve reciprocal actions, for example,

(11) *Tina and Lisa hiked in the mountains.*

When used in a joined-subject construction, as in sentence (13), the verbs connoted that the two participants committed the act simultaneously, but not reciprocally.

For the lexical reciprocals and the reciprocal anaphors, we constructed 24 sentence sets by manipulating whether the test names were the first- versus second-mentioned participants, and whether the test names were joined versus single subjects. For the comitatives, we constructed 16 sentence sets by manipulating whether the test names were the first- versus second-mentioned participants. Table 2 shows examples.

We tested 120 subjects, whose average reaction times to respond to the test names appear in Figure 3. For all three types of sentences, we observed only an Advantage of First Mention: First-mentioned participants were considerably more accessible than second-mentioned participants. So, the Advantage of First Mention is not lost when both the first- and second-mentioned participants are syntactic subjects.

In another experiment, we separated the Advantage of First Mention from an advantage for syntactic subjects. We did this by taking one of the

Table 2

Lexical reciprocals

Joined subjects

__Tina__ and Lisa argued during the meeting.
Lisa and __Tina__ argued during the meeting.

Single subjects

__Tina__ argued with Lisa during the meeting.
Lisa argued with __Tina__ during the meeting.

Reciprocal anaphors

Joined subjects

__Tina__ and Lisa annoyed one another at the conference.
Lisa and __Tina__ annoyed one another at the conference.

Single subjects

__Tina__ annoyed Lisa at the conference.
Lisa annoyed __Tina__ at the conference.

Comitatives

Joined subjects

__Tina__ and Lisa hiked in the mountains.
Lisa and __Tina__ hiked in the mountains.

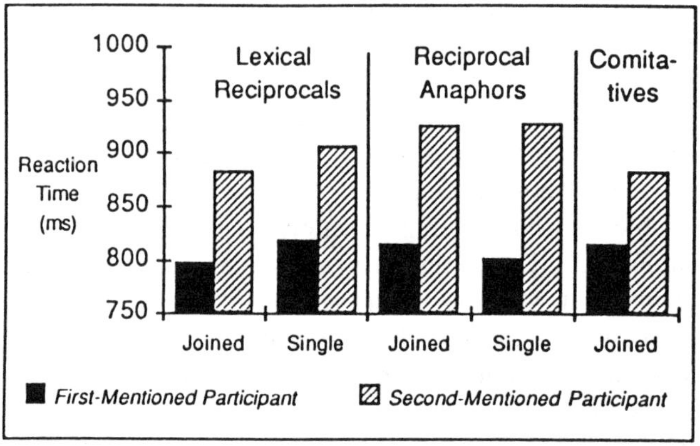

Figure 3. (*From Gernsbacher and Hargreaves 1988*)

participants out of its main clause and placing it in a complex prepositional phrase (Huddleston 1984). These prepositional phrases were either preposed, in which case the first-mentioned participants were not syntactic subjects, as in

(12) *Because of* ***Tina****, Lisa was evicted from the apartment.*

or the prepositional phrases were postposed, in which case the first-mentioned participants were syntactic subjects, as in

(13) ***Tina*** *was evicted from the apartment because of Lisa.*

In addition to manipulating the position of the prepositional phrases, we also manipulated whether the test names were the first- or second-mentioned participants.

We constructed 32 sentence sets. We used four different prepositional phrases: *because of, according to, compared with*, and *except for*. An example sentence set for each is shown in Table 3. We tested 80 subjects, whose reaction times to the test names appear in Figure 4. As Figure 4 illustrates, we observed an Advantage of First Mention: First-mentioned participants were considerably more accessible than second-mentioned participants. As Figure 4 also illustrates, the Advantage of First Mention was nearly doubled when the phrases were postposed. Perhaps the larger advantage in these postposed-sentences is due to the first-mentioned participants seeming to be the sole participants through the majority of their sentences.

Table 3

Preposed preposition	
	Because of ***Tina****, Lisa was evicted from the apartment.*
	Because of Lisa, ***Tina*** *was evicted from the apartment.*
	According to ***Tina****, Lisa was an inspiring teacher.*
	According to Lisa, ***Tina*** *was an inspiring teacher.*
	Except for ***Tina****, Lisa was the oldest member of the club.*
	Except for Lisa, ***Tina*** *was the oldest member of the club.*
	Compared with ***Tina****, Lisa was a tidy housekeeper.*
	Compared with Lisa, ***Tina*** *was a tidy housekeeper.*
Postposed preposition	
	Tina *was evicted from the apartment because of Lisa.*
	Lisa was evicted from the apartment because of ***Tina****.*
	Tina *was an inspiring teacher according to Lisa.*
	Lisa was an inspiring teacher according to ***Tina****.*
	Tina *was a tidy housekeeper compared with Lisa.*
	Lisa was a tidy housekeeper compared with ***Tina****.*
	Tina *was the oldest member of the club except for Lisa.*
	Lisa was the oldest member of the club except for ***Tina****.*

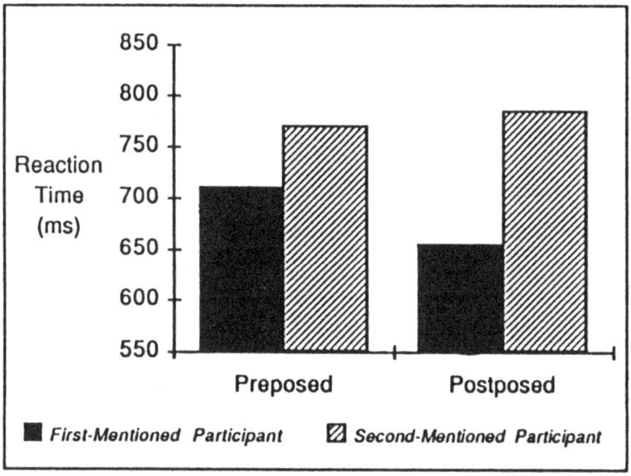

Figure 4. (*From Gernsbacher and Hargreaves 1988*)

From these experiments, we conclude that the Advantage of First Mention is not due to first-mentioned participants being semantic agents or syntactic subjects. Our Structure Building Framework explains the Advantage of First Mention by proposing that comprehension requires building a mental representation or structure. Building a mental structure requires both laying a foundation and mapping subsequent information onto that foundation. First-mentioned participants are more accessible because they form the foundation of their sentence-level representations, and because it is through them that subsequent information is mapped onto the developing representation.

The Advantage of First Mention versus the Advantage of Clause Recency

The Advantage of First Mention seems to contradict a second well-known advantage — what we call the Advantage of Clause Recency. The Advantage of Clause Recency is that immediately after comprehenders hear or read a two-clause sentence, words from the most recently heard or read clause are more accessible than words from an earlier clause (Bever and Townsend 1979; Caplan 1972; Chang 1980; Jarvella 1970, 1971, 1973, 1979; Jarvella and Herman 1972; Marslen-Wilson et al. 1978 ; von Eckardt and Potter 1985).

So, the Advantage of Clause Recency, like the Advantage of First Mention, is also caused by the order in which concepts are mentioned. But the Advantage of Clause Recency is an advantage for the most recent or second-mentioned concept.

How can this discrepancy be resolved? The Advantage of Clause Recency could also be due to structure building. According to the Structure Building Framework, language comprehension often requires shifting to initiate a new substructure. Comprehenders shift to initiate a new substructure when the incoming information is less related to the previous information, for instance, when the topic, point of view, or setting of a passage changes.

Indeed, words and sentences that change the ongoing topic, point of view, or setting take substantially longer to comprehend than words or sentences that continue the topic, point of view, or setting. We suggest that such words and sentences trigger comprehenders to shift and begin laying the foundation for a new substructure.

Comprehenders also have more difficulty retrieving information presented before a change in topic, point of view, or setting than they do retrieving information presented after such a change. According to the Structure Building Framework, information presented before the change is probably represented in one substructure, while information presented after the change is represented in another.

When building their representations of sentences, comprehenders might also shift and initiate a new substructure when speakers and writers signal the beginning of a new clause or phrase. In fact, one of Kimball's (Kimball 1973) seven parsing principles was that "the construction of a new node is signalled by the occurrence of a grammatical function word" (p. 29).

So, as Clark and Clark (1977) suggested, comprehenders might use signals such as determiners and quantifiers to initiate a substructure representing a new noun phrase. And they might use subordinating conjunctions (such as *because, although*) and coordinating conjunctions (*and, but*) as signals to initiate a substructure representing a new clause.

Thus, the Structure Building Framework can account for both of the seemingly contradictory phenomena: the Advantage of First Mention *and* the Advantage of Clause Recency. The Structure Building Framework accounts for these two phenomena by making the following assumptions: Comprehenders represent each clause of a multi-clause sentence in its own substructure. Comprehenders have the greatest access to the information that is represented in the substructure that they are currently developing, in other words, they have the greatest access to the most recent clause. However, at some point, the first clause becomes more accessible than other clauses because the substructure representing the first clause of a multi-clause sentence serves as a foundation for the whole sentence-level structure.

A series of experiments that we performed in collaboration with Mark Beeman tested these assumptions (Gernsbacher, Hargreaves and Beeman 1989). In each experiment, we measured the accessibility of sentence participants in two-clause sentences, for example,

(14) *Tina gathered the kindling, and Lisa set up the tent.*

As in sentence (14), the first-mentioned participants (e.g. *Tina*) were the syntactic subjects of the first clauses, and the second-mentioned participants (e.g. *Lisa*) were the syntactic subjects of the second clauses. By measuring how rapidly subjects accessed these two sentence participants, we investigated how comprehenders build their mental representations of sentence clauses.

Do comprehenders have greatest access to the substructure they are currently building?

In our first experiment we tested the Structure Building Framework's assumption that comprehenders have greatest access to information represented in the substructure that they are currently building. To test this assumption, we wanted to catch comprehenders when they were just finishing building substructures to represent the second clauses. If we could capture that point, we expected to find an Advantage of Clause Recency — in other words, we expected an advantage for the second-mentioned participant.

Because we wanted to present the test names right when our subjects were finishing comprehending the second clauses, we presented the test names coincident with the last words in the sentences. However, we presented the test names at a different location on the computer screen than where we presented the sentences. We supposed that by the time our subjects shifted their eyes and their attention (Posner 1980) from the sentences to the test names, our coincident presentation was comparable to an extremely short delay.

We constructed 48 sentence sets; an example appears in Table 4. Each sentence set resulted from manipulating whether the test name was the first- versus second-mentioned participant (in other words, whether the test name was the subject of the first clause or the subject of the second clause), and whether the test name was the subject of a main, a subordinate, or a coordinate clause.

Because each verb phrase had to serve in a main, subordinate, and coordinate clause, the two verb phrases in each sentence had to be relatively equivalent along several dimensions. For example, their action had to occur at about the same time, last about the same period, and be of equal importance, and neither action could be the impetus for the other.

To construct such sentences, we first selected pairs of verb phrases whose actions were relatively equivalent subcomponents of a larger activity, for example, *sang a song* and *played the guitar, dusted the shelves* and *swept the floor, did aerobics* and *lifted weights*. All verbs were transitive and took direct objects. To reduce temporal asymmetries, we assigned both verbs to the simple past tense (Haiman and Thompson 1984).

Table 4

Main clauses
Tina *gathered the kindling as Lisa set up the tent.*
As Lisa set up the tent, ***Tina*** *gathered the kindling.*
Subordinate clauses
As ***Tina*** *gathered the kindling, Lisa set up the tent.*
Lisa set up the tent as ***Tina*** *gathered the kindling.*
Coordinate clauses
Tina *gathered the kindling, and Lisa set up the tent.*
Lisa set up the tent, and ***Tina*** *gathered the kindling.*

When the sentences appeared in their subordinate clause condition, they appeared with one of the following four temporal subordinators: *as, when, before*, and *after*. Each subordinator was randomly assigned to twelve sentence sets. When the sentences appeared in their coordinate clause conditions, they were joined with *and*.

We tested 120 subjects, whose average reaction times to the test names are displayed in the two left-most bars of Figure 5. As Figure 5 illustrates, when the test names were presented coincident with the last words of their sentences, we observed an Advantage of Clause Recency: Second-mentioned participants were considerably more accessible than first-mentioned participants. This 60 millisecond difference is the same magnitude as the Advantage of Clause Recency observed by others (e.g. Caplan 1972).

So, immediately after a two-clause sentence is comprehended, the second clause — the more recent clause — is more accessible. This finding supports the Structure Building Framework's assumptions that comprehenders have greatest access to information represented in the substructure that they are currently developing.

Do comprehenders represent each clause in its own substructure?

According to the Structure Building Framework, after comprehenders represent the second clause of a two-clause sentence, they must map that sec-

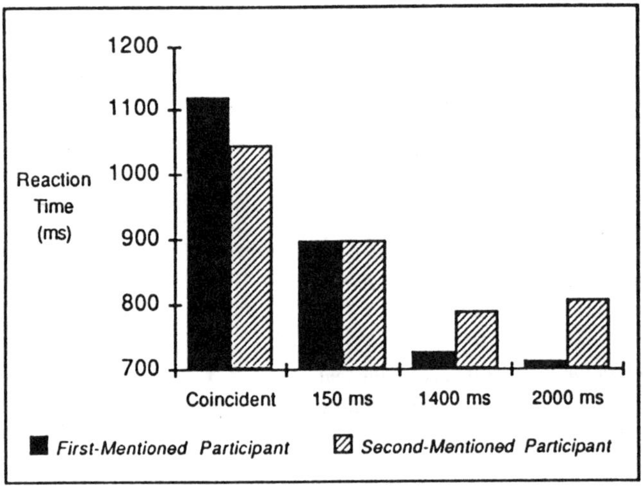

Figure 5. (*From Gernsbacher, Hargreaves and Beeman 1989*)

ond-clause representation onto their first-clause representation. In other words, to fully represent a two-clause sentence, comprehenders must incorporate the two substructures.

The goal in our next experiment was to catch comprehenders after they had built substructures to represent each clause, but before they had mapped the substructure representing the second clause onto the substructure representing the first clause. According to the Structure Building Framework, if we could capture that point, the two clauses should be equally accessible. To capture that point, we presented the test names 150 milliseconds after the offset of the final words of their sentences.

We tested 120 subjects, whose data appear in the third and fourth bars of Figure 5. As Figure 5 illustrates, when accessibility was measured 150 milliseconds after the sentences, the two clauses were equally accessible. That is, first-mentioned participants were just as accessible as second-mentioned participants. We observed the same results in a replication experiment. So, at some point during the comprehension of a two-clause sentence, the two clauses are equally accessible. This finding supports the Structure Building Framework's assumption that each clause is represented in its own substructure.

Do first clauses form the foundation for their sentence-level structures?

According to the Structure Building Framework, to fully represent a two-clause sentence, comprehenders must incorporate the two substructures. Therefore, in our experiments if we measured accessibility a little bit later — say, a little more than a second later — no longer should both clauses be equally accessible.

Instead, if comprehenders have successfully mapped the two clauses together, the first clause should be more accessible than the second clause. In other words, we should observe an Advantage of First Mention. This advantage would suggest that the substructure representing the first clause is serving as the foundation for the whole sentence-level representation.

We tested this prediction by measuring accessibility after we assumed that comprehenders had time to map the substructures representing the two clauses together. More specifically, we presented the test names 1400 milliseconds after the offset of the final words of their sentences.

We tested 96 subjects, whose data appear in the fifth and sixth bars of Figure 5. As Figure 5 illustrates, when accessibility was measured 1400 milliseconds after the end of each sentence we observed an Advantage of First Mention: First-mentioned participants were considerably more accessible than second-mentioned participants. This 60 millisecond Advantage of First Mention is the same magnitude as the advantage typically observed with simple sentences (e.g. those we described earlier in this chapter).

Let us review the three experiments we have just described: At our earliest test point, second-mentioned participants were more accessible; in other words, there was an Advantage of Clause Recency. According to the Structure Building Framework, comprehenders were still developing their substructures to represent the second clauses. When we measured accessibility 150 milliseconds later, the two sentence participants were equally accessible. According to the Structure Building Framework, comprehenders had built their substructures representing both clauses, but they had not begun mapping those substructures together. When we measured accessibility after 1400 milliseconds, we observed an Advantage of First Mention. According to the Structure Building Framework, comprehenders had finished mapping the two substructures together, and the first clause was more accessible because its substructure serves as the foundation for the whole sentence-level representation.

These results support the Structure Building Framework's assumptions about how comprehenders build mental structures to represent clauses: Comprehenders represent each clause of a two-clause sentence in its own substructure. Comprehenders have greatest access to information in the substructure that they are currently developing (i.e., the most recent clause). But at some point, the first clause becomes more accessible because the substructure representing the first clause of a two-clause sentence serves as a foundation for the whole sentence-level representation.

In another experiment, the test names appeared 2000 milliseconds after the offset of their sentences' final words. We tested 120 subjects, whose data appear in the two right-most bars of Figure 5. As Figure 5 illustrates, when accessibility was measured 2000 milliseconds after the end of each sentence, there was still an Advantage of First Mention. That is, first-mentioned participants were still considerably more accessible than second-mentioned participants.

So, two seconds after comprehenders finish reading a two-clause sentence, participants from the first clause are still more accessible than participants from the second clause. In fact, the Advantage of First Mention is even greater 2000 milliseconds after the sentences than it is 1400 milliseconds afterward. The Advantage of First Mention is a relatively long-lived characteristic of the representation of a sentence. In contrast, the Advantage of Clause Recency is relatively short-lived. It is observed only when we measure accessibility immediately after comprehenders finish reading the second clause.

Can the Advantage of First Mentioned and the Advantage of Clause Recency co-occur?

According to the Structure Building Framework, the Advantage of First Mention arises because first-mentioned participants form the foundations for their sentence-level structures, and through them subsequent information is mapped onto the developing structure. The Advantage of Clause Recency arises because comprehenders build a substructure to represent each clause of a two-clause sentence, and they have greatest access to information represented in the substructure that they are currently developing.

Thus, when comprehension is viewed as structure building, these two seemingly contradictory phenomena — the Advantage of First Mention and the Advantage of Clause Recency — are not mutually exclusive. In fact, according to the Structure Building Framework, the two phenomena can occur simultaneously. We demonstrated this in a fifth experiment.

In this experiment, we measured the accessibility of each of four participants, for instance, *Tina, Lisa, Ann*, and *Pam* in

(15) *Tina and Lisa gathered the kindling, and Ann and Pam set up the tent.*

As in sentence (15), two participants were the joined subjects of the first clause (e.g. *Tina* and *Lisa*), and two participants were the joined subjects of the second clause (e.g. *Ann* and *Pam*). In other words, two participants were the first- and second-mentioned participants of the first clause, and two participants were the first- and second-mentioned participants of the second clause.

According to the Structure Building Framework, within both clauses we should observe an Advantage of First Mention: That is, the participants mentioned first in each clause should be more accessible than the participants mentioned second. This is because the participants mentioned first in each clause should form the foundation for their clause-level substructure.

In addition, according to the Structure Building Framework, if we catch comprehenders at the point where they are just finishing building their representations of the second clause, we should also observe an Advantage of Clause Recency: Both participants from the second clause should be more accessible than both participants from the first clause. This is because each clause of a two-clause sentence should be represented in its own substructure, and information should be most accessible from the substructure that comprehenders are currently developing.

To test these predictions, we constructed 32 sentence sets; an example appears in Table 5. Each sentence set resulted from manipulating (a) whether the test name was the clause's first- versus second-mentioned participant, and (b) whether the test name was from the first versus second clause.

The verb phrases for the sentence sets were drawn from the pool of verbs used in the previous four experiments. All verbs were in the simple past tense, and all sentences comprised two main clauses joined with *and*. We tested 80 subjects, whose average reaction times to the test names appear in Figure 6. As Figure 6 illustrates, we observed an Advantage of First Mention: For both clauses, the first-mentioned participants were considerably more accessible than the second-mentioned participants. As Fig-

Table 5

First clause
Tina *and Lisa gathered the kindling, and Ann and Pam set up the tent.*
Lisa and ***Tina*** *gathered the kindling, and Pam and Ann set up the tent.*
Second Clause
Ann and Pam set up the tent, and ***Tina*** *and Lisa gathered the kindling.*
Pam and Ann set up the tent, and Lisa and ***Tina*** *gathered the kindling.*

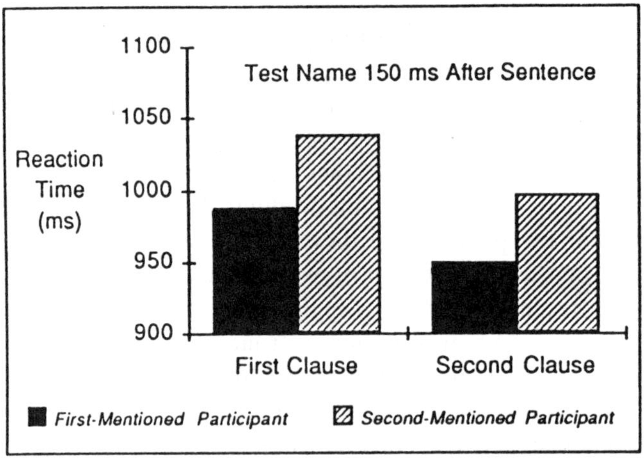

Figure 6. (*From Gernsbacher, Hargreaves and Beeman 1989*)

ure 6 also illustrates, we observed an Advantage of Clause Recency: Participants from the second clause were more accessible than participants from the first clause. No other effects were reliable, including the interaction between the Advantage of First Mention and the Advantage of Clause Recency.

So, this experiment — like the first experiment of this series — demonstrated that immediately after a two-clause sentence, the most recently read clause is more accessible than an earlier clause. According to the Structure Building Framework, this is because each clause of a two-clause sentence is represented in its own substructure, and comprehenders have greatest access to information represented in the substructure that they are currently developing.

This experiment also demonstrated that when two participants are mentioned in the same clause, the first-mentioned participant is more accessible. According to the Structure Building Framework, this is because the first participant in each clause forms the foundation for its clause-level substructure.

The Advantage of First Mention and the Advantage of Clause Recency can occur simultaneously. However, according to the Structure Building Framework, the Advantage of First Mention is a relatively long-lived characteristic of a sentence or clause, whereas the Advantage of Clause Recency is observed only when accessibility is measured immediately after comprehension of the most recent clause. Therefore, if we again presented two-clause sentences that mentioned two participants in each clause, but we measured accessibility a little later, we should no longer observe an Advantage of Clause Recency; instead, we should observe only an Advantage of First Mention. We tested this prediction in our sixth and final experiment.

This last experiment was identical to the experiment just described except that all test names appeared 2000 milliseconds after the offset of their sentences' final words. We tested 80 subjects, whose data appear in Figure 7. As Figure 7 illustrates, with two-clause sentences that mentioned

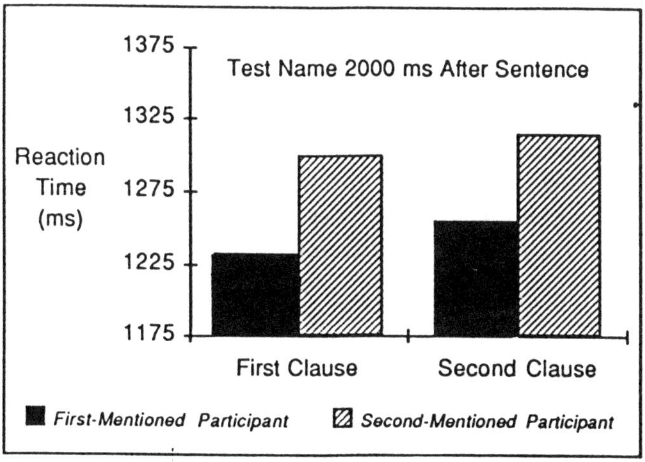

Figure 7. (*From Gernsbacher, Hargreaves and Beeman 1989*)

two participants in each clause, we again observed an Advantage of First Mention: For both clauses, first-mentioned participants were considerably more accessible than second-mentioned participants.

However, as Figure 7 also illustrates, when accessibility was measured 2000 milliseconds after the end of each sentence, as opposed to 150 milliseconds after, we no longer observed an Advantage of Clause Recency. In contrast to our fifth experiment in which the second-clause participants were considerably more accessible than the first-clause participants, in this last experiment the second-clause participants were slightly less accessible than the first-clause participants.

These experiments support the following assumptions made by the Structure Building Framework: Comprehenders represent each clause of a multi-clause sentence in its own substructure. Comprehenders have greatest access to information represented in the substructure that they are currently developing; that is, they have greatest access to the most recent clause. However, at some point the first clause becomes more accessible than later clauses because the substructure representing the first clause of a two-clause sentence serves as a foundation for the whole sentence-level representation.

Do comprehenders build hierarchical structures?

To observe the Advantage of First Mention simultaneously with the Advantage of Clause Recency, we capitalized on intra-clause versus inter-clause relations. We observed the Advantage of First Mention at one level — within a clause — and the Advantage of Clause Recency at another level — between two clauses.

Comprehenders' mental structures and substructures must capture these hierarchical relations. Clauses are represented in their own substructures, and sentences, comprising those clauses, are represented in larger substructures. Consider the four participants in sentence (17):

(17) *Tina and Lisa gathered the kindling, and Ann and Pam set up the tent.*

Because *Tina* and *Lisa* are members of the first clause, they are represented in one substructure, while *Ann* and *Pam*, the members of the second clause, are represented in another substructure. If the four participants were remembered as only four names in an unstructured list, then Figure 6 should resemble a typical serial position curve. The first bar should be short (manifesting the primacy component of the curve); the second bar should be somcwhat longer; the third bar might be equally long as the second or perhaps slightly longer, and the fourth bar should be short, perhaps even the shortest (manifesting the recency component).

But instead, the first bar is shorter than the second bar (manifesting the Advantage of First Mention in the first clause), and the third bar is shorter than the fourth bar (manifesting the Advantage of First Mention in the second clause). Furthermore, the third and fourth bars are shorter than the first and second bars (manifesting the Advantage of Clause Recency).

Comparing Figures 6 and 7, we see that the third and fourth bars change almost as a unit. Both bars become taller with the increased test delay; however, the relationship between the third and fourth bar is maintained. Again, this is not the pattern expected if the four participants are remembered only as four names in an unstructured list. If that were the case, Figure 7 should resemble a serial position curve with only the primacy component: The first bar should be the shortest, and the remaining bars but should be progressively longer. Instead, the third bar is shorter than the fourth bar, just as the first bar is shorter than the second bar. This pattern occurs because the first participant of each clause forms the foundation for its clause-level representation.

In what sense does the first-mentioned participant form a foundation? It is in the sense that a first-born child, a first trip to Europe, or a first romance earns a special status. All other children, trips to Europe, or romances are interpreted with reference to the initial one. So, by definition, later-occurring sentence participants must be understood with reference to the first-mentioned participant. *Lisa* accompanied *Tina* in gathering the kindling, and *Pam* accompanied *Ann* in setting up the tent. First-mentioned participants are not more important; they simply come first, and their precedence affects the subsequent representation.

The same privilege by precedence occurs with clauses — particularly clauses of equal status, like the ones we examined in our experiments. Knowledge that *Ann and Pam set up the tent* is added to the knowledge that *Tina and Lisa gathered the kindling*. Again, the first clauses are not more important; they simply come first, and their precedence affects the subsequent representation.

Primacy effects in sentence production

We have suggested that in language comprehension the privilege of primacy arises from general cognitive processes, those involved in structure building. Mental structures are built sequentially: First, foundations are laid. Because foundations can be based only on the information that comprehenders initially receive, initialized concepts must serve as the foundation for their sentence-level structures. Then, after a foundation is laid, subsequent information is mapped onto that foundation; therefore, first-mentioned concepts achieve even more accessibility because it is through them that subsequent information — including information about later-mentioned concepts — is attached to the developing structure.

Language production also involves sequencing. Speakers must confront what Levelt (1981) calls the *linearization problem*: They must decide "what to say first, what to say next, and so on" (p. 305). In other words, speakers face "the problem of mapping nonlinear meanings onto a highly constrained linear medium" (Bates and MacWhinney, 1989: 8). In this last section, we consider how speakers' placement of lexical items in initial position reflects their cognitive processes.

The demands of real time discourse constrain the ordering of elements in a message. For efficient, fluent production, those parts of the message that occur to the speaker first — for whatever reason — are most likely to be placed first in the sentence (Kempen and Hoenkamp 1987; Levelt 1989). However, the tendency to place more accessible items first is constrained by language-specific grammatical structures (Bates and Devescovi 1989; MacWhinney and Bates 1978). So, placement via accessibility competes with morphosyntactic constraints (Bates and MacWhinney 1989). In short, we would expect "free" word order languages to manifest placement via accessibility more transparently than other languages.

Several factors make lexical items more accessible. Experiments with English speakers demonstrate that perceptually salient, animate, and definite concepts are likely to be mentioned first (Clark and Chase 1974; Costerman and Hupet 1977; Grieve and Wales 1973; Harris 1978; Hupet and LeBoudec 1975; Johnson-Laird 1968a; Johnson-Laird 1968b; Turner and Rommetveit 1967); see reviews by Anisfeld and Klenbort (1973), Bock (1982) and MacWhinney (1977).

Experiments with English speakers also demonstrate that concepts that are explicitly cued or implicitly presupposed are also likely to be mentioned first (Bock 1977; Bock and Irwin 1980; Carroll 1958; Englekamp and Zimmer 1982; Klenbort and Anisfeld 1974; MacWhinney and Bates 1978; Olson and Filby 1972; Prentice 1966; Prentice 1967; Singer 1976; Tannenbaum and Williams 1968; Turner and Rommetveit 1967; Turner and Rommetveit 1968); see reviews by Bates and MacWhinney (1982) and Bock (1982).

What about other languages? Unfortunately, cross-linguistic studies of sentence production are rare. One exception is Sridhar's (1988) study of ten diverse languages (Cantonese, American English, Finnish, Modern Israeli Hebrew, Hungarian, Slovenian, Mexican Spanish, Japanese, Turkish, and Kannada). Across these diverse languages, Sridhar observed reliable preferences for initialization.

When describing scenes, Sridhar's subjects commonly mentioned figures before grounds, and they mentioned near objects before far objects. When describing events, they mentioned sources before goals, and they preserved the chronological order of events. Other things being equal, speakers mentioned humans before animates and animates before inanimates.

Cross-linguistic text studies (as demonstrated by this volume) have analyzed a variety of "free" and "fixed" word orders. These studies demonstrate the discourse factors that favors first mention; that is, important, focused or newsworthy participants are mentioned first (Givón 1989; Mithun this volume). Important, focused or newsworthy items are likely to be more accessible in speakers' mental representations; therefore, they are likely to be mentioned first. Similarly, their discourse status is also likely to make them suitable foundations for comprehenders' mental representations. In the name of parsimony, we suggest that the privilege of primacy observed in language production, like the privilege of primacy observed in language comprehension, derives from general cognitive processes and the demands of sequential ordering.

What about pragmatic motivations?

We have suggested that general cognitive processes in both comprehension and production contribute to a privileged status for first-mentioned concepts. It is not surprsing then that cross-linguistic text studies demonstrate that speakers tend to initialize concepts that are important, focused or newsworthy. Nevertheless, we find it important to distinguish between the general cognitive processes involved in production and comprehension and the pragmatic processes that are associated with word order.

Cooperative speakers presumably have a discourse model of what they think will be communicatively effective and contextually relevant for the listener (Clark and Wilkes-Gibbs 1986). This model could include the knowledge that initial position serves as the basis for comprehenders' mental structures. If speakers have this knowledge, they might intentionally exploit first mention to aid listeners in their structure building.

In addition, cooperative listeners presumably have a discourse model of what they think the speaker intends to communicate (Sperber and Wilson 1986). This model could include the knowledge that initial position reflects those items that are perceptually prominent or contextually salient to the speaker. If so, listeners might interpret initialization as an indicator of the speakers' viewpoint or intent.

Furthermore, in conversation, the role of the participants as speakers and listeners is negotiated via the turn-taking system (Sachs, Schegloff and Jefferson 1974). Thus, the turn-taking system might motivate speakers to initialize items in certain contexts (Duranti and Ochs 1979). Conversely, turn-taking allocation might constrain when and where items may be initialized (Ford 1988). In short, interactional features may also play a role in determining how speakers exploit first position in the clause.

The distinction we want to make is between an account of primacy effects in terms of general cognitive processes (like structure building) and an account of word order pragmatics in terms of discourse motivations and communicative goals. We are not in a position to describe how the complex inferential and intentional processes in discourse (what we would call pragmatics) interact with a general cognitive process like structure building. Indeed, the attribution and characterization of intentional processes is subject to intense debate in philosophy and cognitive science (Brand 1984; Dennett 1987; Fodor 1987; Stich 1983). However, we do suggest that when word order is exploited for communicative purposes, it is the general cognitive processes involved in production and comprehension that mediate the desired effects.

Notes

1. This research was supported by Research Career Development Award KO4 NS-01376 from the National Institute of Health, Air Force Office of Sponsored Research Grants 89-0258 and 89-0111, and the National Science Foundation Grant BNS85-10096 (all awarded to MAG). This chapter is based on research reported in Gernsbacher and Hargreaves (1988) and Gernsbacher, Hargreaves and Beeman (1989).

2. To encourage our subjects to attend to all aspects of the sentences (not just the participants' names), we followed each experimental sentence with a two-alternative question. A third of the questions asked about the setting of the action, for example, *When did Tina beat Lisa?* or *When did Lisa beat Tina?* Another third asked about the action the participants engaged in, for example, *What did Tina do?* or *What did Lisa do?*. And the final third asked about the identity of the agents or patients, for example, *Who did Tina beat?* or *Who did Lisa beat?*

References

Aaronson, D. & S. Ferres. 1983. "Lexical Categories and Reading Tasks." *Journal of Experimental Psychology: Human Perception and Performance* 9.675-699.

Aaronson, D. & H.S. Scarborough. 1976. "Performance Theories for Sentence Coding: Some Quantitative Evidence." *Journal of Experimental Psychology: Human Perception and Performance* 2.56-70.

Anderson, N.H. & A.A. Barrios. 1961. "Primacy Effects in Personality Formation." *Journal of Abnormal and Social Psychology* 63.346-350.

Anisfeld, M. & I. Klenbort. 1973. "On the Functions of Structural Paraphrase: The View from the Passive Voice." *Psychological Bulletin* 79.117-126.

Asch, S.E. 1946. "Forming Impressions of Personality." *Journal of Abnormal and Social Psychology* 41.258-290.

Bates, E. & A. Devescovi. 1989. "Cross-Linguistic Studies of Sentence Production." *The Cross-Linguistic Study of Sentence Processing* ed. by B. MacWhinney & E. Bates, 225-253. Cambridge, UK: Cambridge University Press.

Bates, E. & B. MacWhinney. 1982. "Functionalist Approaches to Grammar." *Language Acquisition: The State of the Art* ed. by E. Wanner & L. R. Gleitman, 173-218. Cambridge, UK: Cambridge University Press.

Bates, E. & B. MacWhinney. 1989. "Functionalism and the Competition Model." *The Cross-Linguistic Study of Sentence Processing* ed. by B. MacWhinney & E. Bates, 3-73. Cambridge, UK: Cambridge University Press.

Bever, T.G. & D. Townsend. 1979. "Perceptual Mechanisms and Formal Properties of Main and Subordinate Clauses." *Sentence Processing: Psycholinguistic Studies Presented to Merrill Garrett* ed. by W.E. Cooper & E.C.T. Walker, 159-226. Hillsdale, N.J.: Erlbaum.

Bock, J. K. 1977. "The Effect of Pragmatic Presupposition on the Syntactic Structure in Question Answering." *Journal of Verbal Learning and Verbal Behavior* 16.723-734.
Bock, J. K. 1982. "Toward a Cognitive Psychology of Syntax: Information Processing Contributions to Sentence Formulation." *Psychological Review* 89.1-47.
Bock, J. K. & D.E. Irwin. 1980. "Syntactic Effects of Information Availability in Sentence Production." *Journal of Verbal Learning and Verbal Behavior* 19.467-484.
Brand, M. 1984. *Intending and acting*. Cambridge, MA: MIT Press.
Bruner, J.S. & A.L. Minturn. 1955. "Perceptual Identification and Perceptual Organization." *Journal of General Psychology* 53.21-28.
Cairns, H. S. & J. Kamerman. 1975. "Lexical Information Processing During Sentence Comprehension." *Journal of Verbal Learning and Verbal Behavior* 14.170-179.
Caplan, D. 1972. "Clause Boundaries and Recognition Latencies for Words in Sentences." *Perception & Psychophysics* 12.73-76.
Carroll, J. B. 1958. "Process and Content in Psycholinguistics." *Current Trends in the Description and Analysis of Behavior* ed. R. Glaser, 175-200. Pittsburgh, PA: University of Pittsburgh Press.
Chang, F. R. 1980. "Active Memory Processes in Visual Sentence Comprehension: Clause Effects and Pronominal Reference." *Memory & Cognition* 8.58-64.
Cirilo, R. K. 1981. "Referential Coherence and Text Structure in Story Comprehension." *Journal of Verbal Learning and Verbal Behavior* 20.358-367.
Cirilo, R. K. & D.J. Foss. 1980. "Text Structure and Reading Time for Sentences." *Journal of Verbal Learning and Verbal Behavior* 19.96-109.
Clark, H. H. 1965. "Some Structural Properties of Simple Active and Passive Clauses." *Journal of Verbal Learning and Verbal Behavior* 4.365-370.
Clark, H. H. & W.G. Chase. 1974. "Perceptual Coding Strategies in the Formation and Verification of Descriptions." *Memory & Cognition* 2.101-111.
Clark, H. H. & E.V. Clark. 1977. *Psychology and Language: An Introduction to Psycholinguistics*. New York: Harcourt Brace Jovanavich.
Clark, H. H. & D. Wilkes-Gibbs. 1986. "Referring as a Collaborative Process." *Cognition* 22.1-39.
Corbett, A. T. & F.R. Chang. 1983. "Pronoun Disambiguation: Accessing Potential Antecedents." *Memory & Cognition* 11.283-294.
Costerman, J. & M. Hupet. 1977. "The Other Side of Johnson-Laird's Interpretation of the Passive Voice." *British Journal of Psychology* 68.107-111.
Cutler, A. & D.J. Foss. 1977. "On the Role of Sentence Stress in Sentence Processing." *Language and Speech* 21.1-10.
Dennett, D. C. 1987. *The Intentional Stance*. Cambridge, MA: MIT Press.
Duranti, A. & E. Ochs. 1979. "Left-Dislocation in Italian Conversation." *Syntax and Semantics: Discourse and Syntax* ed. by T. Givón, 377-414. New York: Academic Press.
Englekamp, J. & H.D. Zimmer. 1982. "The Interaction of Subjectivisation and Concept Placement in the Processing of Cleft Sentences." *Quarterly Journal of Experimental Psychology* 34A.463-478.
Fodor, J. 1987. *Psychosemantics: The Problem of Meaning in the Philosophy of Mind.* Cambridge, MA: MIT Press.

Ford, C. E. 1988. *Grammar in Ordinary Interaction: The Pragmatics of Adverbial Clauses in Conversational English.* Unpublished doctoral dissertation, University of California at Los Angeles, Los Angeles.

Foss, D. J. 1969. "Decision Processes During Sentence Comprehension: Effects of Lexical Item Difficulty and Position Upon Decision Times." *Journal of Verbal Learning and Verbal Behavior* 8.457-462.

Foss, D. J. 1982. "A Discourse on Semantic Priming." *Cognitive Psychology* 14.590-607.

Foss, D. J. & R.H. Lynch Jr. 1969. "Decision Processes During Sentence Comprehension: Effects of Surface Structure on Decision Times." *Perception & Psychophysics* 5.145-148.

Gernsbacher, M. A. 1983. *Memory for the Orientation of Pictures in Nonverbal Stories: Parallels and Insights into Language Processing.* Unpublished doctoral dissertation, University of Texas at Austin, Austin.

Gernsbacher, M. A. 1989. "Mechanisms that Improve Referential Access." *Cognition* 32.99-156.

Gernsbacher, M. A. 1990. *Language Comprehension as Structure Building.* Hillsdale, NJ: Erlbaum.

Gernsbacher, M. A. (1991). "Cognitive Processes and Mechanisms in Language Comprehension: The Structure Building Framework." *The Psychology of Learning and Motivation* ed. by G. H. Bower, 217-263. New York: Academic Press.

Gernsbacher, M. A. & D. Hargreaves. 1988. "Accessing Sentence Participants: The Advantage of First Mention." *Journal of Memory and Language* 27.699-717.

Gernsbacher, M. A., D. Hargreaves, & M. Beeman. 1989. "Building and Accessing Clausal Representations: The Advantage of First Mention Versus the Advantage of Clause Recency." *Journal of Memory and Language* 28.735-755.

Givón, T. 1983. *Topic Continuity in Discourse: A Quantitative Cross-Language Study.* Amsterdam: Benjamins.

Givón, T. 1989. *Mind, Code and Context: Essays in Pragmatics.* Hillsdale, NJ: Erlbaum.

Glanzer, M., B. Fischer, & D. Dorfman. 1984. "Short-Term Storage in Reading." *Journal of Verbal Learning and Verbal Behavior* 23.467-486.

Graesser, A. C. 1975. "Study Times for Sentences in Stories." Paper presented at the annual meeting of Western Psychological Association, Los Angeles.

Greenberg, J. H. 1963. *Some Universals of Grammar with Particular Reference to the Order of Meaningful Elements.* Cambridge, MA: MIT Press.

Greeno, J. G. & D.L. Noreen. 1974. "Time to Read Semantically Related Sentences." *Memory & Cognition* 2.117-120.

Grieve, R. & R.J. Wales. 1973. "Passives and Topicalization." *British Journal of Psychology* 64.173-182.

Haberlandt, K. 1980. "Story Grammar and Reading Time of Story Constituent." *Poetics* 9.99-118.

Haberlandt, K. 1984. "Components of Sentence and Word Reading Times." *New Methods in Reading Comprehension Research* ed. by D. E. Kieras & M. A. Just, 219-252. Hillsdale, NJ: Erlbaum.

Haberlandt, K. C. Berian, & J. Sandson. 1980. "The Episode Schema in Story Processing." *Journal of Verbal Learning and Verbal Behavior* 19.635-650.

Haberlandt, K. & G. Bingham. 1978. "Verbs Contribute to the Coherence of Brief Narratives: Reading Related and Unrelated Sentence Triples." *Journal of Verbal Learning and Verbal Behavior* 17.419-425.

Haberlandt, K. F. & A.C. Graesser. 1985. "Component Processes in Text Comprehension and Some of Their Interactions." *Journal of Experimental Psychology: General* 114.357-374.

Haiman, J. & S.A. Thompson. 1984. ""Subordination" in Universal Grammar." *Proceedings of the 10th Annual Meeting of the Berkeley Linguistics Society*, 510-523. Berkeley, CA: Berkeley Linguistics Society.

Hakes, D.T. 1971. "Does Verb Structure Affect Sentence Comprehension?" *Perception & Psychophysics* 10.229-232.

Hakes, D. T. & D.J. Foss. 1970. "Decision Processes During Sentence Comprehension: Effects of Surface Structure Reconsidered." *Perception & Psychophysics* 8.413-416.

Harris, M. 1978. "Noun Animacy and the Passive Voice: A Developmental Approach." *Quarterly Journal of Experimental Psychology* 30.495-504.

Huddleston, R. 1984. *Introduction to the Grammar of English*. Cambridge: Cambridge University Press.

Hupet, M. & B. LeBoudec. 1975. "Definiteness and Voice in the Interpretation of Active and Passive Sentences." *Quarterly Journal of Experimental Psychology* 27.323-330.

James, C. T. 1972. "Theme and Imaginary in the Recall of Active and Passive Sentences." *Journal of Verbal Learning and Verbal Behavior* 11.205-211.

James, C. T. J.G. Thompson, & J.M. Baldwin. 1973. "The Reconstructive Process in Sentence Memory." *Journal of Verbal Learning and Verbal Behavior* 12.51-63.

Jarvella, R.J. 1970. "Effects of Syntax on Running Memory Span for Connected Discourse." *Psychonomic Science* 19.235-236.

Jarvella, R.J. 1971. "Syntactic Processng of Conneceted Speech." *Journal of Verbal Learning and Verbal Behavior* 10. 409-416.

Jarvella, R.J. 1973. "Co-Reference and Short Term Memory for Discourse." *Journal of Experimental Psychology* 96.426-428.

Jarvella, R.J. 1979. "Immediate Memory and Discourse Processing." *The Psychology of Learning and Motivation* ed. by G. H. Bower, 379-421. New York: Academic Press.

Jarvella, R.J. & S.J. Herman. 1972 "Clause Structure of Sentences and Speech Processing." *Perception and Psychophysics* 11.381-384.

Johnson, M. G. 1967. "Syntactic Position and Rated Meaning." *Journal of Verbal Learning and Verbal Behavior* 6.240-246.

Johnson-Laird, P. N. 1968a. "The Choice of a Passive Voice in a Communicative Task." *British Journal of Psychology* 59.7-15.

Johnson-Laird, P. N. 1968b. "The Interpretation of the Passive Voice." *Quarterly Journal of Experimental Psychology* 20.69-73.

Kempen, G. & E. Hoenkamp. 1987. "An Incremental Procedural Grammar for Sentence Production." *Cognitive Science* 11.210-258.

Kieras, D. E. 1978. "Good and Bad Structure in Simple Paragraphs: Effects on Apparent Theme, Reading Time, and Recall." *Journal of Verbal Learning and Verbal Behavior* 17.13-28.

Kieras, D. E. 1980. "Initial Mention as a Signal to Thematic Content in Technical Passages." *Memory & Cognition* 8.345-353.

Kieras, D. E. 1981. "Component Processes in the Comprehension of Simple Prose." *Journal of Verbal Learning and Verbal Behavior* 20.1-23.

Kimball, J. P. 1973. "Seven Principles of Surface Structure Parsing in Natural Language." *Cognition* 2.15-47.

Klenbort, I. & M. Anisfeld. 1974. "Markedness and Perspective in the Interpretation of the Active and Passive Voice." *Quarterly Journal of Experimental Psychology* 26.189-195.

Kuno, S. & E. Kaburaki. 1977. "Empathy and Syntax." *Linguistics Inquiry* 8.627-672.

Kutas, M. C. van Petten, & M. Besson. 1988. "Event-Related Potential Asymmetries During the Reading of Sentences." *Electroencephalography and Clinical Neurophysiology* 69.218-233.

Levelt, W. J. M. 1981. "The Speaker's Linearization Problem." *Philosophical Transactions of the Royal Society* 295B.305-315.

Levelt, W. J. M. 1989. *Speaking: From Intention to Articulation*. Cambridge, MA: MIT Press.

Lieberman, P. 1984. *The Biology and Evolution of Language.* Cambridge, MA: Harvard University Press.

MacWhinney, B. 1977. "Starting Points." *Language* 53.152-168.

MacWhinney, B. & E. Bates. 1978. "Sentential Devices for Conveying Givenness and Newness: A Cross-Cultural Developmental Study." *Journal of Verbal Learning and Verbal Behavior* 17.539-558.

Mandler, J. M. & M.S. Goodman. 1982. "On the Psychological Validity of Story Structure." *Journal of Verbal Learning and Verbal Behavior* 21.507-523.

Marslen-Wilson, W. L.K. Tyler, & M. Seidenberg. 1978. "Sentence Processing and the Clause Boundary." *Studies in the Perception of Language* ed. by W. J. M. Levelt & G. B. Flores d'Arcais, 219-246. New York: Wiley.

Olson, D. R. & N. Filby. 1972. "On the Comprehension of Active and Passive Sentences." *Cognitive Psychology* 3.361-381.

Olson, G.M., S.A. Duffy, & R.L. Mack. 1984. "Thinking-Out-Loud as a Method for Studying Real-Time Comprehension Processes." *New Methods in Reading Comprehension Research* ed. by D. E. Kieras & M. A. Just, 253-286. Hillsdale, NJ: Erlbaum.

Osgood, G. M. 1971. "Where do Sentences Come From?" *Semantics: An Interdisciplinary Reader in Philosophy, Linguistics, and Psychology* ed. by D. D. Steinberg & L. A. Jakobovits, 497-529. Cambridge, UK: Cambridge University Press.

Posner, M. I. 1980. "Orienting of Attention." *Quarterly Journal of Experimental Psychology* 32.3-25.

Prentice, J. L. 1966. "Response Strength of Single Words as an Influence in Sentence Behavior." *Journal of Verbal Learning and Verbal Behavior* 5.429-433.

Prentice, J. L. 1967. "Effects of Cueing Actor vs Cueing Object on Word Order in Sentence Production." *Psychonomic Science* 8.163-164.

Sachs, H., M. Schegloff, & G. Jefferson. 1974. "A Simplest Systematics for the Organization of Turn-Taking in Conversation." *Language* 50.696-735.

Shields, J.L., A. McHugh, & J.G. Martin. 1974. "Reaction Time to Phoneme Targets as a Function of Rhythmic Cues in Continuous Speech." *Journal of Experimental Psychology* 102.250-255.

Singer, M. 1976. "Thematic Structure and the Integration of Linguistic Information." *Journal of Verbal Learning and Verbal Behavior* 15.549-558.

Sperber, D. & D. Wilson. 1986. *Relevance: Communication and Cognition*. Oxford: Blackwell.

Sridhar, S. N. 1988. *Cognition and Sentence Production: A Cross-Linguistic Study*. New York: Springer-Verlag.

Stevenson, R. J. 1986. "The Time Course of Pronoun Comprehension." *Proceedings of the Eighth Annual Conference of the Cognitive Science Society*, 102-109. Hillsdale, NJ: Erlbaum.

Stich, S. 1983. *From Folk-Psychology to Cognitive Science: The Case against Belief*. Cambridge, MA: MIT Press.

Tannenbaum, P. H. & F. Williams. 1968. "Generation of Active and Passive Sentences as a Function of Subject or Object Focus." *Journal of Verbal Learning and Verbal Behavior* 7.246-250.

Tomlin, R. 1983. "On the Interaction of Syntactic Subject, Thematic Information, and Agent in English." *Journal of Pragmatics* 7.411-432.

Turner, E. A. & R. Rommetveit. 1967. "Experimental Manipulation of the Production of Active and Passive Voice in Children." *Language and Speech* 10.169-180.

Turner, E. A. & R. Rommetveit. 1968. "Focus of Attention in Recall of Active and Passive Sentences." *Journal of Verbal Learning and Verbal Behavior* 7.543-548.

von Eckardt, B. & M.C. Potter. 1985. "Clauses and the Semantic Representation of Words." *Memory & Cognition* 13.371-376.

Zubin, D. A. 1979. "Discourse Function of Morphology: The Focus System in German." *Syntax and Semantics: Discourse and Syntax* ed. by T. Givón, 469-504. New York: Academic Press.

Information Distribution in Ojibwa[1]

Russell S. Tomlin and Richard Rhodes
University of Oregon *The University of California*

Introduction

The limited goal of this paper is to confirm a hypothesis about the distribution of information in Ojibwa texts. That hypothesis is stated in (1):

(1) *In Ojibwa, thematic information comes later in a sentence or clause than non-thematic information.*

Now there are few linguistic universals that are widely accepted by linguists. However, there is at least one. That universal, in its most simplistic form, is that "old information precedes new information".[2] This simplistic generalization has been widely used, for instance, by some sentence grammarians who see the importance of discourse factors to syntax.

However, in the primary literature on discourse analysis, which includes the work of the Prague school (cf. Firbas 1964a, 1964b, 1974; Daneš 1970, 1974; Halliday 1967, 1968; Kuno 1972, 1975, etc.), the simplistic notion of "old information" is split into two parts.[3] One part concerns information which the speaker holds in common with the hearer; what, for example, Halliday calls "given information". The other part concerns information which is central to the development of a particular text or sub-text; again, what Halliday calls "theme" or "thematic information". "Given information" is intimately tied up with noun phrase specification, pronominalization, and definiteness. "Thematic information" is more connected with questions of word order.

Having clarified the distinction between given information and thematic information, a revised and more accurate version of the widely held linguistic universal is that thematic information comes earlier in a sentence or clause, or more simply put, theme comes first. But our hypothesis for Ojibwa is that Ojibwa orders its thematic information in exactly the opposite way. That is, in Ojibwa thematic information comes later in a sentence or clause, or, simply put, in Ojibwa theme comes last.

We shall prove this hypothesis in two steps. First, we will examine some symptoms of Ojibwa syntax which correlate with information distribution in a reasonably clear-cut manner, and which demonstrate a pattern quite distinct from what we see in other languages. Second, we shall do some direct analysis of Ojibwa texts which, when compared to the same sort of analysis of English texts, confirms our initial observations and independently validates our hypothesis.

Symptomatic analysis of Ojibwa syntax

At this point we would like to take up the symptomatic analysis of Ojibwa syntax. The basic idea of symptomatic analysis, like symptomatic diagnosis in medicine, is that certain relatively superficial syntactic features provide reasonably reliable indications of deeper, more significant phenomena. Since symptomatic analysis is relatively superficial, it can be wrong more easily than direct analysis; but if it is done carefully, it can yield useful and reliable results in a short amount of time.

There are several classes of data for Ojibwa which exhibit symptomatic syntactic patterns very different from what we ordinarily see. These classes include the ordering of definite versus indefinite NPs, fronting rules, the position of adverbials, the position of non-referential NPs, and backward pronominalization.

As background to this section we note that the unmarked word order for Ojibwa is VOS. This fact is somewhat obscured by a number of interacting principles. In particular, the normal text medial sentence undergoes zero pronominalization for one or both of its terms, while those sentences which have non-pronominalizable NPs commonly occur in textual positions which adjust word order by principles we will discuss below.[4]

The ordering of definite versus indefinite NPs

In many languages definite and indefinite NPs are not marked overtly. Instead, NPs which occur in their basic word order position or to the left of it are ordinarily interpreted as definite, while NPs which occur to the right of their basic word order position are ordinarily interpreted as indefinite. In Chinese, for example, a postverbal NP is ordinarily interpreted as indefinite and a preverbal NP as definite (Li and Thompson 1976):

(2) a. *Ren lai le.*
people come ASP
'The people have come.'

b. *Lai ren le.*
'Some people have come.'

This pattern does not seem to be peculiar to language families or areas or word order types. However, in Ojibwa just the opposite observation holds. For the order NP V, the NP is ordinarily interpreted as indefinite. For the order V NP, the NP is ordinarily interpreted as definite.[5]

(3) a. (i) *Mookman nglii-mkaan.*[6]
knife I-found-it
'I found a knife.'

(ii) *Ngii-mkaan mookmaan.*
'I found the knife.'

b. (i) *Wiiyaas biijmaagod.* [S243][7]
meat it-smells
'There is a smell of meat.'

(ii) *Mnopgod wiiyaas.* [S244]
it-tastes-good meat
'The meat tastes good.'

These sentences, we should add, are typical and unmarked. There is no peculiar intonation involved, nor do they represent any peculiar stylistic inversion. Thus, the pattern of distribution of definite and indefinite NPs in Ojibwa is reversed from that normally observed. To the extent that definite NPs correlate with thematic information and to the extent that indefinite NPs correlate with non-thematic information, the facts of Ojibwa support our hypothesis.

Fronting rules

In most languages transformations which move phrases to the left usually prefer or even require that the NPs moved be definite (Tomlin 1979). Ojibwa has a rule which moves phrases to the left, but it prefers the NP moved to be indefinite.

(4) English
a. (i) *I was going to buy something at the store.*
(ii) **Something, I was going to buy at the store.*
b. (i) *The bear killed the man/somebody.*
(ii) *The man/*Somebody, the bear killed.*

(5) Ojibwa
a. (i) *Waya gii-yaa.* [S62]
someone he-was-at
'There was someone here.'

(ii) **Gii-yaa waya.*

b. (i) *Waya ngii-waabmaa.*
someone I-saw-him
'I saw someone.'

(ii) ?**Ngii-waabmaa waya.*

The distribution of adverbs

Questions can be used to isolate the unmarked positions of certain constituents in languages in which those constituents do not occur in syntactically fixed positions. Since in many languages adverbs do not have a fixed place in the word order, questions can be used to isolate the unmarked position of rhematic adverbs. In many languages these adverbs will be isolated to the far right. In Ojibwa they are isolated to the far left.

(6)

	English	Ojibwa
a. Q:	*When did he get here?*	*Aanii-sh piichj gaa-bi-dgoshing?* which time he-coming-arrived
A:	*He drove in last night*	?**Gii-bi-bminaazhhige dbikone.* he-coming-drove last-night
	?**Last night he drove in*	*Dbikong gii-bi-dgoshing?*

b. Q:	*Where did you find the pencil?*	*Aapii-sh gii-mkaman zhibiibgaans?* where you-found-it pencil
A:	*I picked it up on the walk.*	**Ngii-ndinaan miiknaansing.* I-got-it-from path-LOC
	?**On the walk I picked it up.*	*Miikaansing ngii-ndinaan.* [S491]

The position taken by non-referential NPs

In many languages non-referential NPs (including generics and indefinite non-specific NPs) pattern with definite NPs. This means sometimes that fronting rules restricted to definites will allow non-referential NPs to be fronted even if they are not definite. In Ojibwa non-referential NPs also pattern with definite NPs, and always come from the right.

(7) English
  a. *I wish I had a newspaper.*
  b. *A newspaper, I wish I had (one/*it).*

(8) Ojibwa
  a. *Endso-dgwaaggin zhaawag zhiishiibag zhaawnong.*
  every-fall they-go ducks south-LOC
  'Ducks head south every fall.'
  b. *Gego wiikaa nsaaken aw en'goonh.* [S842]
  don't ever kill-him-NEG-IMP ant
  'Don't ever kill ants.'

Backwards pronominalization

For the purposes of this paper we will simply state the obvious — that pronominalization constraints are fairly directly connected to principles governing information flow. Assuming this, we then observe another symptom which suggests that Ojibwa and English (and languages like English) differ in how they distribute information in texts.

While English allows leftward pronominalization only under restricted circumstance, namely the controller must command the victim, Ojibwa freely allows leftward pronominalization regardless of command relationships. This is illustrated in (9). We show only the difficult cases — where the victim is upstairs and to the left.

(9) a. *..., wigii-waabmaan widi waawaashkeshwan*
he-saw-him(OBV) there deer(OBV)
niibwinid. [T36.23]
he(OBV)-stands
'..., he looked there and saw a deer standing (there).'

b. *Mii dash gii-ziignamwaad gaa-biindgeyooded maa*
they-poured-it (when)-he-crawled-in there
mdoodoowgamgon, iw mshkikwaaboo wii-mbaabteg.[T21.7]
steam-bath-LOC liquid-medicine it-will-steam-up
'Then they poured the medicine (on the hot rocks), so that when he had crawled into the steam bath, medicine vapors would steam up.'

c. *Gaa wii wgii-gkenmaasiin nmanj ge-kidwen*
not she-knew-him(OBV)-NEG whatever he-might-say
aw noos. [T5.12]
my-father
'She didn't know what my father would say.'[8]

d. *Wedi ge gii gga-miijin, maanda dash ge nii*
that also you you-will-eat-it this also I
nga-miijin waawan. [S174]
I-will-eat-it egg
'You eat that egg, and I'll eat this one.'

The clause constituency of these examples can be shown by various facts of Ojibwa syntax and semantics, including adverb placement, obviation, and the readings assigned to NPs, which are, of course, determined by the order of the NP relative to the verb in its clause.

In each of the symptomatic cases above, a syntactic pattern symptomatic of information distribution in English (and languages like English) is reversed in Ojibwa. This reversal suggests that the organizational principle determining these symptoms is reversed as well.

Direct analysis of Ojibwa text

At this point we would like to take up a second class of data that support our hypothesis about information distribution in Ojibwa: direct analysis of Ojibwa text.

Methodological preliminaries

The approach to direct text analysis we will use here is a further refinement of the approach presented in Bayless and Tomlin (1978) and developed in Tomlin (1978, 1979). Like the traditional approaches of Halliday (1967, 1968) or Daneš (1974), the present approach makes a basic split between two classes of information: shared information and thematic information. And the structure of texts is sensitive to these classes of information.

However, the present approach is different from the more traditional approaches in that it utilizes extralinguistic and non-linguistic factors to define the types of information and to identify phrases as belonging to one class or the other in the analysis of particular texts. Texts are not treated as isolated linguistic units. Rather they are instruments for a larger communicative event which includes both the speaker and the hearer and their knowledge of the world. This larger communicative event is a process through which the knowledge of one person is reconstructed or reconstrued by another for some specific purpose or goal.

We have been using the term "knowledge" a little loosely so far and would like now to use it in a more restricted fashion. Knowledge is viewed here as the embodiment of stored experience; it is grounded in experience, either directly or indirectly. When experience is the same, so is the knowledge; that is, common experience is shared knowledge.

It should be clear that the knowledge that a person has in his head is different from the knowledge contained in a text. We can make this difference explicit by restricting the term "knowledge" to whatever it is that human beings store in their heads, and by using the term "information" to refer to representations of knowledge in texts. At this point we would like to introduce formally the definitions of shared and thematic information:

(10) **Shared information**: that knowledge which the speaker assumes he has in common (through like experience) with the hearer.

(11) **Thematic information**:[9] that knowledge which the speaker assumes is relevant to the goal of the communicative event.

Shared information involves knowledge which all the participants in the communicative event have in common. This commonality of knowledge most frequently involves the identification of referents for the various NPs and phrases in the text. Thematic information involves another dimension — that of relevance to the goal of the communicative event.

The goal of a communicative event is the informational purpose in communicating. It is not to be confused with the metalinguistic or social or personal reasons for communicating. Information is more relevant to the goal of the communicative event if it is more important to the development of the text than other information. For instance, for the play-by-play reporting of sports events like hockey or football, the goal of the communicative event is an accurate description of the action. Such descriptions are framed in terms of critical features of the extralinguistic situation: the players, the ball, and so on, but not pads, or sidelined players, etc. The former are more relevant to the goal of the particular communicative event than the latter. Thus, references to such items would constitute relatively more thematic information than would references to other things.

An example from English

Having briefly described the notions which underpin direct text analysis, it would be useful to illustrate how we do direct text analysis by analyzing a fragment of a text in a familiar language, like English. The text fragment in (12), taken from Tomlin (1978), is a typical example of the kind of text produced orally by sportscasters of the play-by-play action of ice hockey.

(12) English text fragment [Boston-Toronto G219]
1. [***BOSTON***] *bringing* [***the puck***] *up* [*to center ice*].
2. [***THAT***]***'S*** [***Mike Milburry,*** *no. 26*], [*along the boards in the corner*].
3. [***Ø***] *stopped by* [***the Bruins***]. (Ø = *Milburry*)
4. *Standing* [*out in front*] *is* [***Peter McNab***],
5. *and* [***IT***]*'s shot back* [*to* ***Milburry***].
6. [***MILBURRY***] *gets* [*a shot*].
7. [***THAT***]*'s* [*right in front*].
8. [***Ø***] *stopped by* [***Williams***]. *(Ø = the puck/the shot)*
9. [***Ø***] *lost* [***it***] [*to* ***McCann***]. *(Ø = Williams)*

The first step in the analysis is to isolate the relevant phrases for consideration. These will include sentence level phrases — terms and non-terms; it does not include the verb.[10] In (12) the relevant phrases are bracketed.

The second step is to determine which of the relevant phrases represent shared information and which do not and why. In (12) the phrases which represent shared information are in bold. These represent shared information because the viewer and the sportscaster are both watching the game during the production of the text. For this case almost all of the relevant phrases are shared information.

The third step is to establish a working hierarchy of relative thematicity. This is done by considering the relation of the goal of the communicative event to the non-linguistic situation the text is a part of. The goal of this particular communicative event is to describe the action on the ice. Such a description will not be randomly structured. Instead, its structure will reflect those aspects of the non-linguistic real-world situation which are particularly salient for that situation.

In watching hockey there are two particularly salient features, two centers of attention: the puck and the players. Of these, the puck is more relevant. It is the instrument of scoring, and all of the activities of the players are directed to its control. However, when a particular player does take control of the puck, the two centers of attention coincide for a while. To the extent these observations are correct, we can establish a working hierarchy of relative thematicity as shown in (13):

(13) Working hierarchy of relative thematicity for hockey play-by-play (Tomlin 1978).
player with puck > puck > player without puck

Having established — without reference to the text — a working hierarchy of relative thematicity, each clause is examined, and the NPs representing the most thematic information identified. In (12) these NPs are in CAPITALS. Once the most thematic NPs are identified, one can proceed to investigate their syntactic treatment. This example, and others like it, support a generalization that more thematic information is ordered earlier in a sentence or clause.[11]

An examination of an Ojibwa text

We can perform the same sort of step-by-step text analysis on Ojibwa texts. Let us consider a fragment from an expository text on what Indians do to earn money. This can be found in (14). Such expository texts are common (though not in Bloomfield's collection), and this one is typical of such texts.

(14) Ojibwa text fragment [Bloomfield T15.9-17]

9\. [*Kina bebkaan*] *namkiiwag* [***NISHNAABEG***]
all different they-work-thus Indians
zwii-debnamwaad [***ZHOON'YAA***].
for-them-to-get-it money
'The Indians do all kinds of different things to earn money.'

10a. *Ge go* [*mtigoon*] *wgiishkboodoonaawaan.*
and wood-PL they-saw-them-down
'They cut down wood.'

10b. *Mii dash daawewaad* [***oodenaang***] *ge go* [***maa Island***].
they-sell-it town-LOC and there
'Then they sell it in Detroit and on the Island.'

11\. [*Bgiishenh*] *ge* [***nii***] *ndayaan* [*MTIGWAAKINNS*
small also I I-have-it small-stand
MAA ENDAAYAAN.]
there where-I-live
'I, too, have a small stand of trees at my place.'

12\. *Aapji dash go nzaagtoon.*
very I-am-stingy-with-it
'I'm very stingy with it.'

13\. *Gaa wii ndoo-glishkhanziin* [***AAPJI GEGOO***].
not I-go-and-cut-it-NEG very something
'I don't cut very much of it.'

14a. *Baamaa niigaan wii-aabjitooyann,*
later future I-will-use-it
'I plan to use it in the future.'

14b. *ge zhoon'yaamsiwaan, ji-giishpnadooyaambaa*
and (if)-I-have-money-NEG I-will-sell-it
[***IW MTIG***].
wood
'If I ever run out of money, I'll sell wood.'

14c. *Mii baamaa iw daa-giishkwag* [***AW MTIG***].
later I-might-cut-him tree
'That's when I would cut down my trees.'

15. *Eshkam* *znagad* *wii-debnaming*
more-and-more it-is-difficult for-one-to-get-it
[*IW BOODWENG*].
one-burns
'It's becoming increasingly difficult to get stuff to burn.'

16. *Wjaaggahaanaawaan* [*niibna* *wdakiimwaan*]
$they_i$-clear-$them_j$ much $their_i$-$lands_j$
[*GIW NISHNAABEG*].
$Indians_j$
'The Indians are clearing much of their land.'

17. *Ge go* *eshkam* [*niibna*] *nagndenoon*
and *more-and-more* *much* *they-cost-thus*
[*MTIGOON*].
wood-PL
'Consequently, wood costs more and more.'

The first step, in this case, as above, is to identify the relevant phrases for consideration. In (14) they are bracketed. The second step is to determine which of the relevant phrases represent shared information. In (14) these phrases are in bold. The justification for each is presented in (15):

(15) Identification of phrases as shared or non-shared information

a. **Shared** (some source(s) of common experience)

Prior mention	Culturally shared	Inferable
9. *Nishnaabeg*	10b. *oodenaang*	11. *nii*
9. *zhoon'yaa*	10b. *maa Island*	17. *mtigoon*
13. *aapji gegoo* (paraphrase)	16. *niibna wdakiimwaan*	
14b. *iw mtig*		
14c. *aw mtig*		
15. *iw boodweng* (paraphrase)	16. *giw Nishnaabeg*	

b. Non-shared (does not fit above categories, and no other source of common experience)

9. *kina bebkaan*
10a. *mtigoon*
11. *bgiishenh*
11. *mtigwaakinns maa endaayaan*
16. *niibna*

The third step is to set up a working hierarchy of relative thematicity for this sort of text. To do this we asked native speakers what they believe this text is about. Native speakers, untrained in linguistics and thus without theoretical insights to bias their opinions, have quite strong opinions about which information in a text is more important. For this text, native speakers agree uniformly that the overall text deals primarily with Indians and what they do to earn money. Secondly, they agree that this portion of the text deals with wood. Thus we can set up a working hierarchy of relative thematicity for this text (though not in as clearly an empirical way as with the hockey example). This hierarchy is given in (16).

(16) Working hierarchy of relative thematicity for Indian livelihood text.
Indians > money > wood > other

With this hierarchy we can identify those phrases which show a higher degree of thematicity in this text. In (14) those phrases are in CAPITALS. Finally, we can observe the distribution of the more thematic versus less thematic information. Information which we identify as more thematic tends to come last in the sentence or clause. Thus, all of the mentions of 'wood' come last in their clauses except the first (10a). That particular mention occurs in a position in a clause which indicates a subject change, which (as we discuss below) is a grammatical means in Ojibwa of starting a new sub-theme in the overall text. In addition to the mention of wood, the two mentions of 'Indians' and 'money' also come at the end of their respective clauses, (9) and (15).

In contrast, we can see that those phrases lower on the hierarchy tend to occur earlier in their clauses. Thus, it seems clear, at least for this text, that the more thematic some bit of information is, the closer it will come to the end of the sentence or clause in Ojibwa. We have performed the same sort of analysis on the remaining 37 texts in Bloomfield (1957), and see the same pattern in each one of them.

In our investigation of all of these texts it is quite clear that in Ojibwa, more thematic information comes later in a sentence or clause. Thus, direct text analysis also confirms our initial hypothesis.

Further observations

To this point we have made it sound like the facts of Ojibwa word order are quite simple. But, as with any language, there are a number of complicating factors which may, at first glance, obscure the basic generalization. These are of two types: those cases in which indefinites appear to the right of the verb instead of to the left, and those cases in which definites appear to the left of the verb.

Indefinites to the right of the verb

There are two major types of indefinites which appear to the right of the verb. The first involves quantifier verbs, *baatiinak* 'be much, many', *niizhig* 'be two', etc. The appearance of indefinite NPs to the right of exactly this class of verbs follows from two facts: 1) with such verbs there is prototypically no contrast between definite and indefinite subject, and 2) the unmarked word order is VS.

The second type of indefinite NP appearing to the right of the verb includes those which are thematically irrelevant. Thematically irrelevant NPs have several different syntactic properties which enable us to identify them directly. For example, while thematically relevant postverbal NPs float their quantifiers leftward to clause initial position, as in (17), thematically irrelevant NPs do not, as in (18).

(17) *Ge dash mii kina gii-maajiidwaawaad iw wziisbaakdomni.*[T32.5]
all they-took-from-them their-sugar
'And they took all their sugar from them.'

(18) *Mii dash gii-wiindmaadwaad kina giw ninwag,...* [T31.40]
they-discussed-it-all men
'Then all the men discussed what ...'

This analysis of postverbal indefinites as thematically irrelevant receives strong support from the fact that in some text variants a thematically irrelevant indefinite may receive treatment as thematically relevant, in which case it is, as predicted by our analysis, fronted. Compare (19) and (20).

(19) *Gye gii-wiiwkwejiinid aanind iw wdgawwin.* [T4.6]
she-wrapped-me-up some her-clothes
'And she wrapped me up in some of her clothing.'

(20) *Mii dash bekaanak* *gii-wiiwjiinid.* [T5.8]
that-which-is-different she-wrapped-me
'Then she wrapped me in other clothes.'

There are a few other classes of postverbal indefinites (e.g., counterfactual 'if' clauses), but a discussion of such subtleties of Ojibwa word order syntax is beyond the scope of this paper.

Definites to the left

Having shown that indefinites appearing post-verbally are not a problem for our analysis, let us now discuss those cases in which definite NPs appear preverbally. There are three classes of such preverbal definite NPs: (1) quantifiers, (2) contrastive NPs, and (3) "T-fronted" NPs.

As discussed above, there is a rule which floats quantifiers off of post-verbal NPs to the front of the clause (immediately following any clause initial adverbs), as shown in (17). For now we will treat this as an ad hoc extension of our analysis, although we believe it is only a special case of the principle which fronts contrastive definite NPs.

As for contrastive NPs, they are fronted for the following reason. There are facets of contrastive NPs which are both "old" or thematic information and "new" or rhematic information. Consider the use of contrastive constructions to repair texts. In such cases the contrastive NP represents rhematic information in that it adds information to the text which corrects the hearer's error. But it is thematic in that the contrastive element must be drawn from a limited set previously shared. Thus, perhaps a language can choose to class contrastive NPs syntactically either with thematic or with non-thematic NPs. Ojibwa classes its contrastive NPs with non-thematic NPs. But even this is not an accidental choice on the part of Ojibwa. Since there are no suprasegmental devices, nor special morphemes for marking contrastive NPs, Ojibwa is essentially forced to use its word order to mark the contrastiveness of NPs, treating its contrastive definites like indefinites in order to distinguish them from ordinary definites.

The final class of definite NPs which occur preverbally are those which we are calling "T-fronted". Such NPs are fronted for one purpose and one purpose only, and that is to establish the referent of the NP as the theme of the local section of text. Such T-fronted NPs, both definite and indefinite, can be identified by the fact that they occur in section initial sentences. Two short excerpts can serve to show how this mechanism works. The first has *nookmis* 'my grandmother' as its theme. In (21) we cite all relevant clauses containing relevant NPs.

(21) Fragment from Grandmother story [T2].

1a. *Nookmis* *wde-gkendaan...*
my-grandmother she-remembered-it
'My grandmother could remember when...'

2a. *Zhangsimdana shi niiwin gii-dso-bboon'gizi*
ninety and four she-was-that-old
aw nookmis,...
my-grandmother
'My grandmother was ninety-four...'

3. *Ngii-zaaghaa nookmis gye go nmishoomis.*
I-loved-her my-grandmother and my-grandfather
'I loved my grandmother and grandfather.'

The second text does not have an overt nominal theme, and it has no T-fronted NPs. In (22) we cite all clauses containing relevent NPs.

(22) Fragment from Rice-gathering story [T4].

1a. ..., *ngii-maajiinig aw ngashi gye bezhig kwe,*
she-took-me mother and one woman
'..., my mother and this other woman took me along,'

1b. *gii-wa-yaamwaad iw bgoji-mnoomin.*
(when)-they-went-and-got-it wild-rice
'when they went to get wild rice.'

2b. ..., *waa-dzhi-bwahmowaad iw bgoji-mnoomin.*
(to)-where-they-would-harvest-it wild-rice
'...where they would harvest the wild rice'

3. *Aana dash go ngii-kawaabmig aw ngashi,...*
in-vain she-watched-me my-mother
'My mother watched me..., but...'

6. *Wewiib dash ngiizkon'yebnig aw ngashi,...*
quickly she-undressed-me my-mother
'My mother quickly undressed me,...'

7b. ..., *bngii miin'waa gii-bwahmowaad iw bgoji-mnoomin.*
little again they-harvested-it wild-rice
'..., they harvested a little more wild rice.'

9. *Aapji gii-zegzi maaba ngashi.*
very she-was-scared my-mother
'My mother was very scared.'

10b. ..., *nmaj ge-kidgwen maaba noos.*
whatever he-would-say my-father
'..., what my father might say.'

While there are some further subtleties of the use of T-fronting in sections of text without overt nominal themes, they are beyond the scope of this paper. It is enough to note that we can account for the position of all NPs in Bloomfield's texts, assigning them the correct readings for definiteness (sharedness) and, where independently determinable, thematicity.

As a final note on the predictions our hypothesis makes about Ojibwa texts, we want to mention that there are 19 sentences in Bloomfield's texts which contain two or more postverbal NPs in the same clause. Of these, our analysis directly accounts for the relative order of the two NPs in all but one case. And that case deviates in the direction of the unmarked word order.

Conclusions

We feel that we have shown that Ojibwa provides a clear counterexample to the claim that information is distributed in text in such a way that thematic information precedes rhematic information. In Ojibwa texts, nominals expressing thematic information occur further right in sentences than nominals expressing rhematic information.

The discovery of languages which distribute information in the order rheme-theme raises a number of questions, some of which we have ideas about and some of which we do not, but we raise two here as directions for future inquiry. First, what is it about Ojibwa that makes it organize its information in this unusual way? We feel that this fact is directly related to questions about the unmarked word order, some of which proceed, we feel, from discourse level principles, and some of which, we feel, proceed from sentence level principles (cf. Tomlin 1979).

The other question we would like to mention has to do with the whole approach to doing language universals. We, of course, recognize the theme-rheme ordering is the "normal" case for languages, but then what does it mean when we find the opposite order in a language like Ojibwa? Our feeling is that it is, in fact, a metatheoretical question regarding how one does universals, and what one takes universals to be.

In some sense we feel that linguistic universals are truths with the same kind of states that generic assertions have. For example, just because there a few types of owls, like the Burrowing Owl, that are diurnal, does not nullify the validity of the generic assertion: Owls are nocturnal birds. Instead, there's something we'd like to know about Burrowing Owls which doesn't throw out our observation about the habits of owls in general. In the same way, we'd like to know why Ojibwa orders its information in what appears to be such an unusual way, rheme before theme, without having to discard the well-established universal that languages in general order information theme before rheme.

Notes

1. We would like to thank Reta Sands, our primary language consultant, for her patient and careful assistance. This paper is a reprint of our paper which appeared in CLS 15 (Tomlin and Rhodes 1979). We have made only a few corrections to that paper, leaving it otherwise as originally published.

2. There are, to the best of our knowledge, only two references in the literature that claim that a "new-old" ordering is possible as the unmarked order in a language: Hockett (1966: 23) and Creider (n.d.). It is worth noting that Hockett edited Bloomfield's Algonquian materials, including Bloomfield (1957), which is the source of our texts.

3. See Prince (1979) for some further distinctions in kinds of information for discourse analysis.

4. Bloomfield's (1957: 131) comment is: "Word order is decidedly flexible."

5. Our informants uniformly reject indefinite readings on postverbal NPs from Bloomfield's sentence elicitation, with the exception of certain classes of clauses which we will discuss below. It is likely that Bloomfield's elicitation was embedded in more elaborate discussions which would affect the word order of individual sentences by the principles that are the point of this paper.

6. As is becoming increasingly popular, we will cite our examples in practical orthography rather than in Bloomfield's linguistic orthography.

7. We cite examples from Bloomfield's sentence elicitation with a capital S, and examples from his texts with a capital T, followed by the text number and sentence number (derived from his punctuation).

8. The Ojibwa verb *gkendang* 'know (it)' raises complement subjects to object, but the complement remains an island with respect to obviation.

9. Originally, Bayless and I (Tomlin) chose "expected information" as our term, because we wanted our extralinguistic text-independent approach to "theme" to be distinguished from the semantic text-bound approaches of others. We wanted to avoid certain connotations of the term "theme" or "thematic" in a linguistic universe of discourse. However, numerous friends and colleagues have found the connotations of "expected" at least as distracting. So, since the ideas are obviously related to others in the area, though also quite distinct, I have decided to change the term "expected information" to "thematic information".

10. At this point in time we are ignoring the verb. We are convinced that the position of the verb is determined by a lot more than information structure, although at this point we are not certain what those factors are.

11. If we were doing a specifically synchronic description of English, a more precise statement of the facts would be that syntactic subject takes thematic information (cf. Tomlin 1978). However, for a more generalized task like this, English serves to illustrate the tendency for thematic information to come early, since its subjects tend to come first anyway.

References

Bayless, Richard & Russ Tomlin. 1978. "The Role of Expected Information in the Analysis of English Texts." *University of Michigan Publications in Linguistics* Vol. 3:2.1-16.

Bloomfield, Leonard. 1957. *Eastern Ojibwa: Grammatical Skitch, Texts, and Word List.* Ann Arbor: The University of Michigan Press.

Creider, Chet. n.d. "Thematicization and Word Order." Unpublished University of Western Ontario paper.

Daneš, Frantisek. 1970. "One Instance of Prague School Methodology: Functional Analysis of Utterance and Text." *Methods and Theory in Linguistics*. ed. by P. Garvin, 132-146. The Hague: Mouton.

Daneš, Frantisek. 1974. "Functional Sentence Perspective and the Organization of the Text." *Papers on Functional Sentence Perspective* ed. by F. Daneš, 106-128 . The Hague: Mouton.

Firbas, Jan. 1964a. "From Comparative Word Order Studies. (Thoughts on V. Mathesius' Concept of the Word Order System in English Compared with that of Czech)". *Brno Studies in English* 4.11-26.

Firbas, Jan. 1964b. "On Defining the Theme in Functional Sentence Analysis." *Travaux Linguistique de Prague* I.267-280.

Firbas, Jan. 1974. "Some Aspects of the Czech Approach to Problems of FSP." *Papers on Functional Sentence Perspective* ed. by F. Daneš, 11-37. Academy Publishing House of the Czechoslobak Academy of Sciences.

Halliday, M.A.K. 1967. "Some Aspects of the Thematic Organization of the English Clause." Memorandum RM-5224-PR. Santa Monica: Rand Corp.

Halliday, M.A.K. 1968. "Notes on Transitivity and Theme in English, part 3." *Journal of Linguistics* 4.179-215.

Hockett, Charles. 1966. "The Problem of Universals in Language." *Universals of Language*, second edition, ed. by J. Greenberg, 1-29. Cambridge and London: MIT Press.

Kuno, Susumu. 1972. "Functional Sentence Perspective." *Linguistic Inquiry* III:3.269-320.

Kuno, Susumu. 1975. "Three Perspectives in the Functional Approach to Syntax." *Functionalism* ed. by R. Grossman, et al., 276-336. Chicago: Chicago Linguistic Society.

Li, Charles & Sandra Thompson. 1976. "On the Issue of Word Order in a Synchronic Grammar: A Case Against Movement Transformations'." *Lingua* 39.169-181.

Prince, Ellen. 1979. "On the Given/New Distinction." *Papers from the Fifteenth Regional Meeting of the Chicago Linguistics Society* ed. by P. Clyne et. al., 267-278. Chicago: Chicago Linguistics Society.

Rhodes, Richard. 1978. "Topic Chains in Ojibwa Discourse." Paper presented to the Algonquian Seminar, University of Montral. Montreal, Quebec.

Rhodes, Richard. to appear. "Some Aspects of Ojibwa Discourse." *Proceedings of the 10th Algonquian Conference.* Ottawa: Carleton University Press.

Tomlin, Russell. 1978. "The Relation of Expected Information to Syntactic Subject in English: Some Evidence from Descriptive Texts." Unpublished University of Michigan paper.

Tomlin, Russell. 1979. *An Explanation of the Distribution of Basic Constituent Orders.* University of Michigan PhD dissertation. Ann Arbor: University of Michigan.

Tomlin, Russell & Richard Rhodes. 1979. "An Introduction to Information Distribution in Ojibwa." *Papers from the Fifteenth Regional Meeting of the Chicago Linguistics Society* ed. by P. Clyne et. al., 307-321. Chicago: Chicago Linguistics Society.

Nonidentifiable Information and Pragmatic Order Rules in 'O'odham

Doris L. Payne
University of Oregon & Summer Institute of Linguistics

1. Introduction

By definition, the order of words and phrases is a syntactic phenomenon: it involves putting phrases together (**syn**) in certain allowable orders (**taxis**), and not in others. Along with linear order, several theories of syntax have maintained that constituency, dominance, government, and grammatical relations are equally parts of syntax. Although certain phenomena have sometimes been taken as primes (e.g. constituency) and others as derivative (e.g. grammatical relations), all have been said to pertain to the syntactic part of grammar.[1] These phenomena were unified in the Standard and Extended Standard Theories partially by the premise that a single device such as phrase structure rules could, and therefore should, model them all. For instance, Chomsky (1965) argued that it would be redundant to independently specify both grammatical relations and constituency since the former supposedly could be predicted on the basis of the latter. Linear order came along for the ride in the modelling of constituency.[2] Most generative theories of syntax have specifically excluded discourse-pragmatic factors from grammar. Such factors are presumably outside of strictly linguistic competence because they are concerned with the knowledge of how to use grammatical sentences, and not with the knowledge of simply what are grammatical sentences.

The current paper is primarily concerned with pragmatic factors that govern order of nonidentifiable information in 'O'odham (or Papago), and with the extent to which an association between such pragmatic factors and order may be rule governed, and thus grammaticized. If such an association is grammaticized, then it is not clear why discourse-pragmatic factors should a priori be excluded from "grammar". The lack of any necessary relationship between order and grammatical relations should be obvious at this point in our knowledge of language. Numerous languages from Australia and the Americas have very strong links between discourse-pragmatic categories and order, and relatively weaker or nonexistent links with GRs (cf. the articles in this volume; Scancarelli 1987; Givón 1988; Aberdour 1985; C. Jensen 1980 and A. Jensen 1982, *inter alia*).

The basic descriptive facts of 'O'odham syntax can be found in Saxton 1982, Zepeda 1983, and a number of specialized articles by numerous authors. As these works point out, all orders of subject (both transitive and intransitive subject), object, oblique and verb occur in 'O'odham. This is despite the absence of overt case marking. The literature shows considerable controversy over what is the "basic" order. The controversy is crucially dependent on the theoretical presuppositions one adopts and how one defines "basic order". Hale (this volume) argues that SOV or NP-NP-V order is the d-structure basic order within a Government Binding framework. His arguments are based on tonal phrasing, determiner allomorphy, and extraction possibilities. In a 1983 paper, Hale posits phrase structure rules which indicate that non-clausal complements [NPs] are prenuclear. In these works, he is concerned with "underlying" order, and notes that this order is not always true at surface structure and that Papago makes use of extraposition to derive alternative orders. Saxton and Saxton (1969) and Langacker (1977) identify 'O'odham as VSO. Saxton (1980) describes it as predicate non-final. Saxton (1982) describes it as predicate-initial. However, as Payne (1987) shows, 'O'odham surface order is only weakly associated with grammatical relations. It instead depends almost completely on the identifiability and pragmatic markedness of the information expressed in a particular phrase.

Languages like 'O'odham lead me to make three assertions. First, theories of grammar should separate the more visible syntax of (a) linear order, marking on noun phrases (including case), marking on verbs (including agreement), and other overt morphosyntax (possibly also including constituency and aspects of intonation), from the less visible syntax of (b) grammatical relations (GRs), head-dependent relations, and function-argument relations. The two lists are different in kind. Further, the more visible syntax may express discourse-pragmatic categories and relations, just as well as it may express the kinds of relations listed in (b). Such a separation between "more visible syntax" and "less visible syntax" has been quite clearly articulated, I believe, by Lexical Functional Grammar (cf. Mohanan 1983; Bresnan and Mchombo 1987), and by Givón (1984). One strong motivation for the separation comes precisely from the fact that linear order can be as closely tied to discourse-pragmatic factors as it can be to the kinds of relations articulated in (b). However, if GRs are included in "grammar" on the traditional grounds that they are intimately tied to surface morphosyntax, it would also seem to follow that discourse-pragmatic categories which intimately determine surface morphosyntax should also be included in grammar.

Second, because linear order can be determined by discourse-pragmatic categories as surely as it can be by the expression of GRs, a larger research typology is called for which takes this into account. The intersecting parameters in a broader order typology should include: (1) the range of discourse-pragmatic phenomena which are empirically found to correlate with order, (2) the extent to which order correlates with discourse-pragmatic categories in any given language, (3) the range of syntactic relations which are found to correlate with order, and (4) the extent to which order correlates with various types of syntactic relations in any given language. At this stage in our understanding it is clear that an order typology in terms of subject, object, and verb is not the only interesting one.

Third, this research framework will allow better exploration of word order change. Because linear order is equally adept at expressing both discourse-pragmatic categories and GRs, pragmatic order stages can serve as crucial stepping stones between GR order stages, and vice versa.

Relevant terminology

In this paper I will use the term **function** to refer both to traditionally syntactic functions, such as GRs, and to grammaticized discourse-pragmatic functions. This use of the term "function" corresponds rather well to what is called "functional structure" in Lexical Functional Grammar. A discourse-pragmatic function is **grammaticized** when particular features of the morphosyntax are required in order to express the category. This definition of **grammaticized (discourse-pragmatic) function** is fairly synonymous with what Tomlin and Pu (1991) call "structural coding", i.e. where

> there is a production requirement on the speaker to automatically use that [linguistic] form whenever that function obtains and if the hearer automatically derives the function from the heard form... Structural codings are part of the knowledge of a particular language which is represented in the grammar directly.

Tomlin and Pu cite use of {/s/, Ø} for semantic number [singular, plural] in English as an example of structural coding.[3] For our present concerns, what is grammaticized may be either a traditionally syntactic function, such as a GR,[4] or a traditionally pragmatic function having to do with speaker-hearer presuppositions and context.

A grammaticized discourse-pragmatic function differs from what has sometimes been referred to as "pragmatic signalling" or coding. For instance, Tomlin (1985: 95-96; see also Tomlin and Pu 1991) defines "pragmatic coding" as a case in which:

> some fragment of form co-occurs with some class of semantic or pragmatic information with such regularity that when the syntactic form occurs the hearer can infer the semantic/pragmatic information... The syntactic form retains any other syntactic coding function, but the high frequency of co-occurrence creates an association between form and function which the hearer can use with some, but less certain, reliability.

Tomlin and Pu (1989) cite use of English *and* to signal temporal order or causality as an example of pragmatic signalling (the semantic meaning of *and* is simply conjunction). I am adopting different terminology here precisely because my point is to underscore that the same type of form can equally well code either traditionally syntactic or traditionally discourse-pragmatic functions.

A simplistic understanding of "required" in the definition of a grammaticized discourse-pragmatic category may quickly lead one to doubt the validity of such a category. This is because a 100% relationship between a grammaticized function and a single linguistic form can be obscured in at least two ways. First, due to the on-line nature of unplanned discourse there may be numerous sentence fragments and other "performance errors" that can still in some way or another be repaired communicatively; but such on-line phenomena can obfuscate a 100% encoding pattern. Second, and more importantly, a given function can be encoded in more than one way, depending on the interaction of factors. This is certainly true even for traditionally syntactic functions, as shown by Lee and Thompson's (1987) discussion of Korean direct object marking. The Korean direct object can be encoded with *-ka*, but there are four conditions under which *-ka* does not occur. One situation is when a single phrase simultaneously expresses both object and Topic. However, a less than 100% relation between the direct object function and use of *-ka* does not mean that direct object is not a grammaticized category in Korean.

The term **focus** has often been used in the literature to include non-presupposed asserted new information, as well as contrastive information. However, languages most neutrally express new and/or nonidentifiable asserted information simply as an object or oblique in a run-of-the-mill sentence type (Du Bois 1987). Such information is communicatively distinct from what I term **pragmatically marked** information. Either given or new information can be pragmatically marked. Briefly, information is highly pragmatically marked when the speaker assumes that the information, or the informational network in which the speaker wishes to establish the information, will directly contradict the hearer's current expectations or presuppositions. In such a situation the speaker may perform a speech act which attempts to override the hearer's supposed expectations. This act may be performed by expressing the contrastive, potentially contradictory information in a marked structure, which particularly calls it to the hearer's active focus of attention. In contrast, if the speaker assumes that information will be entirely consonant with the hearer's current expectations (even though it may be "new" information not previously activated), then the speaker assumes that information is relatively unsurprising or unmarked. As a consequence, it may be expressed in relatively unmarked surface morphosyntax (this is a language-specific question).[5]

Thus, pragmatic markedness is grounded in both knowledge structures or networks (script, frame, or schema structures; Schank and Abelson 1977; Fillmore 1982; Lehnert 1980; *inter alia*), plus the speaker's goals vis-a-vis the hearer's knowledge structure. The use of a pragmatically marked structure is essentially a type of speech act in which the speaker says: "I hereby instruct you, the hearer, to change what I assume are your current expectations deriving from the current state of your knowledge network".

From an etic perspective, degrees of pragmatic markedness need to be considered. The etic cline is basically one of the degree to which the speaker assumes the information will be expected by the hearer, relative to the hearer's current presuppositions about what is true, likely, possible, impossible, etc., and how certain pieces of information are related to other pieces. At the most extreme end of the etic cline are focus of contrast situations. Specifically included are single and multiple (usually double) foci of contrast situations (Chafe 1976; Dik et al. 1981). Answers to information questions share much of the same pragmatic makeup as do single focus contrast situations (Dik et al. 1981, Payne 1990).[6] Also similar are the information questions themselves, though here there is no assertion of unknown or unexpected information but rather a solicitation of information against the background of an otherwise presupposed proposition. A further type of pragmatic markedness involves contrastive new topics. In discourse the unmarked situation is to expect continuity with what has preceded, with what has already been cognitively activated. This is partially seen in the use of various conversational move devices such as *Speaking of X....* or *A similar thing happened to me*, etc. The new turn-taker claims that his or her assertions are somehow relevant to the content of previous turns — even when they are actually not very relevant. When a contrastive new topic occurs, however, the speaker is explicitly conveying to the hearer 'expect discontinuity; I as speaker am no longer talking about X as topic, but Y' (cf. Lee 1984 and Iwasaki 1987 for some discussion).

Information is **identifiable** if the speaker assumes that the hearer will be able to pick out and establish reference for it, based on information already available within the universe of discourse. As Du Bois (1980) and Hawkins (1984) have discussed, it is only necessary that the hearer be able to pick out a referent that is "close enough to count" for the speaker's current pragmatic purposes. For example, if I say *My daughter scribbled on the living room wall*, I am treating *living room wall* as identifiable (signalled by the definite article *the*). I probably do not expect that my hearer can, on the basis of such an assertion, identify exactly which wall; all that matters is that the hearer identify this as one (of probably four or less) walls in a living room that most likely belongs to me (unless otherwise indicated by the context). As speaker, I assume that the hearer can identify the referent of *the living room wall* with sufficient accuracy for my present pragmatic purposes. If it mattered that it was the east wall (e.g. because we had already planned to paint that one wall), I might instead have specified it further for the hearer by saying *My daughter scribbled on the living room wall where the piano is*. Certain entities and concepts, such as culturally unique items, are permanently identifiable. Information is **nonidentifiable** if the speaker assumes that the hearer will not be able to pick out and establish reference, based on information already available within the universe of discourse.

When introducing information which is nonidentifiable and referential (Section 3.2), speakers are most commonly requesting their hearers to open an **active discourse file** for it; afterwards, it is treated as identifiable. An active discourse file is a mental entry that is created, "lit up", or activated for an entity or concept within a language user's active focus of consciousness (Chafe 1987). Once a file is activated for an entity, this entity becomes available for future deployment as a participant or prop within the discourse. It can then be referred to as the **same** entity, often by anaphoric devices, and is normally treated as identifiable and referential within the universe of discourse. Once the entity fades into background awareness or is de-activated (because of non-mention for a time, discourse discontinuity, or limits on how much information can be held in active memory at once), then a new cognitive file need not be established in order for it to be rementioned. However, some discourse-pragmatic device is often employed in order to reactivate an already existing file.

2. 'O'odham constituent order

Here we will review the major findings reported in Payne (1987), and then examine in more detail the behavior of nonidentifiable mentions. The following discussion is based on a subsample of the corpus used in the Payne (1987) sample. This sample consists of nine texts taken from Saxton and Saxton (1973), comprising nearly 800 clauses (incomplete clause fragments and copular clauses were excluded from consideration).[7]

Text data first make it apparent that clauses tend to express fewer than their full allowable complement of arguments via overt NPs or pronouns. This is true for both transitive and intransitive clauses (Table 1).

Table 1. Number of overt arguments relative to transitivity

	transitive		**intransitive**		**total**
2 overt arguments	22	9%	—		22
1 overt argument	141	60%	166	32%	307
0 overt arguments	73	31%	357	68%	430
Total	236		523		759

Table 2. Pre- vs. postverbal order of A, S, and O arguments

	A	S	O	Total
Preverbal	15	33	44	92
Postverbal	22	136	108	266
Total	37	169	152	358

$\chi^2 = 8.46$, $p < .025$, d.f. 2; $\phi = .15$

Second, pre- versus postverbal order of noun and adpositional phrases is only weakly associated with GRs. This is shown for subject and object relations in Table 2 (A = transitive subject, S = intransitive subject, O = object). These data also show that the majority of all nominal references are postverbal (74%). The χ^2 statistic only indicates whether a particular association is significant. The ϕ statistic measures strength of association: a value of zero indicates no association, while a value of 1.0 indicates an association of 100%. The .15 value of ϕ indicates a very weak association between GR and pre- versus postverbal order. Rather than being expressed by order, GRs are expressed via a second-position "auxiliary" system (though these are not auxiliary verbs), a verbal prefix showing person and number of object, and by a limited switch reference or "discontinuity" system (cf. Scancarelli 1989).

The significance of the association seen in Table 2 results primarily from the stronger placement of intransitive subjects (S) and objects (O) in postverbal position than would be expected if order were simply random. One factor contributing to the more strongly postverbal placement of intransitive subjects appears to be the presence of floated quantifier constructions (Section 3.1), in which the quantifier appears before the verb, but the rest of the co-referential NP occurs after the verb (such phrases were counted as postverbal). If sentences with floated quantifiers are factored out, order of GRs vis-a-vis the verb is nearly random. If just A and O are considered, the distribution in pre- versus postverbal position is random.

Order is strongly associated with the discourse-pragmatic status of information encoded in a particular phrase. The general hypotheses discussed in Payne (1987) are given in 1 and 2. These can be viewed as processing rules, either from a coding (speaker's) perspective or from building of a cognitive representation (hearer's) perspective.

(1) Information occurs in preverbal position when it is:
   a. **pragmatically marked**. This includes information which is contrastive, questioned, and other similar statuses.
   b. **nonidentifiable and the hearer is instructed to open a new active discourse file for it**. The speaker may instruct the hearer to open an active discourse file for certain information because he or she anticipates that the information is potentially **important**.
   c. Some nonreferential mentions also occur preverbally.

(2) Information occurs in postverbal position when it is:
   a. identifiable or nonidentifiable, but destined to be unimportant or ancillary to subsequent action.
   b. Some nonreferential mentions also occur postverbally.

These hypotheses were tested for subject, object, and oblique phrases. Preverbal vs. postverbal position relative to identifiability status is shown in Table 3 (taken from Payne 1987).

The data of Table 3 show that the hypotheses in 1 and 2 are supported as strong tendencies; the figures for pragmatically marked and identifiable mentions reflect essentially grammaticized discourse-pragmatic categories. Relative to pragmatically marked mentions, there are several etic subtypes (Table 4). The etic subtypes do not matter for purposes of order, as essentially all correlate with preverbal phrasees. The two exceptions seen in Table 3 are third person free pronouns. In most cases, 'O'odham free pronouns occur in contexts of single or double focus contrast; however, some cannot be accounted for by contrastiveness in the strong sense. Nevertheless, ordinary referent tracking is accomplished by the switch reference (or

Table 3. Cross-tabulation of order with discourse-pragmatic status

	Preverbal		Postverbal		Total	
Nonidentifiable	125	83%	26	17%	151	100%
Identifiable	6	2%	278	98%	284	100%
Pragmatically marked	38	95%	2	5%	40	100%
Other (including some nonreferentials)	1		4		5	
Total	170		310		480	

χ^2 with Yates' correction calculated over nonidentifiable and identifiable information = 304.6, $p < .001$, 1 d.f.

Table 4. Pragmatically marked subtypes

Non-pronominal mentions	
Single focus contrast	5
Double focus contrast	4
Fronting of contrastive new topic	7
Free pronoun	24
Total	40

discontinuity) system, the second position auxiliary system, and a limited system of verb agreement; thus any use of a free pronoun is in some way non-neutral.

Table 3 shows that the majority of all nonidentifiable (usually referential) mentions occur in preverbal position (83%). However, 17% still occur in postverbal position. Thus, in and of itself identifiability (for pragmatically non-marked phrases) is a weaker predictor of order than we might hope for. In a complete analysis we should like to have closer to a 100% solution. If identifiability is a relevant factor driving surface order, what other factors are interacting with, and thus appear to confound, the identifiability factor?

3. Nonidentifiable mentions

Although the hypotheses presented in (1) and (2) above are well supported, there are some remaining questions surrounding nonidentifiable information. As (1b) and (2a) indicate, nonidentifiable mentions are split between pre- and postverbal position. In Payne (1987) I suggested that placement depends on subsequent "importance" of the referent, but did not evaluate this in any objective way. Second, certain nonidentifiable mentions have preverbal floated quantifiers (Q); in the earlier study I suggested that postverbal position may be largely grammaticized for such NPs from which Qs had been floated. Although quantified NPs can be identifiable, most are not. Third, nonreferential mentions remained largely unexplored in the 1987 study. In the following sections we will explore NP placement in floated quantifier sentences, the placement of a class of words which most commonly expresses nonreferential information ("*h*-words"), and attempt to objectively evaluate "importance" of nonidentifiable mentions.

3.1 Floated quantifier sentences

Contrary to the earlier suggestion that postverbal position may be largely grammaticized for NPs from which Qs have been floated, closer examination suggests that position of such NPs vis-a-vis the verb is also pragmatically determined. In the corpus used here there are 27 instances of quantified NPs in which both the Q and head noun are overtly present. A simple quantified NP is first illustrated in 3; the Q is structurally part of the NP and has not been floated off and incorporated into the verb phrase.[8]

(3) *Ku-t* ***mu'i hemajkam*** *'ia 'e-hemapaḍ*
DS-PFV many people here REFL-gather.IMPFV
'And many people gathered.' (SS118)

Noun phrases with nonfloated Qs occur both before and after the verb, though they appear to be dominantly preverbal; there are 14 such NPs in the corpus (Table 5).

When a Q has been floated off an overt NP, the Q precedes the verb. The rest of the NP with which it is coreferential may occur either before the verb (as in exs. 4-6), or after it (7-8). Floated Qs may be interpreted with a subject, a direct object, a semantic dative or recipient, or with the object of an incorporated postposition (cf. Munro 1984 for discussion of the syntax of Pima floated Q sentences; Pima and 'O'odham are very closely related dialects).

(4) *Ku-ṣ g* ***'uwpio*** *'am haha waṣ* ***hema***
DS-QT ART skunk AM afterward just an/one
oimmed.
walk.around.distributive
'Suddenly there was a/one skunk going about.' (SS118)

(5) *m-a-t g* ***'uupad mamhadag hema*** *wo ṣonc*
ITR-AUX-PFV ART catclaw branch one mod chop.PFV
'by cutting a/one catclaw branch' (SS219)

(6) *Ku-ṣ* ***hegam 'O'oḍham wees*** *e wepo kaiḍam*
DS-QT those people all themselves equal loudly
neneok.
talk
'And the people all spoke alike'. (SS349)

(7) *c* ***wees*** *ha-gegosiḍ* ***hegam*** ***'O'oḍham.***
ss all 3PL-feed those people
'and fed all the people' (SS349)

(8) *m-a-ṣ* *hebai* ***ha'i*** *wo* *ku'ago* ***g*** ***'u'uwi***
ITR-AUX-QT somewhere some MOD get.firewood art women
'It's said that when some women would go for firewood...' (SS221)

Although the total sample is fairly small, Table 5 might initially suggest that floated Q sentences stand as an exception to principle 1b above: NPs from which Qs have been floated appear to be dominantly postverbal (10 out of 13 instances), even though the information is consistently nonidentifiable in this situation. However, closer examination suggests that placement of such NPs is not exceptional. The referential persistence (RP) in discourse of preverbal floated-Q NPs is much higher than that of postverbal floated-Q NPs. Preverbal floated-Q NPs have an average RP value of 7.0 (range 4-10), while postverbal floated-Q NPs have an average RP of 2.6 (range 0-7).[9] Thus, if we take the number of re-mentions as an objective measure of "importance", principle 1b still may hold for floated-Q NPs. However, the size of the sample is too small to make this much more than a suggestion. The RP value of postverbal floated-Q NPs is roughly equivalent to that of both pre- and postverbal quantified NPs with nonfloated Qs. The potential significance of these data will be revisited at the end of Section 3.

Table 5. Quantified NPs

	NPs w/ **Nonfloated** Qs				NPs w/ **Floated** Qs			
	Preverbal		**Postverbal**		**Preverbal**		**Postverbal**	
	AV		VA		AQV		QVA	1
	SV	7	VS		SQV	2	QVS	3
	OV	2	VO	3	OQV	1	QVO	6
	OblV	1	VObl	1	OblQV		QVObl	
Total		10		4		3		10
AVG RP:		2.8		3.0		7.0		2.6
RP Range:		0-9		0-9		4-10		0-7

Q = quantifier; RP = referential persistence

3.2 *H*-words and referentiality

Principles (1b) and (2c) indicate that nonreferential mentions also occur on both sides of the verb (the definition of referentiality will be elaborated shortly). In 'O'odham there is a special set of nominal words which tend to be used both for nonreferential mentions and for concepts which do not persist in discourse. These include *hema* 'one, someone',[10] *has* 'how, what', *hebai* 'where, somewhere', *ha'icu* 'what, thing, something', *haschu* 'what', *ha'i* 'some, someone', *hedai* 'who', *hekid* 'sometime', *he'ekia* 'how many, that many', *hasko* 'somewhere'. There are also shortened forms of some of these. I subsequently refer to these as *h*-words. In a so-called "flexible" word order language like 'O'dham, it is important to empirically determine to what extent order does, or does not, depend on such factors as referentiality. In what follows we will see that regardless of referentiality and "importance", nearly all *h*-phrases are preverbal.

3.2.1 *Uses of* ***h****-words*

H-words have three major uses. They elicit information in questions, they are used for referential-indefinite mentions, and they are used for nonreferential mentions. They are of interest in evaluating the adequacy of principles (1c) and (2b) because the last function is their most common usage.

Information questions

Information questions elicit informative answers, beyond just 'yes' or 'no'. In all 'O'dham information questions, the grammaticized position for phrases eliciting information is before the verb. In the sample studied, there were 6 instances of nonreduced *h*-words used in information questions. All were nonreferential, as illustrated in exs. 9-10:

(9) a. *M-ac-s* ***has*** *wo juu iiḍa*
ITR-1-DUB how FUT do this
'What will we do with this thing?

b. *n-at-t-pi pi pi has wo juu*
NEG-1-PFV-COND NEG NEG something FUT do
'If we don't do something

c. *ku-t wo t-hugio.*
DS-PFV FUT 1PL-do.away.with
'it will do away with us'. (SS308)

(10) ***Hascu*** *wo i mea g al I'itoi?*
what FUT PCT cause.to.die ART little I'itoi
'What could little I'itoi kill?' (SS309)

According to Jane Hill (p.c.) it is considered quite impolite to ask information (as well as yes/no) questions. Partly for this reason, information questions have low frequency in ordinary conversation.

*Referential uses of **h**-words*

At the risk of oversimplifying what many scholars have said, definitions of referentiality fall into two broad types depending on whether one views referentiality as belonging to the domain of how a speaker manipulates language, or to the domain of how language maps onto the "real world". The first approach is a pragmatic one; the second is a logico-semantic objectivist approach (hereafter I will refer to this simply as "semantic").

In a strict semantic approach, a phrase is considered referential if it is used to refer to an existing entity in the real world. However, most philosophers who have discussed referentiality allow that referential status may be extended to entities which are set up as if they actually existed within the "world" created in a particular discourse.

In a pragmatic approach, a phrase is considered referential if the speaker **intends** the hearer to mentally tag the information as denoting a particular objectified entity which will (potentially) have continuous identity over time (Du Bois 1980). Objectified concepts, such as "the institution of marriage", or "the peace process" can, under this view, also be treated as referential. Thus, this approach allows for the metaphorical extension of referentiality according to the speaker's pragmatic purposes. From a pragmatic viewpoint, a nonreferential expression is one which is used to speak about an attribute or quality of an object or objectified concept, or to mention some information which has not been objectified as a bounded entity, or when the speaker simply does not care that the hearer tag the information as denoting some particular entity (cf. Wright and Givón 1987).

Thus, a pragmatic approach to referentiality includes both more and less than a semantic approach. It includes less in the sense that semantically referential entities can be treated as pragmatically nonreferential simply because the speaker does not care that the hearer tag them as particular entities (even though logically both the speaker and hearer may know that "some particular entity x must exist"; cf. example 11b below). On the other hand, a pragmatic view of referentiality includes more in that phrases which are nonreferential from a semantic perspective may take on referentiality if the speaker intends that the hearer treat the information as if it were an objectified concept. For example, an initial (technically) nonreferential mention may evoke a concept and act as if it had established an objectified, bounded referent in that subsequent references to this same concept can be expressed with whatever devices the language uses for clearly referential identifiable mentions. Thus, the first mention in effect behaves as if it were "pragmatically referential" (cf. example 15 below).

Examples (11-13) illustrate the use of *h*-phrases to refer to entities which are semantically referential. Some of these would be judged as pragmatically nonreferential, and others as pragmatically referential. Example (11) is an excerpt from a Coyote story. Clauses (b) and (d) both express semantically referential entities. In clause (b) the Coyote must have built the house in some actual location (within the universe of discourse). However, what that particular location might be is completely immaterial to the story plot. In clause (d) *ha'icu* also denotes something which must be taken as referential from a semantic viewpoint, relative to what the Coyote intends his hearers to understand. However, the subsequent text makes it clear that the content of what was said is also immaterial to the story. From the story-teller's perspective, the Coyote's only aim is to get all the people together in one spot. (The text is continued at points in just the English translation.)

(11) a. *Ṣ 'am 'i mee g Ban*
QT AM PCT run ART coyote
'Coyote ran on

b. *k 'aṣ 'am huu* ***hebai*** *hema kii-t*
SS 3.QT AM REM somewhere one house-make
and made a house somewhere,

and when he finished, he stood on top of it and announced and said, "My relatives,

c. *meek jewed ḍaam 'ani memelhim*
far dirt over 1SG was.running.around
I've been running around all over the earth

d. *c naanko* ***ha'icu*** *kaa.*
SS various something hear
and hearing various things.

Now let's gather together facing this way and hear". So the people came from all around and crowded into his house. The wise men spoke. After awhile coyote said, "I'm going outside and I will stretch a bit." So he went and stood in the doorway and stooped over and tried to spray the people with odor and then watched them. They ran off in all directions...' (SS119-120)

The following excerpt illustrates the semantically referential use of an *h*-phrase which is also pragmatically referential. *Ha'icu* 'something' occurs first in a quote, referring to some entity which is making a noise. The referent, which turns out to be the speaker's niece, continues on both within and after the quote.

(12) a. *'Ab 'o* ***ha'icu*** *has kaij Cemmo'oḍ ḍaam.*
there AUX something what say Cloud.stopper.Peak on
'"Something is making a sound up on Cloud-stopper peak

b. *T-p hems wud wa ñ-ma'i*
PFV-COND maybe COP MOD 1SG-older.sister's.child
Maybe it's my niece

c. *c 'an ḍaha*
SS there sitting
sitting there.

(d) We'll find out tomorrow." (e) In the morning they went, (f) and when they arrived they found

g. *m-o ga huu ḍaha g 'uwi*
ITR-AUX LOC REM sitting ART woman
that the woman was up there

h. *m-o 'ab 'i si pi apkog*
ITR-AUX there PCT INT NEG even
and that the mountainside was very rough.

i. *ṣ ṣoak*
QT crying
(It is said that) She was crying

j. *c pi 'e-'amicuḍ*
SS NEG RFV-understand
and didn't know

k. *m-a-s has 'e-juu*
ITR-AUX-DUB what RFV-do
what to do

l. *k wo 'i hud.*
SS MOD PCT descend
to get down'. (SS17)

The following example is an even clearer case where the *h*-phrase has both semantic and pragmatic referentiality. No quoted material is involved and *ha'icu* persists for more than ten following clauses.

(13) a. *m-a-t 'am* ***ha'icu*** *wuuṣ 'amai*
ITR-AUX-PFV LOC something come.out there
'Something came out there.

b. *'a-ṣ-p gd huu jewed weco amjed 'i him*
AUX-QT-COND LOC REM earth under from PCT go
It must have come from a long way underground

c. *k 'am wuuṣ 'am hebai 'amai*
SS LOC come.out LOC somewhere there
and come out somewhere there

d. *ge'e wud ha'icu*
big COP something
It was a big thing

e. *c 'am wo'iwua*
SS LOC lie
and lay there

f. *'am wuuṣ 'amai*
LOC come.out there
it came out and lay there

g. *k 'am wo'iwua*
SS LOC lie

h. *k 'amjed hab 'e-wuui.*
SS from thus REFL-lie.PFV
and it lay there thus

i. *m-a-ṣ g hemajkam ha-howicṣulig*
ITR-AUX-QT ART people 3PL-inhale
(the one that?) inhaled people

j. *'am wo'iwua*
LOC lie.IMPFV
it was lying there

k. *k 'ab wo si 'iibhuiwua 'ihab ha'ag*
SS toward MOD INT breathe this.point other.side
and would inhale towards the other side

It's breath was like a strong wind that drew (people) from a long way off...' (SS305-306)

Nonreferential uses of ***h****-words*

By far the most frequent use of *h*-words in the Saxton and Saxton texts is for nonquestioned information which is semantically nonreferential. Two simple instances are given in 14:

(14) *T* ***has*** *wo cei p-t 'ia wo ñ-aagi.*
PFV what FUT say 2SG-PFV here FUT 1SG-tell
'What he says tell me'.

N-t wenog 'am ***has*** *wo juu.*
1SG-PF then there something FUT do
'Then I'll know what to do'. (SS12)

In a very few cases an *h*-phrase may introduce a semantically nonreferential concept which is referred to again and can even have considerable continuity. Example (15) comes from a text about how women play field hockey. In a global sense all participants and props are nonreferential since this is a procedural text and no particular instance of playing field hockey is being referred to. However, once the world of discourse has been created, certain information may take on referentiality within (some subportion of) that discourse. The following first illustrates how the entity 'women' takes on referentiality. In this particular instance *ha'i...g 'u'uwi* 'some women' is a discontinuous reference with a floated Q. (*Ha'i* 'some' was therefore not included in the data reported in Section 3.2.2 below.)

(15) 'Field hockey was played in various ways.

a. *m-a-ṣ* ***hebai*** ***ha'i*** *wo* *ku'ago*
ITR-AUX-QT somewhere some MOD get.firewood

g ***'u'uwi***
ART women

It's said that when some women would go for firewood or water, they would start from home tossing the puck and racing to see who would be the first to get

b. *m-a-t* ***hebai*** *wo* *'i* *ku'a*
ITR-AUX-PFV somewhere MOD PFV get.firewood.PFV
to where they were going for wood

or water. Then they would race back the same way carrying their wood or water on their heads. What skill!' (SS221)

A second point of interest in the preceding example is the phrase *hebai* 'somewhere' in clause a. No particular location is being referred to, and yet the concept of that same location is rementioned in clause (b). However, *hebai* 'somewhere' has a lower degree of pragmatic referentiality in the text compared with *ha'i* ... *g 'u'uwi* 'some women', most probably because the speaker does not care that the hearer mentally tag *hebai* as some particular location with continuous identity over time. Thus, in contrast to the concept of 'women', the location is explicitly rementioned in clause (b) with the form *hebai* and is not referenced with anaphoric devices.

The following is another example of a semantically nonreferential *h*-phrase which does have continuity into a second structural clause; however, it is arguable that it is pragmatically referential in the discourse from which it is taken.

(16) a. *T* ***hedai*** *wo* *'e-nakog*
PFV who MOD RFV-be.able
'Whoever is able

b. *k* *wo* *gewickwua* *'am* *'e-weemkam* *ha-wui*
SS MOD strike.down there RFV-companion 3PL-to
hits it there to her companions'. (SS220)

The majority of *h*-phrases are like those in exs. (14) and (16).

3.2.2 *Order distribution and 'importance' of* ***h****-referents*

Principles (1c) and (2b) correctly state that nonreferential mentions can occur in either pre- or postverbal position. They do not, however, predict when which order will be chosen for nonreferential mentions. Here we will consider just the class of *h*-words which dominantly (though not exclusively) encode nonreferential information.[11]

Information which is (treated as) nonreferential within a given universe of discourse is relatively incidental or "unimportant" to the development of the narrative at hand. Thus, in 'O'odham we might predict that the majority of nonreferential mentions would occur postverbally in accord with the "unimportant information last" principle given in (2). This is decidedly not the case for *h*-words, even though the vast majority of them do not occur in questions (for which preverbal position is grammaticized), and even though the vast majority encode semantically nonreferential incidental information which does not persist in the discourse.

In the text sample used, there are 91 instances of *h*-words that function essentially as some type of pronoun.[12] Referentiality, pre- versus postverbal order, and the number of references (including references made via zero forms) in the ten clauses immediately following each *h*-phrase were evaluated.

Determinations about referentiality were made from a semantic perspective within the universe of discourse. This was done in order not to prejudice the results from potentially fuzzy intuitions about "importance" (which doubtless are closely tied to degree of persistence). Table 6 gives the results. The first horizontal line of figures in Table 6 indicates that there were 10 preverbal referential instances of *h*-phrases, and 56 preverbal nonreferential instances, all of which never reappeared in the next ten clauses (i.e. persistence = zero). There was 1 postverbal referential instance of an *h*-phrase, and 3 postverbal nonreferential instances of *h*-phrases, again with persistence values of zero.

From Table 6 it is immediately apparent that the majority of *h*-phrases occur in preverbal position, regardless of whether they express referential or nonreferential information. Second, when these *h*-words express semantically nonreferential information, that information strongly tends **not** to persist in discourse. The few cases discussed earlier are exceptional.

A significant observation is in order, namely, that one of the *h*-words has a markedly different behavior relative to referentiality and persistence

Table 6. Referential persistence of **h***-phrases cross-tabulated with pre- vs. postverbal position and referentiality*

RP	**preverbal**		**postverbal**	
	REF	NONREF	REF	NONREF
0	10	56	1	3
1	3	6	–	1
2	2		1	
3	2			
4	–			
5	2			
6	1			
7	2			
8	–			
9	–			
10	1			
Totals				
RP :	53	6	2	1
Mentions:	23	62	2	4
Average RP:	2.30	.10	1.0	.25

than do other *h*-words. This is *hema* 'one, someone'. In the sample used here, when not quantifying another noun, *hema* always refers to a human or anthropomorphized participant. Second, *hema* accounts for seven of the 25 referential instances of *h*-words and only one of the 66 nonreferential instances (counting both pre- and postverbal instances). Third, referential uses of *hema* have an average persistence of 4.4 clauses. In contrast, referential uses of other *h*-words have an average persistence of 1.4. These data are summarized in Table 7.

Although the referential instances of *hema* are few (N = 7), it is striking that all have a persistence value greater than zero. Information expressed via other h-words can have a high degree of continuity,[13] but participants expressed with *hema* are much more likely to have a high degree of continuity than are participants expressed with other *h*-words. In sum, although *h*-words as a group tend to encode nonreferential mentions, *hema* is largely specialized for introducing referential mentions that are likely to be continuous.

*Table 7. Referential persistence cross-tabulated with pre- vs. postverbal order and type of **h**-word; referential mentions only*

	hema		other *h*-words	
RP	PREVERBAL	POSTVERBAL	PREVERBAL	POSTVERBAL
0	–	no postverbal	10	1
1	1	instances of	2	
2	1	*hema*	1	1
3	1		1	
4	–		–	
5	1		1	
6	1		–	
7	2		–	
8	–		–	
9	–		–	
10	–		1	
Totals				
RP:	31		22	2
Mentions:	7		16	2
Average RP:	4.4	—	1.4	1.0

3.2.3 *Conclusions regarding **h**-words and order*

In preceding sections we have seen that *h*-words strongly tend to be used for nonreferential mentions which do not persist in the discourse. Although they may be used in information questions and for referential mentions, these uses are infrequent. *Hema* is exceptional in that it is dominantly used for referential mentions that do have some degree of continuity. However, total instances of *hema* are few in proportion to the whole sample.

Regardless of the job they do in any particular clause, *h*-words have a strongly uniform distribution in preverbal position. Only six out of 91 instances occurred postverbally. Of these six, two mentions were referential, four nonreferential, and four had zero cataphoric continuity. Since nonreferential mentions are "relatively unimportant" for the development of a narrative, we might have initially predicted that they would tend to follow the order pattern dictated by principle 1a. However, this is decidedly not true for nonreferential *h*-phrases. Conceivably, the preverbal placement of nonreferential *h*-phrases is reinforced by two salient — albeit infrequent — uses of *h*-words, namely their role in information questions and the use of *hema* to introduce important animate or anthropomorphized participants. That is, even in their nonreferential function, *h*-words may occur preverbally due to analogical pressure from their marked functions.

3.3 Other nonidentifiable mentions

In a revised count of the main corpus used in Payne (1987), there are 60 nonidentifiable mentions that do not belong to the set of *h*-words just discussed, that are not pragmatically marked, and that do not belong to floated Q sentences. For these nonidentifiable mentions, referential persistence was also evaluated in the ten clauses following first mention. When entities from this group are introduced in preverbal position, they have higher continuity in the subsequent discourse than when they are introduced in postverbal position (Table 8).

Table 8. Referential persistence of indefinite mentions cross-tabulated with pre- vs. postverbal position

Referential Persistence	*Preverbal (No. of instances)*		*Postverbal (No. of instances)*	
0	11	26%	13	76%
1	6	14%	1	6%
2	7	16%	–	
3	7	16%	1	6%
4	–		1	6%
5	4	9%	1	6%
6	3	7%	–	
7	3	7%	–	
8	1	2%	–	
9	1	2%	–	
10	–		–	
Totals				
RP:	117		13	
Mentions:	43	100%	17	100%
Average RP:	2.72		.76	

The data in Table 8 also show that the range of cataphoric persistence is, in absolute measures, broader for preverbal nonidentifiable mentions than for postverbal ones: the preverbal mentions had values as high as 9, while the highest persistence value for a postverbal mention was 5.

Table 8 further shows that 76% of all postverbal mentions do not persist in the discourse. In contrast, this is true for only 26% of preverbal mentions. This skewing is statistically significant. The null hypothesis in this case is that there is no association between cataphoric continuity and placement of information in pre- versus postverbal position. Position upon first mention is the dependent variable, and cataphoric remention versus non-mention is the independent variable. Table 9 presents data for evaluating this null hypothesis. The Ø score is .47, indicating a relatively strong, though non-absolute, correlation.

These figures establish more strongly that identifiability alone does not determine pre- versus postverbal position of non-pragmatically marked phrases. Rather, the postverbal position of both nonidentifiable mentions which have very low cataphoric persistence, and of identifiable mentions suggests that the function of postverbal position as a whole is to direct the hearer NOT to establish a "new active discourse file" for the entity mentioned — either because such a file already exists, or because it will not be needed. Although the item may momentarily enter the hearer's active consciousness, the hearer is not specifically instructed to open a cognitive file for anaphoric purposes since the item is so incidental to the story.

Let us now put these data together with that from our study of quantified NPs (*h*-phrases are excluded here). These data suggest that the following constructions are on a cline for coding nonidentifiable information, depending on importance of a referent in the subsequent discourse:

Table 9. Cross-tabulation of zero, vs. greater than zero persistence values, with pre- vs. postverbal position; nonidentifiable mentions only

	zero subsequent mentions		**one or more subsequent mentions**		**total**	
Preverbal	11	26%	32	74%	43	100%
Postverbal	13	76%	4	24%	17	100%
Total	24		36		60	

χ^2 with Yates' correction = 11.1, $p < .001$, 1 d.f.; $\phi = .47$

(17)	*Higher Importance of Referent*				*Lower Importance of Referent*
	preverbal floated-Q NP	<	postverbal floated-Q NP		
			nonfloated-Q NP (either order)		
			preverbal nonquantified NP	<	postverbal nonquantified NP
Avg RP:	7.0		2.6, 2.8, 3.0		.76

Pragmatically, preverbal NPs with floated Qs appear to express a high degree of importance. Postverbal floated-Q NPs appear to express essentially the same degree of importance as any nonfloated-Q NP, and as preverbal nonidentifiable mentions without quantifiers. Postverbal nonidentifiable mentions without Qs are quite unimportant in subsequent discourse. Thus for both NPs with floated Qs and nonquantified NPs, preverbal placement is associated with a comparatively higher degree of importance than is postverbal placement of the same construction.

4. Conclusions

Excluding the special category of *h*-words, Tables 8-9 bring us to a near-100% accounting for the data along the lines suggested in principles 1 and 2 above. In particular, only 4 out of 17 nonidentifiable postverbal mentions even have any persistence in the discourse, and these have less absolute persistence than do preverbal nonidentifiable mentions (Table 8). Principle (1c) should be modified as:

(1c) Some nonreferential mentions, including nearly all *h*-phrases, occur preverbally.

Finally, appropriate qualifications need to be made about order of quantified NPs. The persistence values for postverbal NPs with both floated and nonfloated Qs may constitute minor exceptions to the claim that the overall function of postverbal position is to direct the hearer not to establish a "new active discourse file" for the entity mentioned. As exceptions, they may mark a subtle move towards verb initial structure. In fact, we might speculate that if the quantifier itself signals a measure of the referent's importance, then the speaker need rely less on other morphosyntax — such as order — for indicating importance. Thus, precisely because the quantifier may be an alternative means of signalling pragmatic status, quantified NPs can move early to postverbal position.

In sum, it appears that the discourse-pragmatic categories laid out in (1a-b) and (2a) above have been essentially grammaticized and are expressed via order. Because this relationship is **rule governed** (revealed by the near 100% nature of the revised principles 1-2), there is as much or as little a priori reason to exclude grammaticized discourse-pragmatic categories from the domain of "grammar" as there is to exclude grammatical relations. To exclude such pragmatic categories from grammar may lead us to treat pragmatic order languages as if they were more like English than they really are, positing a "basic" order of subject and object vis-a-vis the verb.

Given that the bulk of pronominal and noun phrase references are instances of (1b) and (2a), we could legitimately (though somewhat imprecisely) characterize 'O'odham as a fairly rigid "Nonidentifiable-V-Identifiable" (or Indefinite-V-Definite) language. If the first linguists had been 'O'odham speakers, and if they were predisposed to assume that all reasonable languages operate on the basis of the same function-structure mappings as does their native language (as have the majority of scholars of language to date), then English would be viewed as a "free" word order language. That is, in English any order of identifiable and nonidentifiable phrases is allowed: *This man/A man* [nonidentifiable] *showed up at my door* [identifiable] *this morning* vs. *Tom* [identifiable] *saw a guy* [nonidentifiable] *lurking in the backyard*. But clearly, such a claim misses the real function of constituent order in English. In 'O'odham, the weak association that is seen between order and GR in Table 2 appears to be an epiphenomenon of how GRs are related to informational statuses; and it is the informational status that is really relevant.[14]

Dominantly pragmatic order languages may contain relics of a time when order was driven by grammatical relations. Such relics may be either robust or moribund and may co-exist for centuries with now-dominant pragmatic functions. In many cases these relics lead to positing a certain order as "underlyingly basic", despite the fact that this "underlyingly basic" order rarely surfaces; pragmatic factors are simply said to allow other orders. The gaining of either regularity or syntactic purity by appealing only to "grammatical" evidence or by developing a "purely syntactic" analysis appears to be a simple recreating of history in the guise of abstract synchronic analysis. It is time that linguistics address how abstract synchronic analyses of syntax should be; it is also time to recognize that the relation between pragmatic functions and morphosyntactic structure can be just as intimate as that between traditionally syntactic functions and morphosyntax.

Notes

1. That is, they are distinct from phonology, (much of) morphology, much of semantics, and especially pragmatics.

2. In at least some current Government Binding work, linear order is also tightly tied to syntactic relations. This is reflected in claims that case assignment (on the basis of government) must be done in a leftward direction (or in a rightward direction) in a given language.

3. See also Tomlin's (1985) definition of "syntactic coding", in which "some unit of form signals to the hearer some class of semantic or pragmatic information whenever that semantic or pragmatic information is part of the message."

4. Even though I take grammatical relations as primes for the purposes of this discussion, whether some information is expressed as subject, object, or oblique ultimately derives from the pragmatic and semantic status of the information.

5. The following discussion might suggest that in 'O'odham there is a single emic focus category encompassing both highly marked information and non-presupposed asserted new information. The form coding this etic range of functions would be "preverbal position". However, nonidentifiability, rather than non-presupposed new status, turns out to be (closer to) one of the relevant factors for preverbal position.

6. More in depth discussion of pragmatic markedness is found in Payne (1987, 1988 and 1990), which draw heavily on the works of Chafe (1976) and Dik et al. (1981). Other types of markedness explored in those works include information which is not expected on cultural grounds, added detail restatement, simple restatement, threats, and heightening the degree of a quality or attribute.

7. The help of Etheleen Rosero, Dean Saxton, Pamela Munro, Lynn Gordon, Hyo Sang Lee, Janine Scancarelli, Olivia Tsosie, and Charles Ulrich in better understanding the data is gratefully acknowledged. I also thank Janine Scancarelli and Matthew Dryer for comments on an earlier version of this paper. The same procedures are followed here as were used in the 1987 study for dividing the texts into clauses, identifying subject and object, and categorization of information as identifiable, etc. Though these methodological decisions are crucial in evaluating the adequacy of the findings, in the interests of space I will not repeat them here.

8. The orthography used here is an adaptation of that developed for 'O'odham by Albert Alvarez, Ken Hale, and others. Abbreviations are as follows: AM the particle *'am* which sometimes has locative/directional functions, ART article, COND conditional, DS different subject, DUB dubitive, INT intensity, ITR initiator, MOD modal, PCT punctual, QT quotative mood, REM remote. Examples are from Saxton and Saxton (1973), identified by SS plus the page number from that volume.

9. Referential persistence was counted within the next ten clauses following the floated-Q NP.

10. *Hema* also functions as a quantifier. Its quantificational uses are filtered from the data discussed in this section.

11. In the 1987 study (cf. Table 3), most instances of *h*-words were counted in the "nonidentifiable" category rather than in the "other" category.

12. Here I exclude *h*-words which function as quantifiers, such as *he'ekia* 'how many' in *he'ekia 'i 'u'uwi* 'any number of women', or *ha'icu* 'some' in *g si ha'icu s-a'amicuddam* 'some wise men'. Further, *h*-phrases are excluded if they function as one of the constituents of a predicate locative or predicate nominal construction. *H*-words functioning as information question words are included. There were only six instances of the latter; all were preverbal and nonreferential. If they were excluded, the average persistence values (Table 6) would not be appreciably different.

13. In fact, in this corpus the particular h-word with the highest degree of continuity was *ha'icu* (RP = 10), given in example (13).

14. The 1987 study similarly suggested that a correlation between activation status ("given/new") and order was an epiphenomenon due to the way that activation status is associated with identifiability. It is noteworthy, however, that the correlation between activation status and order was still much, much stronger than that between GR and order.

References

Aberdour, Cathie. 1985. "Referential Devices in Apurinã Discourse." *Porto Velho Workpapers* ed. by David Lee Fortune, 43-91. Brasilia: Summer Institute of Linguistics.

Bresnan, Joan and Sam McChombo. 1987. "Topic, Pronoun, and Agreement in Chichewa." *Language* 63.741-782.

Chafe, Wallace. 1976. "Givenness, Contrastiveness, Definiteness, Subjects, Topics, and Point of View." *Subject and Topic* ed. by Charles Li, 25-55. New York: Academic Press.

Chafe, Wallace. 1987. "Cognitive Constraints on Information Flow." *Coherence and Grounding in Discourse* ed. by Russell S. Tomlin, 21-51. Amsterdam: J. Benjamins.
Chomsky, Noam. 1965. *Aspects of the Theory of Syntax.* Cambridge: M.I.T. Press.
Dik, Simon, et al. 1981. "On the Typology of Focus Phenomena." *Perspectives on Functional Grammar* ed. by Teun Hoekstra et al., 41-74. Dordrecht: Foris.
Du Bois, John. 1980. "Beyond Definiteness, the Trace of Identity in Discourse." *The Pear Stories: Cognitive, Cultural, and Linguistic Aspects of Narrative Production* ed. by Wallace Chafe, 203-274. Norwood, N.J.: Ablex.
Du Bois, John. 1987. "The Discourse Basis of Ergativity." *Language* 63.805-855.
Fillmore, Charles. 1982. "Frame Semantics." *Linguistics in the Morning Calm* ed. by the Linguistic Society of Korea, 111-137. Seoul: Hanshin.
Givón, T. 1984. *Syntax, a Functional-Typological Introduction, 1.* Amsterdam: J. Benjamins.
Givón, T. 1988. "The Pragmatics of Word Order." *Studies in Syntactic Typology* ed. by Michael Hammond, Edith Moravcsik and Jessica Wirth, 243-284. Amsterdam: J. Benjamins.
Hale, Kenneth. 1983. "Papago *(k)c.*" *International Journal of American Linguistics* 35.302-312.
Hawkins, John. 1984. "A Note on Referent Identifiability and Co-Presence." *Journal of Pragmatics* 8.649-659.
Iwasaki, Shoichi. 1987. "Identifiability, Scope-Setting, and the Particle *wa*: A Study of Japanese Spoken Expository Discourse." *Perspectives on Topicalization, the Case of Japanese 'wa'* ed. by John Hinds, Senko Maynard and Shoichi Iwasaki, 107-141. Amsterdam: J. Benjamins.
Jensen, Allen. 1982. "Análise Formal do Discurso de Dois Textos Didáticos na Língua Wayapí (Oiampí)." *Anais do VII Encontro Nacional de Linguística.* Divisaõ de Intercámbio e Edicoẽs. PUC — Rio de Janeiro.
Jensen, Cheryl. 1980. "Word Order in Oiampi." MS.
Langacker, Ronald. 1977. *Studies in Uto-Aztecan Grammar, 1: An Overview of Uto-Aztecan Grammar.* Dallas: Summer Institute of Linguistics.
Lee, Hyo Sang. 1984. Discourse Presupposition and Discourse Function of the Topic Marker *nɨn* in Korean. UCLA Master's thesis.
Lee, Hyo Sang and Sandra Thompson. 1987. "A Discourse Account of the Korean Accusative Marker." *Korean: Papers and Discourse Data.* (= *Santa Barbara Papers in Linguistics 1.*)
Lehnert, W. G. 1980. "The Role of Scripts in Understanding." *Frame Conceptions and Text Understanding* ed. by D. Metzing, 79-95. Berlin: Mouton de Gruyter.
Mohanan, K. P. 1983. "Move NP or Lexical Rules? Evidence from Malayalam causativisation." *Papers in Lexical-Functional Grammar* ed. by Lori Levin, et al., 47-111. Indiana University Linguistics Club.
Munro, Pamela. 1984. "Floating Quantifiers in Pima." *The Syntax of Native American Languages* (= *Syntax and Semantics 16.*) ed. by Eung-Do Cook and Donna Gerdts, 269-287. New York: Academic Press.
Payne, Doris L. 1987. "Information Structuring in Papago Narrative Discourse." *Language* 63.783-804.

Payne, Doris L. 1988. "Meaning and Pragmatics of Order in Selected South American Languages." MS. [A preliminary version of this paper was presented at the Wenner Gren Symposium on the Relation of Theory to Description, Ocho Ríos, Jamaica, November 1987]

Payne, Doris L. 1990. *The Pragmatics of Word Order: Typological Dimensions of Verb Initial Languages*. Berlin: Mouton de Gruyter.

Saxton, Dean. 1980. "Evidence for Basic Word Order in Papago-Pima." MS.

Saxton, Dean. 1982. "Papago." *Studies in Uto-Aztecan Grammar, 3* ed. by Ronald Langacker, 93-266. Dallas: Summer Institute of Linguistics.

Saxton, Dean and Lucille Saxton. 1969. *Papago and Pima to English Dictionary*. Tucson: University of Arizona Press.

Saxton, Dean and Lucille Saxton. 1973. *O'othham Hoho'ak A'agitha: Legends and Lore of the Papago and Pima Indians*. Tucson: University of Arizona Press.

Scancarelli, Janine. 1987. Grammatical Relations and Verb Agreement in Cherokee. UCLA doctoral dissertation.

Scancarelli, Janine. 1989. "Marking Discontinuity in Pima and 'O'odham (Papago)." *Southwest Journal of Linguistics* 9:1-22.

Schank, Roger and R. P. Abelson. 1977. *Scripts, Plans, Goals and Understanding*. Hillsdale, N.J.: Lawrence Erlbaum.

Tomlin, Russell. 1985. "Foreground-Background Information and the Syntax of Subordination." *Text* 5.85-122.

Tomlin, Russell and Ming Ming Pu. 1991. "The Management of Reference in Mandarin Discourse." *Cognitive Linguistics* 2.65-95.

Wright, S. and T. Givón. 1987. "The Pragmatics of Indefinite Reference: Quantified Text-Based Studies." *Studies in Language* 11.1-33.

Zepeda, Ofelia. 1983. *A Papago Grammar*. Tucson: University of Arizona Press.

Word Order in Klamath

Karen Sundberg Meyer
University of Oregon

Word order in Klamath, a Penutian language of southern Oregon, has been described as "almost completely free" (Barker 1964: 341). Barker demonstrates that major arguments within the clause can occur in all logically possible combinations. This paper will demonstrate, however, that in discourse the occurrence of NPs in preverbal or postverbal position is not random, but is greatly influenced by pragmatic factors.[1] This paper examines the effect of the topicality of arguments on their position preceding or following the verb. Topicality is determined using five measures of topic continuity developed by Givón (1983) and one additional measure.

The data base consists of seven Klamath texts from Barker (1963): five traditional myths and two ethnographic and procedural texts,[2] altogether comprising 761 usable clauses. In this study, the position of subject, object, and locative noun phrases is analyzed as to topic status. Unstressed pronouns, though restricted to clause second position, are also analyzed for their topic properties in relation to other categories. The prediction, based on the results reported in Givón (1983), that postverbal position tends to code highly continuous topics, and preverbal position discontinuous topics, is confirmed for all noun phrase categories in Klamath.

We will first briefly outline the methodology followed in this study. Succeeding sections will then describe the Klamath constructions which were investigated, the quantitative results, and the conclusions which can be drawn about the function of word order in Klamath.

1. Methodology

The methodology devised by Givón (1983) for assessing topicality of NPs in text was applied to Klamath texts. In addition, a count of the number of new referents introduced into the text was made for each noun phrase category.

The texts were first divided into individual constituent clauses, each containing a single finite verb. Relative clauses and tightly-bound complement clauses (i.e. those with their subject coreferential to that of the main verb) were not counted as separate clauses; e.g. (1) is counted as a single clause:

(1) *coy solwo:lgis saȟa:Wawli ʔat, na:nok*
and gather.together.clothlike.OBJ want now, all
wičo:L-as
fishnet-OBJ
'Then [they] all wanted to gather together the fishnet.' (26: 47)[3]

Clauses repeated for emphasis or other stylistic reasons, as in (2), were not counted as separate clauses:

(2) *coy sa honk ʔat gena, gena, doscȟa, doscȟa*
and they now go, go, run, run
'Then they went and went, ran and ran.'

Elements within quotations were not measured for topic continuity, but the quotative margin and quoted portion were counted together as a single clause. If no quotative margin was present, the quoted portion counted as an instance of subject zero-anaphora for the speaker (see below).

Occasional interruptions and background interpolations by the narrator were deleted for purposes of the study, and resumption of the narrative counted as a thematic break except when the interruption occurred clause-medially, as in:

(3) *coy honk*[4] *cew — dam mat cew q̓ay ni sˀaywakta*
and Antelope — INT EVID Antelope NEG I know
— kani ʔa gatba
— someone DEC arrive
'And then Antelope — did they say Antelope? I don't know — someone arrived.' (3:109)

Thus counted, the data base totalled 761 clauses.

The measurements which were applied to the texts are as follows:

In determining referential distance, absence of a referent within direct quotation was not counted as a gap, but its presence within quoted material was counted as an occurrence. Indefinites were not subject to this measurement, as by definition they represent the first occurrence of a referent in the text.

In determining potential referential interference, if referents occur in the preceding 3 clauses which are semantically compatible with a referent in the predication for which counts are being made, this is taken as a measure of potential ambiguity of the referent in the clause in question. A value of 0 indicates no potential for ambiguity; a value of 1-3 indicates high potential for ambiguity. (This measure likewise cannot be applied to indefinites.)

Persistence is a measure of the importance of a referent in the discourse. In this study persistence was measured as the number of occurrences of a given referent in the 10 clauses following the clause in which the token occurs. For subjects, only subsequent occurrences as subject were counted; for objects and locatives, occurrence in any role was counted. The minimum possible value of 0 suggests low discourse importance (except for paragraph-final occurrences); the maximum value of 10 suggests high discourse importance of the referent. Occurrences within direct quotation were counted, while absence within a quote was not counted as a gap. As this measurement is cataphoric, it can be applied to indefinites as well as to definites.

To determine the switch-reference functions of SV and VS patterns, the subject of the preceding clause was evaluated for whether it was the same (SS) or different (DS) from the subject of the clause in question. An example of a SS pattern occurs in the second clause of (4); an example of DS occurs in the second clause of (5):

(4) *coy* *detdeye:mi-pk-s* *papakpakkanga,* *hok-t*
and (DIST)hungry-DUR-NOM (DIST)(INT)bark.around that-REF

w̓awka
little.coyotes

'Then, being hungry, those little coyotes barked around here and there.' (3:106)

(5) ... *hontba, hehji:ƙa-lam-ksi.*
land, Hehji:ƙa-GEN-place.

hehji:ƙa cawaltk mna wqepl̓aqs-dat
Hehji:ƙa.sitting.on.top his summer.house-LOC
'... [it] landed at Hehji:ƙa's place. Hehji:ƙa had been sitting on top of his summer house.' (8:2-3)

The paragraph boundaries indicated by Barker in the texts were taken as major thematic breaks, in addition to breaks occasioned by interpolated comments by the narrator. If a referent occurred in the initial clause of a thematic unit, it was counted as paragraph initial. All other occurrences were classified as paragraph non-initial. However, if two referents were introduced in separate clauses at the beginning of a unit, both occurrences were counted as paragraph initial, as in the beginning of the story of Old Bear and Antelope:

(6) *wil̓e:m la:b-a wewe:ʔas gitk.*
Black.Bear two-OBJ children have

cew l:ab-a wewe:ʔas gitk.
Antelope two-OBJ children have
'Black Bear had two children. Antelope had two children.' (1:1-2)

Finally, for each initial occurrence of a referent, the particular order in which it was introduced was determined ("introduction of new referents"). This is another type of discontinuity which overlaps somewhat with contiguity at thematic junctures and with referential distance. This count was applied to all noun phrase categories.

2. Object of investigation

The grammatical forms investigated in this study are unstressed third person pronouns, subject and object noun phrases, both definite and referential-indefinite, in pre- and postverbal positions; and locative noun phrases both preceding and following the verb.

Zero anaphora is the most frequently used subject-coding device in Klamath; it is also used for objects, though less often. The following exemplifies both subject and object zero anaphora:

(7) *coy s̓lo:los-dat pnipno:Goga*
and elder.twig-LOC (DIST)blow.into.a.container
'Then [he] blew [them] into an elder twig.' (1:141)

Anaphoric zeros were not measured for topic continuity but were counted as references in determining the continuity of the categories which were measured.

Unstressed pronouns

Unlike most languages with free word order, Klamath has no obligatory agreement system. Pronouns, when they do occur, are in clause-second position. The following examples illustrate subject and object pronouns:

(8) *coy sa na:nok waytas ge:sˀalca*
and 3PL every day go.to.gather.ipos
'And every day they went to gather ipos.' (1:3)

(9) *coy honk sa-s dom p̓as se:w̓a*
and 3PL-OBJ much food think
'And [she] thought they ate a lot.' (1:49)

Klamath has no noncontrastive third person pronoun as such; instead, demonstratives are used with third person anaphoric reference. (No examples of the contrastive third person pronoun occurred in the seven texts examined.) In order to distinguish pronominal from other functions of the demonstratives, only demonstratives marked with the "referential" suffix *-t* were counted as tokens; an example of a third person pronominal object is:

(10) *coy honk honk-t poLq̓ank, ˀat no:q̓lank,*
and that-REF having.plucked, now having.roasted,

coy sa p̓an
and 3PL eat
'And having plucked it, then having roasted [it], then they ate.' (8:27)

Subject noun phrases

Definite subjects

Klamath also lacks an elaborate case-marking system for nouns. There is no morphological subject marking, and a single object marker marks datives obligatorily and transitive patients optionally. (Factors governing object marking will be discussed below.) Subject NPs may precede or follow the verb:

(11) *hehji:ka cawaltk mna wqeplaqs-dat*
Hehji:*ka* *sitting.on.top his summer.house*-LOC
'*Hehji:*ka had been sitting on top of his summer-house ...' (8:3)

(12) *coy be:n hak hottGičapga hehji:ka*
and again EMPH come.running.down.off Hehji:ka
'And again Hehji:ka came running down.' (8:78)

Often subject NPs are preceded and/or followed by a demonstrative or personal pronoun, which may modify the noun or count as a double mention. If these occurred on the same side of the verb, as in (13), they were counted in this study as a single mention:

(13) *coy honk hok-t časga:y čigatk-damna ʔambo*
and that-REF Weasel fetch.liquid-HAB water
'And that Weasel used to go fetch water ...' (10:8)

However, if the noun and the coreferential demonstrative occurred on opposite sides of the verb, as in (14), neither was counted, as the position of the NP relative to the verb cannot be determined as uniquely preverbal or postverbal:

(14) *ma:ns hok q̓e:gi, hok w̓aka*
long that be.absent, that Little.Coyote
'And he was gone a long time, that Little Coyote.' (3:92)

The few occurrences of this latter pattern in the texts (a total of 4) did not warrant the creation of a separate category.

Referential-indefinite subjects

Referential-indefinite noun phrases include first mention of inanimates, as well as occasional animates which were either preceded by a quantifier, as *la:ba wewe:ʔas* in (15), or were not proper names of well-known mythical characters, as *Ga:q* in (16):

(15) *wil̓e:m la:b-a wewe:ʔas gitk*
Black.Bear two-OBJ children have
'Black Bear had two children.' (1:1)

(16) *coy honk Ga:q honk kiko:ch̓a*
and crow that (DIST)poke.w..sharp.instr.
'Then a crow speared them with its beak.' (2:27)

All referential-indefinite subjects in the texts precede the verb, as in ex. (16).[5]

Object noun phrases

Definite objects

There is only one object marker on nouns in Klamath; this always occurs on datives and generally occurs on animate patients of transitive verbs.[6] In this study all object-marked NPs were treated as belonging to a single category.

Object NPs occur in both pre- (17) and postverbal (18) position:

(17) *coy honk ʔat gaba:tis ce:, sdaynas honk s̓loGi*
and now go.to.shore upon, heart that(OBJ) swallow
'And upon reaching the shore, [he$_i$] swallowed his$_j$ heart.' (3:26)

(18) *gmok̓am̓c sal̓wa:ya maqlaqs-as*
Gmok̓am̓c help people-OBJ
'Gmok̓am̓c helped the Indians.' (26:61)

As with subject phrases, a small number of object references straddle the verb (4 in the sample). Again, these were not counted.

Referential-indefinite objects

This category can occur preverbally (as in ex. 15); unlike referential-indefinite subjects, they can also occur postverbally, as in:

(19) *wil̓e:m̓am̓c c̓aGi: Ge:s*
Old.Bear put.handful.in.mouth ipos
'Old Bear put a handful of ipos into her mouth.' (1:14)

Locative noun phrases

The majority of locative NPs follow the verb, as in:

(20) *coy ksembli wqeplaqs-dal mna*
and take.living.OBJ..back summer.house-to his
'Then [he] took [it] back to his summer-house.' (8:25)

Less often they precede the verb, as in:

(21) *coy honk ʔat go:s-dat dalmi*
and now tree-LOC look.up
'Then [he] looked up in the tree.' (3:109)

3. Quantitative results[7]

Topic continuity properties of subjects

Table 1 presents the average values of referential distance for the various categories of subject NP. The categories rank predictably from the most continuous with the lowest referential distance, the PRO category, to the least continuous with the highest average RD value, the preverbal full NP subjects. The value for postverbal full NP subjects ranks approximately halfway between the others, tending to code topics of higher continuity than the SV category, but not so high as the PRO category.

Table 2 presents the variation of tokens within each category. A full 82% of all occurrences of PRO subjects are seen to cluster at the 1 clause range; 77% of all VS occurrences fall in the 1-3 clause range; while the SV category shows clustering at the two extreme ends of the scale, with 64% occurring within 1-7 clauses, and 30% showing maximal RD at the 20+ clause range.

Table 1. Average referential distance (in number of clauses) for subjects

	N	RD
PRONOUN	132	1.30
VS order	36	3.92
SV order	89	7.82

Table 2. Percent distribution of referential distance within subject categories

no. of clauses	PRO		VS		SV	
	N	%	N	%	N	%
1	108	82	18	50	34	38
2	11	08	7	19	9	10
3	5	04	3	08	5	06
4	3	02	1	03	3	03
5	3	02	1	03	1	01
6	1	0.7	–		4	05
7	–		1	03	1	01
8	–		1	03	–	
9	1	0.7	–		1	01
10			–		2	02
11			–		–	
12			–		3	03
13		–		–		
14			–		–	
15			–		–	
16			–		1	01
17			1	03	–	
18			–		–	
19			1	03		
20+			2	06	25	30
Totals	132		36		89	

The average values for the number of potentially interfering referents in the clause in question are recorded in Table 3. These results again follow the predicted pattern, with pronouns occuring when there is the least potential for ambiguity; the VS category in turn has fewer interfering referents than the SV category; thus, the SV ordered NPs code more discontinuous topics.

Table 4 presents the distribution of potential interference across the categories. The highest percentage of pronouns (61%) has no interfering referents in the preceding clauses; the majority of full NP subjects in both VS and SV patterns has one interfering referent; SV also has the only tokens with 3 such interfering referents.

Table 3. Average potential referential interference (PRI) for subjects

	N	PRI
PRO	132	0.40
VS	36	0.86
SV	89	1.02

Table 4. Percent distribution of tokens with 1, 2, and 3 potentially interfering referents (PIR) in the preceding three clauses

PIR	PRO		VS		SV	
	N	%	N	%	N	%
0	80	61	10	28	18	20
1	51	39	21	58	53	60
2	1	0.75	5	14	16	18
3					2	02
4+						

Persistence measurements are given in Table 5 and are taken as a measure of discourse importance. Pronouns show the highest persistence, the SV/DEF category persists longer than the VS/DEF category, while the REF-INDEF category (all SV) decays most rapidly in the discourse register. The average values obtained for the definite categories reflect their position within thematic units: pronouns nearly always occur in paragraph medial and final clauses, and, being the most continuous category (as reflected in the results for RD and PRI), are most likely to be a major form used in long equi-subject clause chains.[8] The SV category, more often found in paragraph initial clauses, is most likely to initiate such chains. Referents expressed by both PRO and SV tend to persist throughout the thematic unit. Referents expressed by VS tend to persist for a shorter duration than those expressed by either the PRO or SV categories. Thus, the VS category encodes less important referents, and rarely occurs in paragraph initial clauses (which are more typically SV).

All referential-indefinite subject NPs occur in the preverbal position; by far, this category has the lowest persistence.

The distribution within categories is presented in Table 6. At least 70% of the tokens in each category occur in the 0-1 clause range. The REF/

Table 5. Average persistence (in number of clauses across subject categories

	N	Persistence
PRONOUN	132	2.13
VS DEFINITE	36	1.36
SV DEFINITE	89	1.98
VS REF/INDEF	0	N/A
SV REF/INDEF	15	0.53

Table 6. Percent distribution of persistence within subject categories

no. of clauses	PRO		VS		SV		SV/REF-INDEF	
	N	%	N	%	N	%	N	%
0	38	29	17	47	30	34	9	60
1	35	27	8	22	22	25	4	27
2	19	14	4	11	11	12	2	13
3	12	09	3	08	8	09		
4	7	05	1	03	8	09		
5	6	05	1	03	2	02		
6	4	03	1	03	2	02		
7	3	02	–		2	02		
8	2	02	–					
9	–		1	03	–			
10+	6	05			4	04		
Totals	132		36		89		15	

INDEFINITE category has 100% of its tokens within this range; the VS category has 80%; the SV category has 71%; and the PRO category has 70%, with the largest number of tokens in the 3-10+ clause range.

The relative distribution of same subject and different subject occurrences for the definite categories is presented in Table 7. As expected, the PRO category shows the highest ratio of SS to DS occurrences (69% vs. 31%), the VS category shows an intermediate ratio (53% vs. 47%), and the SV category shows the lowest ratio (24% vs. 76%). As yet another measure of topic continuity, the categories rank in the same order as in the RD and PRI measurements; pronouns show the highest degree of continuity to the preceding clause, VS ordered NPs show the next highest degree, and SV ordered NPs show the lowest degree.

Table 8 presents the relative distribution of occurrences at thematic junctures, as opposed to thematic continuations for each category. As noted above, the great majority of PRO occurrences (93%) are in paragraph non-initial clauses; to a somewhat lesser extent this distribution is replicated by the VS category which has 81% of its tokens in non-initial clauses. In contrast, over half the SV tokens (54%) are in paragraph initial clauses.

Almost all of the referential-indefinite NPs (93%) occur in paragraph non-initial clauses. This correlates with the results obtained for the persistence measurement: as highly unimportant referents, they are unlikely to initiate equi-topic chains; rather, they are non-topical and thus are most often introduced in the middle or toward the end of the thematic unit, decaying almost immediately in the discourse.

*Table 7. Relative distribution of SS vs. DS occurrences within subject categories (*definite NPs only)*

	SS		DS		TOTAL	
	N	%	N	%	N	%
PRO	91	69	41	31	132	100
VS*	19	53	17	47	36	100
SV*	21	24	68	76	89	100
TOTAL	131	51	126	49	257	100

Table 8. Relative distribution of contiguity to thematic break vs. thematic continuation within subject categories

	BREAK		CONTINUATION		TOTAL	
	N	%	N	%	N	%
PRO	9	07	123	93	132	100
VS-DEF	7	19	29	81	36	100
SV-DEF	48	54	41	46	89	100
VS-R/I	0		0		0	
SV-R/I	1	07	14	93	15	100
TOTAL	65	24	207	76	272	100

Topic continuity properties of objects

Table 9 presents the average values for referential distance for the definite object categories. As with the subject categories, these are ranked as expected from the most continuous, the PRO category, to the least continuous, the OV category; the VO category has an intermediate degree of continuity.

Table 9. Average referential distance (in number of clauses) for objects

	N	RD
PRONOUN	44	1.70
VO order	45	6.04
OV order	30	9.97

Table 10. Percent distribution of referential distance within object categories

no. of	PRO		VO		OV	
clauses	N	%	N	%	N	%
1	33	75	15	33	10	33
2	5	11	11	24	3	10
3	1	02	1	02	–	
4	2	05	2	05	1	03
5	1	02	3	07	1	03
6	–		1	02	–	
7	–		–		–	
8	2	05	–		–	
9			–		2	07
10			3	07	–	
11			–		–	
12			–		–	
13			1	02	–	
14			–		–	
15			–		–	
16			–		1	03
17			–		–	
18			–		–	
19			–		–	
20+			8	19	12	40
TOTALS	44		45		30	

The distribution within categories is given in Table 10. A full 75% of all PRO occurrences are within the 1 clause range. 71% of the VO occurrences are between 1-5 clauses, with 19% at the 20+ clause range. Like SV, the OV category exhibits clustering at the two extreme ends, with 43% in the 1-2 clause range, and a relatively high 40% at the 20+ clause range. This indicates that objects as well as subjects are most likely to be introduced or reintroduced in preverbal position, as will be demonstrated further below.

Tables 11 and 12 present the average values for potential interference and the distribution within the definite object categories. Both the pronouns and the VO ordered NPs show no interfering referents in the preceding 3 clauses. The average PRI value for the OV category is higher, with 54% of the tokens having 1 or 2 interfering referents in the preceding 3 clauses. Thus, the OV category is the preferred order in potentially ambiguous predications.

Table 13 presents the average values of persistence for the object categories. The VO-ordered definite NPs, with the highest average value, tend to code both highly continuous and important referents; in contrast,

Table 11. Average potential referential interference (PRI) for objects

	N	PRI
PRO	44	0.25
VO	45	0.22
OV	30	0.70

Table 12. Percent distribution of tokens with 1 or 2 potentially interfering referents (PIR) in preceding three clauses

PIR	PRO		VO		OV	
	N	%	N	%	N	%
0	34	77	35	78	14	47
1	9	20	10	22	11	37
2	1	02			5	17
3+						

the OV-ordered definite NPs code referents which decay more quickly in the discourse register. The PRO category has a relatively low persistence, as this category is not used to code new topics and is most often found in paragraph non-initial clauses.

The majority of referential-indefinite objects occur in the OV order. This category has a lower persistence than the definite categories, indicating the lesser importance of the topics encoded by them. Lowest of all, however, is the VO ordered referential-indefinite category, which nearly always expresses a unique mention in the discourse. These are extremely unimportant referents, the action of the verb itself usually being the most salient in the predication, which thus tends to precede the object, as in ex. (22):

(22) *coy honk ˀat noło:łle:Gi, waGe:nha cacga:lam*
and now throw.round.OBJ.across, maybe pine.cone
'And then [he] threw [something] across, maybe a pine cone.' (1:130)

The distribution within categories is recorded in Table 14. 72% of the PRO category shows a low persistence in the 0-1 clause range; the majority of the OV-DEF category (76%) occurs in the 0-2 clause range; and the VO-DEF category again shows the greatest persistence, with 76% distributed in the 0-5 clause range; these are also the only tokens that have the maximum persistence of 10+ clauses. 80% of the VO-REF/INDEF category decays immediately at 0 clauses, and 78% of the OV-REF/INDEF NPs occur in the 0-2 clause range. The REF/INDEF categories also have the least dispersed distribution, with no tokens occurring beyond 2 clauses and 4 clauses, respectively.

Table 13. Average persistence (in number of clauses) across object categories

	N	Persistence
VO REF/INDEF	15	0.27
OV REF/INDEF	27	1.22
PRONOUN	44	1.36
OV DEFINITE	45	1.60
VO DEFINITE	30	2.80

Table 14: Percent distribution of persistence within object categories

no. of	VO-R/I		OV-R/I		PRO		OV-DEF		VO-DEF	
clauses	N	%	N	%	N	%	N	%	N	%
0	12	80	13	48	20	45	13	43	18	40
1	2	13	4	15	12	27	6	20	5	11
2	1	07	4	15	3	07	4	13	3	07
3			3	11	3	07	1	03	3	07
4			3	11	3	07	3	10	2	04
5					–		2	07	3	07
6					1	02	–		3	07
7					1	02	–		3	07
8					1	02	–		3	07
9							1	03	–	
10+									2	04
Totals	15		27		44		30		45	

Topic continuity properties of locatives

The referential distance results for locatives are recorded in Tables 15 and 16. The majority of locative NPs are postverbal, showing lower referential distance. A smaller number of locatives occur preverbally; most of these are highly discontinuous, first-mention referents, as can be seen from their distribution in Table 16. The V-LOC occurrences show a more scattered distribution throughout the 1-20 clause range, indicating their somewhat greater continuity.

Tables 17 and 18 present the average values for persistence and their distribution within the locative NP categories. The majority of occurrences for both the V-LOC and LOC-V orders have no persistence. The V-LOC order, however, contains 30% which persist for 1 clause, and a few tokens which persist for 2-5 clauses. Therefore, although the locative NP category in general tends to code relatively unimportant referents, the more important of these occur postverbally.

Table 15. Average referential distance (in number of clauses) for locative NPs

	N	Rd
V-LOC NP	30	10.93
LOC NP-V	9	17.55

Table 16. Percent distribution of referential distance within locative NP categories

no. of clauses	V-LOC N	NP %	LOC-V N	NP-V %
1	5	17	–	
2	2	07	–	
3	1	03	–	
4	3	10	–	
5	–		–	
6	1	03	–	
7	–		–	
8	2	07	–	
9	2	07	2	22
10	1	03	–	
11	–		–	
12	–		–	
13	–		–	
14	1	03	–	
15	–		–	
16	–		–	
17	–		–	
18	–		–	
19	–		–	
20+	12	40	7	78
TOTALS	30		9	

Table 17. Average persistence for locative NPs

	N	Persistence
V-LOC NP	30	0.67
LOC NP-V	9	0.22

Table 18. Percent distribution of persistence within locative NP categories

no. of	V-LOC		LOC-V	
clauses	N	%	N	%
0	18	60	7	78
1	9	30	2	22
2	1	03		
3	–			
4	1	03		
5	1	03		
6				
7				
8				
9				
10+				
TOTALS	30		9	

Introduction of new referents into the discourse

Table 19 presents the number of first-mention referents occurring in the postverbal and preverbal order for each NP category. 98% of the new subject NPs, both definite and referential- indefinite, are introduced in preverbal order; this is another strong indication of the discontinuity of the referents expressed in that order. For the two object categories, 67% are also introduced in preverbal order. This again suggests the discontinuity of that order. For locative NPs, numerically more referents are introduced in postverbal position (59%). However, as the great majority of all locative NPs occur in this order, this amounts to only 33% of all the postverbal NPs; whereas the number of first-mention referents amounts to 78% of all preverbal NPs. Preverbal order, then, is the preferred mode for introducing new referents of all major case roles into the discourse.

Table 19. Introduction of new referents into discourse

	V NP		NP V		TOTAL	
	N	%	N	%	N	%
SUBJECT						
DEFINITE NP	1	03	28	97	29	100
REF/INDEF NP	0		11	100	11	100
TOTAL SUBJECT	1	02	39	98	40	100
OBJECT						
DEFINITE NP	7	35	13	65	20	100
REF/INDEF NP	12	32	25	68	37	100
TOTAL OBJECT	19	33	38	67	57	100
LOCATIVE	10	59	7	41	17	100

Word order distribution

The distribution of the NP categories in the preverbal and postverbal orders is summarized in Table 20. Order distribution across the major cases is at first glance surprising, relative to the general tendencies exhibited by the major case-roles discussed above; we will return to this in the last section of this paper. The preverbal order, which codes discontinuous referents both within and across categories in terms of all 6 measurements, has the highest percentage of subject NPs and the lowest percentage of locative NPs; the percentage of object NPs in preverbal position ranks midway between the two.

For the subject categories, the skewed distribution results in part from the greater functional load of the SV order: it is used for introducing and re-introducing referents, in potentially ambiguous predications, following DS clauses, and at the start of thematic units. The VS order, on the other hand, is most often used when none of the above conditions is present, i.e. when the referent is predictable and expected. Furthermore, use of the VS order is complemented by the use of zero-anaphora and unstressed pronouns to code more continuous referents, thus decreasing its overall frequency of occurrence. There are simply more discourse environments in which the preverbal, SV, order is preferred for coding referents.

Table 20. Distribution of word order

	V NP		NP V		TOTAL	
	N	%	N	%	N	%
SUBJECT						
DEFINITE NP	36	29	89	71	125	100
REF/INDEF NP	0	0	15	100	15	100
TOTAL SUBJECT	36	26	104	74	140	100
OBJECT						
DEFINITE NP	45	60	30	40	75	100
REF/INDEF NP	15	36	27	64	42	100
TOTAL OBJECT	19	33	38	67	57	100
LOCATIVE	30	77	9	23	39	100

For locative NPs the skewed distribution is explained by the degree of continuity. As we have seen, V-LOC order codes more continuous NPs than does LOC-V order. In fact, 60% of the references had been previously mentioned, and 40% persist for at least 1 clause, as compared to only 22% of previously mentioned referents in the LOC-V category and 22% which showed no persistence whatever. The greater number of postverbal locative NPs, then, is due to the greater number of continuous referents within that category.

Animacy

Klamath shows a cross-linguistically expected correlation between case role and the percentage of animate vs. inanimate topics (Table 21). In particular, subjects are overwhelmingly animate, reflecting the importance of the referents encoded as subject. Objects are roughly equally divided between animate and inanimate. Locatives are nearly always inanimate, indicating the relative unimportance of the referents expressed as locative NPs. As will be discussed below, the animacy associations closely parallel those obtained for both the Persistence and PRI measurements.

Table 21. Percent of animate vs. inanimate NPs in the major case-role categories

	ANIMATE		INANIMATE		TOTAL	
	N	%	N	%	N	%
SUBJECT	135	96	5	04	140	100
OBJECT	61	52	56	48	117	100
LOCATIVE	1	06	16	94	17	100

4. Discussion

RD and topic continuity within case-roles

The average values of referential distance within the major case roles are repeated here for convenience:

	SUBJ	OBJ	LOC
PRO	1.30	1.70	—
V-NP	3.92	6.04	10.93
NP-V	7.82	9.97	17.55

In Table 22, the topic continuity encoded by the grammatical devices is expressed as the percentage of tokens in each category having a referential distance of 1-2 clauses; this is the range of maximally continuous referents. 89% of the PRO category has a low RD of 1-2 clauses; 53% of the entire postverbal category and 44% of the entire preverbal category have a RD of 1-2.

Table 22. Percentage of tokens of each type with RD of 2.0 or lower

	TOTAL SAMPLE		RD of 2.0 or less	
	N	%	N	%
PRO	176	100	157	89
V-NP	111	100	58	52
NP-V	128	100	56	44

Thus, within all case roles the grammatical devices can be ranked from most to least continuous as follows:

(23) PRO > V-NP > NP-V

This gradation confirms the predictions resulting from the studies in Givón (1983). Pronouns clearly code the most continuous referents, postverbal NPs code referents of intermediate continuity, and preverbal NPs clearly code the least continuous referents, which are often the most inaccessible to the speaker and hearer.

PRI and topic continuity

The percentage of subject and object tokens which have no potential for ambiguity is presented in Table 23. This distribution also reflects the hierarchy in (23) above: the PRO category, having the highest percentage of noninterference, is also the most continuous category with respect to the previous discourse. The postverbal category shows a moderate potential for ambiguity; nearly half of its tokens show a PRI value of greater than 0. The preverbal category clearly has the most interference from competing referents. As the potential for ambiguity within the clause increases, the more likely it is that the referent will be coded in the preverbal order: to increase the ease of recoverability of the referent, it is fronted in the clause, making it more salient in the discourse.

Topical importance, animacy, and persistence of referents

The distribution of animate vs. inanimate referents in the major case roles is a more or less direct measurement of the topical importance the case roles typically express. From Table 21, we see that 96% of subjects, 52% of objects, and 6% of locatives are animate.

Table 23. Percentage of subject or object tokens with PRI value of 0

	TOTAL SAMPLE		PRI of 0.00	
	N	%	N	%
PRO	176	100	114	65
V-NP	81	100	45	56
NP-V	119	100	32	27

Discourse importance is also measured in terms of the persistence of the referent in the subsequent discourse. Due to differences in methodology, the results obtained for the subject categories cannot be directly compared with those of the object and locative categories. However, the values obtained show that the object category outranks the locative in topical importance: the object categories consistently show higher persistence values than do the locative categories (Table 13), thus coding more topically important referents.

Of the two ordering patterns, V-NP and NP-V, the postverbal order overall codes more continuous and important topics than does the preverbal order.

All referential indefinite subjects occur in preverbal position. For referential indefinite objects, the postverbal order codes extremely unimportant referents which die out immediately in the register, while the preverbal order codes the relatively more salient referential-indefinite objects.

Subjects were measured for persistence as subject only. The results obtained correlate to some extent with the positioning of the referent in the thematic unit, though not exactly as predicted in Givón (1983). Pronouns show the highest persistence, though they occur overwhelmingly in paragraph non-initial clauses (93%). As discussed above, this results from their being a major component in equi-subject chains. The postverbal NP category shows the lowest persistence, as expected for paragraph non-initial occurrences. The persistence of the preverbal NP category is close to that of the PRO category; both show a relatively high average value, as expected for theme-initial occurrences which initiate equi-subject chains.

SS vs. DS, thematic continuity, and continuity of subjects

The hierarchy expressed in (23) is also supported by the additional measures of SS vs. DS and contiguity of subjects to thematic junctures. The largest percentage of both SS and thematic non-initial subjects are unstressed pronouns. The VS-ordered NPs again rank as intermediary, and the least continuous category, the SV-ordered NPs, contain the smallest percentage of both SS and thematic non-initial occurrences.

A direct measure of topic discontinuity: the entry of referents into the register

The preverbal NP order is highly preferred for introducing referents across all case roles. As the entry of a referent into the register is the most discontinuous function in terms of topic continuity, this strongly confirms the preverbal order as the most discontinuous of all grammatical devices. As can be seen by the total number of new topics for each case role (Table 19), referents are most often introduced into the register as objects (N=57) and least often as locatives (N=17). First mention referents in the subject role (N=40) are intermediate.

In conclusion, word order in Klamath is pragmatically controlled, with the postverbal NP order coding continuous referents, and the preverbal NP order coding discontinuous referents. This conclusion is supported by several functions: for subjects, preverbal order is used most often for entry and re-entry of referents into the discourse; in potentially ambiguous situations it aids in the recoverability of the referent by increasing saliency; it also occurs at points of switch of reference; and at thematic junctures. Pronouns and the postverbal NP order occur in the absence of the above conditions. Similarly, for objects and locatives, the preverbal order is used more often for introducing and re-introducing referents, and, for objects, when there are interfering referents in the preceding discourse. The postverbal position for the two non-subject roles codes continuous referents, and topically important referents which persist in the subsequent discourse. Referential-indefinite subjects and objects tend to precede the verb unless they are extremely unimportant in the discourse; extremely unimportant referential indefinite objects can occur in postverbal position, typically as an afterthought construction. In summary, word order in Klamath is syntactically "free"; but as a general pragmatic rule, unpredictable, potentially ambiguous information is fronted in the clause.

Notes

1. There are other problems of Klamath word order which will not be dealt with in this paper, most notably the fact that noun modifiers occasionally occur on the opposite side of the verb from their head, as in the following example from Barker 1964:315:

nanqa ʔa de:Wi wokas p̓aLa-tdat
some INDIC leave wokas tray-LOC
'[He] left some wokas on a tray.'

2. The texts are: (1), Old Bear and Antelope, (2), Coyote and Badger, (3), Little Porcupine and Coyote (all by Mrs. Pansey Ohles), (8), Hehji:k̓a (Mr. Grover Pompey), (10), The Crater Lake Myth, (26), Killing Fish (both by Mr. Robert David), and (27), Some Historical Incidents (Mrs. Aggie Butler).

3. Citations are to text number and line in Barker (1963).

4. The *honk* of *coy honk* occurring here and in many other examples, although morphologically identical to the object form of the demonstrative, apparently functions as a discourse connective and will not be glossed.

5. One VS existential-presentative construction was omitted from the counts.

6. See Barker (1964:240). Exceptions to marking all and only animate objects do occur, but none were found in the texts studied.

7. N in the tables represents the total number of tokens of that type in the data base.

8. Zero anaphora is the other major form.

References

Barker, M.A.R. 1963. *Klamath Texts.* (= *University of California Publications in Linguistics 30.*) Berkeley: University of California Press.

Barker, M.A.R. 1964. *Klamath Grammar.* (= *University of California Publications in Linguistics 32.*) Berkeley: University of California Press.

Givón, T. 1979. *On Understanding Grammar.* New York: Academic Press.

Givón, T. ed. 1983. *Topic Continuity in Discourse: Quantitative Cross-Language Studies.* (= *Typological Studies in Language 3*). Amsterdam: Benjamins.

Greenberg, Joseph. 1966. "Some Universals of Grammar with Particular Reference to the Order of Meaningful Elements." *Universals of Language* ed. by J. Greenberg, 73-114. Cambridge: MIT Press.

Mithun, Marianne. 1987. "Is Basic Word Order Universal?" *Coherence and Grounding in Discourse* (= *Typological Studies in Language 11*) ed. by R. Tomlin, 281-328. Amsterdam: Benjamins.

Word Order and Topicality in Nez Perce

Noel Rude
University of Oregon

0. Introduction[1]

This paper investigates the discourse function of word order in Nez Perce, an American Indian language of the Pacific Northwest of the United States. Nez Perce and its sister language Sahaptin together comprise the Sahaptian language family. The paper treats word order in the broader context of the general coding of participants: noun, independent pronoun, and verbal agreement. The methodology is that first employed in the studies in Givón (1983a). In this methodology, measurements for topic continuity are correlated with various grammatical strategies (which, in this paper, mean verbal agreement, independent pronouns, and various word orders). The assumption is not that it is the topic continuity which is being coded, but that both the topic continuity and the grammatical strategies reflect some deeper discourse function. The procedure is useful because topic continuity is a measurable entity and discourse function is not. The paper begins with examples of Nez Perce word order, and then follows with comments on the use of pronouns and verbal agreement; lastly, the discourse/pragmatic context for these phenomena are considered. The conclusions drawn are that the pre-verbal position tends to mark less continuous or less expected participants, and that more continuous or expected referents are encoded as nouns in the post-verbal position. The most continuous or expected referents are marked simply by verbal agreement. The pre-verbal position is by far the most frequent with independent pronouns, a fact befitting their usual contrastive function. This study recognizes two primary discourse functions; that of establishing referent identity, and that of directing attention. In Nez Perce, word order serves the first function (word order never distinguishes subject from object in Nez Perce), and various voicing strategies serve the second function. For a description of Nez Perce morphology and morphosyntax, see Aoki (1970), and Rude (1986a, 1986b, 1988) which also comment on discourse function.

1. Flexible word order

According to Aoki (1979: 1), the favored word order in Nez Perce is VSO. In the texts analyzed for this paper,[2] however, post-verbal and pre-verbal nouns (whether S or O) occurred in almost exactly equal proportions: 137 post-verbal and 130 pre-verbal nouns were counted. On the basis of text frequency, Nez Perce might better be classified as a free word order language. All possible word orders are encountered, e.g. VSO:

(1) *yox̣ koná pó-opci'yaw-c-an-a*
that there 3→3-kill-IMPFV-SG.NOM-PAST

he'yúuxs-nim kaa quyéesquyes-nim wi-wéet'u
cottontail-ERG and bluejay-ERG REDUP-NEG

neke'és-nim himeq'íis-ne cikaw'íis-na x̣áx̣aas-na
distinguished-ERG big-OBJ horrible-OBJ grizzly-OBJ
'Thereby the not very distinguished cottontail and bluejay killed the big horrible grizzly' (Aoki 1979: 1:37-38)

SVO:

(2) *kaa háatya-nm páa-'nahna-m-a 'iceyéeye-ne*
and wind-ERG 3→3-carry-CSL-PAST coyote-OBJ
'And the wind carried coyote here' (Aoki 1979: 4:14)

SOV:

(3) *kawó' kii háama-pim 'áayato-na pée-'nehnen-e*
then this husband-ERG woman-OBJ 3→3-take.away-PAST
'Now then the husband took the woman away' (Phinney 1934: 392:5-6)

VOS:

(4) *kii pée-ten'we-m-e qíiw-ne 'iceyéeye-nm*
this 3→3-talk-CSL-PAST old.man-OBJ coyote-ERG
'Now the coyote talked to the old man' (Phinney 1934: 145:11-12)

OVS:

(5) *kaa wáaqo' weptées-ne simées pée-x-yuu-'ey-s-en-e*
and now eagle-OBJ bed 3→3-go-DIR-GEN-IMPFV-SG.NOM-RM
wex̣weqé-nm
frog-ERG
'And now the frog was going to the eagle's bed' (Phinney 1934: 229:4)

and OSV:

(6) *la'ám-na 'éete 'ilcwéw'cix-nim hi-nes-we-'nek-eynéek-e*
all-OBJ surely monster-ERG 3NOM-PL.OBJ-mouth-carry-into-PAST
'Surely the monster sucked in everyone' (Aoki 1979: 4:3)

One encounters numerous examples where subject or object are separated from the verb, e.g. SXV in (7) and VXS in (8).

(7) *kaa* ***'ipí 'iceyéeye*** *'awíixno-nm silúu-ki ká'la*
and he Coyote curlew-GEN eye-INSTR just
hi-tqa-sayóox̣o'-s-a
3NOM-suddenly-see-IMPFV-SG.NOM
'And Coyote just suddenly sees with the curlew's eyes' (Phinney 1934: 68:10-11)

(8) *'ée* ***hi-waptamáawn-a*** *máat'atkin'ika* ***seewi'ís-nim***
you 3NOM-kill-PAST upriver musselshell-ERG
'Musselshell killed you upriver' (Aoki 1988: 527:18-19)

VXO appears in 9, and OXV in 10.

(9) *kíimet koná* ***pe-tqe-p'ni-yúu-ye*** *téekin-pe*
then there 3→3-suddenly-pierce-DIR-PAST meadow-LOC
'iníi-ne
lodge-OBJ
'Then he suddenly discovered a lodge there in a meadow' (Phinney 1934: 78:2-3)

(10) ***yu'ús-ne*** *q'o' wéet'u'* ***pée-leq'eyn-e***
poor-OBJ INTENS NEG 3→3-leave.alone-PAST
'He would not leave the poor one alone at all' (Phinney 1934: 92:8-9)

There is, for example, no fixed order between "shifted" object and demoted patient, e.g. the benefactive object precedes the demoted patient in (11):

(11) *wáaqit ki-x 'e-'wi-'eni-s* ***yú's-ne*** *tu'yé*
now REL-EXCL 3←SAP-shoot-BEN-IMPFV poor-OBJ grouse
'Now let me shoot a grouse for the poor one' (Phinney 1934: 137:14)

And in (12) the benefactive object follows the patient:

(12) *kee páa-nya-'y-s-an-a hípt* ***'istuk'ées-ne***
HORT 3→3-make-BEN-IMPFV-SG.NOM-RM food guest-OBJ
'Let them[3] prepare food for the guest' (Phinney 1934: 322:6-7)

The problem of order is compounded by discontinuous references to a single participant. Note the separation of *yu'úsne* ... *na'tóotap* 'my poor father' in (13).

(13) ***yu'ús-ne*** *taxc ki-nm ta'c 'iyéext 'a-anyáa-'n-yo'*
poor-OBJ soon this-GEN good broth 3SAP-make-BEN-FUT
na'-tóota-p
my-father-OBJ
'Soon I will make of this a good broth for my **poor father**' (Phinney 1934: 268:14-15)

In (13) as in (14), concord in case marking is all that links modifier and noun.

(14) *netíitelwi-**ne*** *'a-pó-opci'yawn-o'* *la'ám-**na***
myth.people-OBJ 3←SAP-PL.NOM-kill-FUT all-OBJ
'You (PL) will kill all the myth people' (Aoki 1988: 384:52-53)

An unmarked modifier and noun are discontinuous in (15).

(15) *kaa* ***'iléxni*** *wáaqo' 'e-w-s-íix* ***núkt***
and much now 3GEN-be-IMPFV-PL.NOM meat
'And now they have much meat' (Aoki 1988: 540:63)

Word order never distinguishes subject from object in Nez Perce, not even in the antipassive where no disambiguating noun case markers exist. There, however, semantic roles are distinguished by discourse/pragmatic/semantic factors. Note the VSO word order in (16), where humanness specifies the agent (which is also the grammatical subject).

(16) *hi-tulúu-m-e* *háacwal* *wá'wa*
3NOM-cast.into.water-CSL-PAST boy hook
'The boy cast the hook into the water' (Phinney 1934: 350:5-6)

There is SVO word order in the antipassive in (17), where context reveals the 'wolf' to be dead:

(17) *kii* *'iceyéeye* *hi-'náx-payk-a* *hímiin*
this coyote 3NOM-carry-arrive-PAST wolf
'Now the coyote brought the [dead] wolf' (Phinney 1934: 146:16)

The word order is SOV in (18), where the antipassive is triggered by a coreferentially possessed kinship term (see Rude 1986b). In such a construction, the kinterm is interpreted as the object because of the oddity of e.g. 'Now the nephew took his weasel to the stream'.

(18) *kii* *c'íƚiƚe* *peqíyex̣* *hi-'néhnen-e* *wéelee-px*
this weasel nephew 3NOM-take-PAST stream-ALL
'Now the weasel took his nephew to the stream' (Phinney 1934: 197:5)

Once again, humanness determines the agent (which is the grammatical subject) in the VOS clause in (19). Context also reveals this to be a coreferential antipassive.

(19) *hi-wéwluq-s-e* *c'oláakstimt* *x̣áx̣aac*
3NOM-want-IMPFV-SG.NOM hand.drum grizzly
'Grizzly wants his hand drum' (Phinney 1934: 83:12)

In the OVS clause in (20) (as in the SOV clause in 18), a coreferentially possessed kinship term is the object.

(20) *kii* *qáaca'c* *hi-weye-weyik-úu-ye* *háacwal*
this mother's.mother 3NOM-running-cross-DIR-PAST boy
'Now the boy ran across to his maternal grandmother' (Phinney 1934: 148:9)

In (21) the OSV word order is disambiguated by animacy.

(21) *ti'nxn-íin* *wáaqo'* *'áayat* *hi-'néhnen-e*
die-STAT now woman 3NOM-take-PAST
'The woman now took the dead' (Phinney 1934: 45:7-8)

Thus, all six possible word orders are found in the antipassive, where subject and object must be disambiguated by semantic or discourse/pragmatic criteria.

2. Independent pronouns

All 3rd person arguments, except for demoted patients, are obligatorily coded by verbal prefixes. When the argument is a noun or stressed pronoun, these verbal pronominals serve as agreement markers. Thus the constructions available in Nez Perce for the coding of 3rd person arguments are (1) full noun (with verbal agreement), (2) independent pronoun (with verbal agreement), and (3) pronominal marking in the verb.

It is to be expected[4] that a full noun generally functions to identify a less easily recoverable referent, and that pronouns serve to point out more easily recoverable referents. Because verbal pronouns are obligatory in Nez Perce, it is therefore the function of the independent personal pronouns that concerns us here.

The independent pronouns serve a contrastive function in Nez Perce. In the texts, this generally means a switch in topic, as is illustrated in (22), (23), and (24). Note that in (22) when the topic continues into the next clause, it is coded in that clause only by the obligatory verbal pronouns. In all three examples, a stressed pronoun is introduced when the topic switches.

(22) *kawó' kii wáaqo' 'óykala pe-'túu*
then this now all DST-what

ti-tá'c ke 'ú-u-s
REDUP-good REL 3GEN-be-IMPFV
'Then here now all good things which **she** has'

***hi**-wce-'séepe-m-e*
3NOM-standing-pack-CSL-PAST
'**she** packed up'

*kaa **hi**-kú-ye*
and 3NOM-go-PAST
'and **she** went'

ke konmá 'ilx̣níi-we-ne titóoqa-na
REL there many-HUM-OBJ person-OBJ

***hi**-nées-cuxwe-c-e.*
3NOM-PL.OBJ-know-IMPFV-SG.NOM
'where **she** knows many people.'

*kii wáaqo' **'ipí** héenek'u' konó' pée-'wi-ye máci-na*
this now 3SG again then 3→3-shoot-PAST several-OBJ
'Here now then **he** again shot several.' (Phinney 1934: 36:8-11)

(23) *kawó' kii pepyúumes te'éx̣et hi-ckilíin-e;*
then this sea.monster youth 3NOM-go.home-PAST
'Here then the sea monster youth went home.'

*taxláy **'ipn-ím** 'iwéepne 'e-tqée-w-s-e*
exchange 3SG-GEN wife 3GEN-suddenly-be-IMPFV-SG.NOM
'On the other hand **he** (Young Coyote) came to have a wife.' (Phinney 1934: 40:10-12)

(24) *kaa pée-mun-e'nixn-e tiwéeti-ne*
and 3→3-call-HAB.PL.NOM-RM shaman-OBJ
'And **they** used to call the shaman,'

*kaa **'ipn-ím** hi-nas-payn-óo-qan-a*
and 3SG-ERG 3NOM-PL.OBJ-arrive-DIR-HAB.SG.NOM-RM
'and **he** used to come to them.' (Aoki 1979: 13:26-27)

An independent personal pronoun may even mark a topic switch when it co-occurs with a noun. The non-direct quotes in (25) are in the antipassive voice, and consequently their subjects and objects are unmarked for case. In the first clause *háama* 'man/husband' is the object and *'áayat* 'woman' is the subject, but in the second clause the topic switches and the subject is *háama*. This switch is marked by the 3rd person independent pronoun *'ipí*.

(25) *'áayat kaa háama hi-hín-e,*
woman and husband 3NOM-say/tell-PAST
'The woman then told her husband,

"ku'ús na'-tóota-m hi-i-c-áa-qa."
thus my-father-ERG 3NOM-say/tell-IMPFV-SG.NOM-PAST
"Thus my father was telling me."

*kaa **'ipí** háama hi-hín-e,*
and 3SG husband 3NOM-say/tell-PAST
And *the husband* said to her,

"'éetee-nm-u' 'ew-'néhne-c-ix."
surely-INCL-INTENS SAP→3-take-IMPFV-PL.NOM
"Very surely we are taking him."' (Phinney 1934: 71:9-10)

With a noun not marked for case and without the independent pronoun there is typically no switch in topic, as in (26).

(26) *páa-mc'i-ya* *'áayato-m*
3→3-hear-PAST woman-ERG
'The woman heard it,'

kaa *píst* *hi-hín-e,* "..."
and father 3NOM-say/tell-PAST
'and said to her father, "..." ' (Phinney 1934: 71:4-5)

A case marked noun often functions to code a shift in topic. In (27) the subject of the first clause is continuous with that in the previous sentence (not shown here) and therefore is marked only by the verbal pronominals (3rd person nominative *hi-* and singular nominative *-e*); in the second clause the case marked noun switches the topic.

(27) *konó'* ***hi**-wqsu'ú-c-e*
there 3NOM-sit-IMPFV-SG.NOM
'She is sitting there,'

kaa *pée-n-e* *háama-**nm**,* "..."
and 3→3-say/tell-PAST man-ERG
'and the man said to her, "..." ' (Phinney 1934: 35:4)

3. Results of topicality measurements

The first 50 pages of Archie Phinney's (1934) *Nez Percé Texts* comprise the data used in this study. All the texts are narrative; no claim is made for any other type of discourse.

For this study, two topicality measurements were taken and then averaged separately for each construction under consideration. The measurements are referential distance (RD) and topic persistence (TP). The RD measurement has to do with referent recoverability, or **anaphoric** continuity. It is the number of clauses since the last recoverable mention of a referent. It measures the **gap** between present mention and last mention. The number 20 has been arbitrarily selected as a cut-off point. First mention and any referential distance over 20 clauses is given the value of 20. For the RD measurement, the smaller the number, the greater the topic continuity.

The topic persistence measurement represents the number of clauses that a referent continues to have recoverable mention. It is a measurement of **cataphoric** continuity, having to do with the persistence a referent has in discourse when coded by a particular structure. Unlike the RD measurement, the larger the TP, the greater the topic continuity. I assume that any structural contrast that correlates with a high TP measurement marks the "importance" of a referent in the narrative ahead.

In this study, both topicality measurements (RD and TP) were taken for all 3rd person personal pronouns, pre-verbal and post-verbal nouns (S and O), and the contrasting coding of participants by verbal agreement alone. Quotes were skipped and not counted as gaps. However, 3rd person referents that occurred in these quotes were counted. Referents in non-finite verbal complements were counted, but not as if they represented separate clauses. Dependent clauses with finite verbs were counted as separate clauses. The word orders SXV and OXV were counted as simply SV and OV, and VXS and VXO as simply VS and VO.

The results of the measurements are presented in Tables 1 and 2. Though these measurements are suggestive, it must be noted that topic continuity does not invariably predict the word order in individual clauses. These measurements are nevertheless useful because they correlate post- and pre-verbal word orders in a so called free word order language with the measurements of referential distance. As predicted by previous studies (see Givón 1983b; Cooreman 1987; Payne 1987; and Sundberg 1987 and this volume), the pre-verbal NP position averages a significantly greater referential distance than the post-verbal position. And, as predicted, there is no significant difference in the averages for the measurement of topic persistence.

The most easily recoverable referents are typically encoded by verbal pronominals alone. The average referential distance for arguments coded by verbal pronominals alone (with no coreferent noun or independent pronoun) was 2.07, while that for post-verbal nouns was 5.90, a difference of nearly 4 clauses. And the difference between the average measurements for post-verbal and pre-verbal nouns approached 3 clauses. Thus, the more expected or continuous topics tend to go to the right of the verb, while the more discontinuous, unexpected topics, or indefinites tend to go to the left of the verb. For example, in (28) the definite *qóotqot* 'feather' sits to the right of the verb, and the non-referential subject complement *wéeptes* 'eagle' sits to the left of the verb.

(28) *q'o' túus-kex hi-kúu-kik-e,*
INTENS up-ALL 3NOM-go-TRL-PAST

q'o' túus-kex hi-weke'éyk-e ***qóotqot***
INTENS up-ALL 3NOM-fly-PAST feather

kaa ***wéeptes*** *hi-wc'ée-ye*
and eagle 3NOM-become-PAST
'Right on up it went, **the** feather flew right up and became **an** eagle' (Phinney 1934: 143:2-3)

The same principle holds in the single clause in (29).

(29) *kaa tim'úune hi-wc'ée-ye háama*
and bow 3NOM-become-PAST man
'And the man became [i.e. turned into] a bow' (Aoki 1988: 135:15)

There are two types of definites; a referent may be definite because it has already been introduced into a particular discourse, or it may be definite because its referent is somehow unique. For this study I have not attempted to distinguish the two. By defining **indefinite** as first mention in a discourse, 32% of the 130 nouns in pre-verbal position were indefinite, versus 19% for those in post-verbal position. Even though an indefinite noun is more likely to occupy the pre-verbal position, the majority of nouns in pre-verbal position were still definite. Thus the pre-verbal position is not primarily a marker of indefiniteness.

There were not enough examples of independent personal pronouns to make any safe predictions. For the most part, their RD measurements lay between those for the verbal pronominals and full nouns. Although there were only three examples of post-verbal independent personal pronouns, it may be significant that all their measurements for TP were high. Two examples of post-verbal indefinite pronouns also occurred and were likewise high in TP. Until further studies are made, it is safe only to suggest that a post-verbal independent pronoun functions, at least in part, to mark a referent of high topic continuity cataphorically.

Tables 1 and 2 give the measurements for subject and object in intransitive, transitive, and antipassive clauses. There are expected differences in the measurements for both RD and TP, e.g. the largest measurements for both RD (and thus least topic continuity anaphorically) and the smallest measurements for TP (and thus topic continuity cataphorically) were for

Table 1. Average measurements for referential distance

	Agreement No./RD	PRO V No./RD	V PRO No./RD	N V No./RD	V N No./RD
Intransitive SUBJ	26/1.34	4/4.00	1/1.00	30/8.67	55/6.69
Transitive SUBJ	113/1.8	10/3.00	2/1.50	42/5.38	39/3.44
OBJ	117/2.46	3/1.00	30/10.00	23/6.70	
Antipassive SUBJ	41/1.95			8/5.00	6/1.67
OBJ	10/2.90			20/14.50	14/10.15
Averages	307/2.07	17/2.88	3/1.33	130/8.59	137/5.90

Table 2. Average measurements for topic persistence

	Agreement No./TP	PRO V No./TP	V PRO No./TP	N V No./TP	V N No./TP
Intransitive SUBJ	26/1.34	4/3.00	1/5.00	30/0.500	55/2.44
Transitive SUBJ	113/2.35	10/1.40	2/5.50	42/2.02	39/2.18
OBJ	117/3.07	3/4.33		30/1.90	23/2.57
Antipassive SUBJ	41/3.49			8/3.38	6/1.83
OBJ	10/0.50			20/1.85	14/1.21
Averages	307/2.63	17/2.29	3/5.33	130/2.16	137/2.24

the antipassive object. Figure 1, which graphs the average measurements for RD, illustrates the correlation between structure and referent recoverability, e.g. verbal agreement (plus the few examples of post-verbal independent pronouns) correlate with the lowest average RD measurement (and thus code the most easily recoverable referents), and full nouns correlate with higher average RD measurements (and thus code less recoverable referents). With full nouns, the pre-verbal position is the most marked in that it correlates with a lower average RD measurement than the post-verbal position. The pre-verbal position correlates with less recoverable, less expected referents.

The measurements presented in Figure 1 do not reveal the topic switch function of pre-verbal independent pronouns. Fortunately, however, this function is readily observable in the texts.

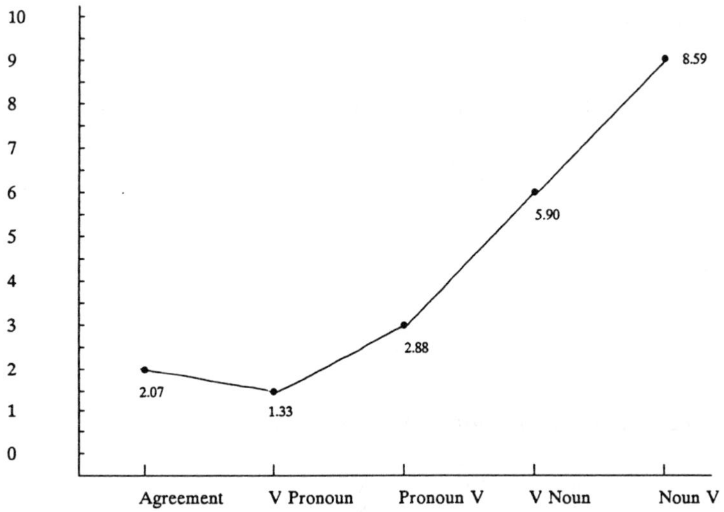

Figure 1. Average measurements for referential distance

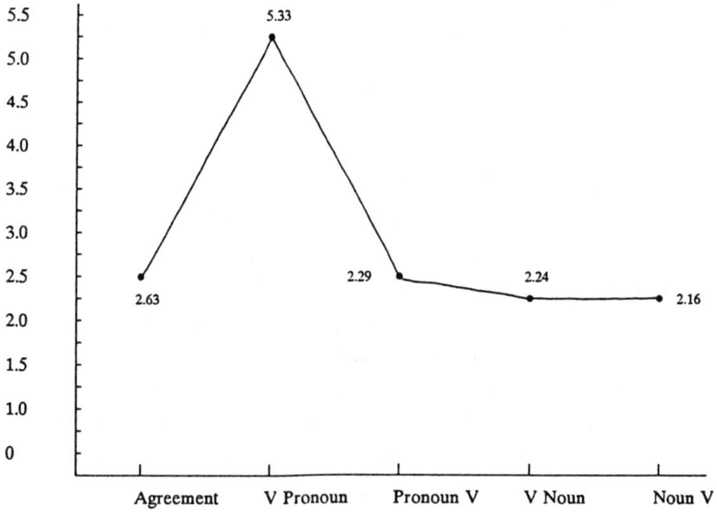

Figure 2. Average measurements for topic persistence

The average TP measurements are graphed in Figure 2, and suggest a lack of correlation between TP and word order. Except for the possible cataphoric function of post-verbal independent pronouns (suggested by the large average TP measurement of 5.33), all TP measurements are nearly the same (2.63, 2.29, 2.24, 2.16). There is not enough variation to suggest any contrastive function. This is in keeping with my findings presented elsewhere (see Rude 1986a, 1986b, 1988) which show a strong correlation between the Nez Perce voicing mechanisms and TP.

In sum, word order functions entirely on a discourse/pragmatic basis in Nez Perce, its main function having to do with referent recoverability. And since the Nez Perce voicing mechanisms (ergative construction, antipassive, passive, various object selection strategies, and strategies which make genitives into subjects or objects) correlate with TP measurements, their function has to do with the relative "importance" a particular referent has in discourse.

Table 3 compares the numbers of occurrence for each argument type (verbal agreement only, personal pronoun, and full noun) and word order possibility. For each, the percent of the total is given. The percentages for

Table 3. Frequencies of occurrence

	Agreement No./%	Personal Pronoun No./%	Full Noun No./%	Totals No./%
V	307/50.5%			307/50.5%
SV		14/2.3%	80/13.1%	94/15.4%
VS		3/0.5%	100/16.4%	103/16.9%
OV		3/0.5%	50/8.2%	53/8.7%
VO		0	37/6.0%	37/6.0%
VSO		0	0	0
SVO		0	5/0.8%	5/0.8%
SOV		0	5/0.8%	5/0.8%
VOS		0	0	0
VS0		0	3/0.5%	3/0.5%
OSV		0	1/0.16%	1/0.16%

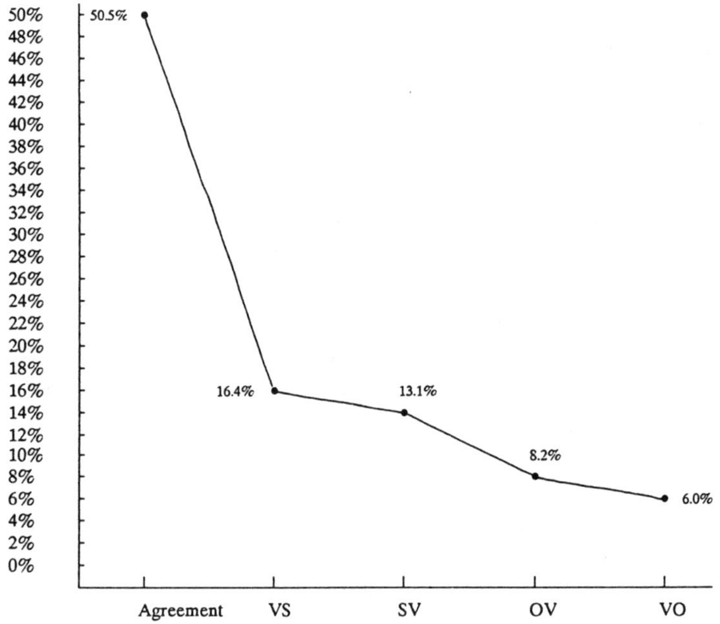

Figure 3. Percentage of occurrence of frequent word orders

verbal agreement alone, in contrast with full nouns, are graphed in Figure 3 (the number of clauses in which both subject and object were full nouns was not sufficient for inclusion). On average, post-verbal nouns tend to be more topical than pre-verbal ones. And, on average, subjects tend to be more topical than objects. Therefore, the ranking evident in Figure 3 should not be surprising; slightly more subject nouns were post-verbal than pre-verbal, with the reverse being true of objects.[5] If all languages have at least a basic (or underlying) word order, then Nez Perce might be classed better as OVS than VSO. This is, of course, based on discourse function, and cannot be justified syntactically.

Notes

1. Funding for this project was provided by a grant from the National Science Foundation, BNS-8919577. The discourse measurements originally appeared in Rude

(1985). I wish to thank T. Givón and Doris Payne for their valuable suggestions. In the Nez Perce orthography, *e* = [æ], *c* = [ts], ' = the glottal stop and *C'* a glottalized consonant, *ł* is a voiceless lateral fricative, and the contrast between *x* and *x̣* is one of velar versus uvular. Special abbreviations, are as follows:

1	=	First person
2	=	Second person
3	=	Third person
CSL	=	Cislocative
DIR	=	Directive object
DST	=	Distributive
HORT	=	Hortative
HUM	=	Human classifier
INTENS	=	Intensifier
PRO	=	Pronoun
RD	=	Referential Distance
REDUP	=	Reduplication
RM	=	Remote tense
SAP	=	Speech Act Participant
TP	=	Topic Persistence
TRL	=	Translocative
V	=	Verb

2. The first 50 pages of Phinney (1934).

3. In the remote tense a plural subject often expresses singular agreement (i.e. with the singular *-en* instead of the plural *-in* in ex. 12).

4. See the studies in Givón (1983a).

5. One might have expected there also to have been a larger percentage of object nouns over subject nouns because of the overall greater likelihood of arguments of lower average topicality surfacing as nouns. This was not the case, perhaps because intransitive subjects were figured in the averages.

References

Aoki, Haruo. 1970. *Nez Perce Grammar*. (= *University of California Publications in Linguistics*, 62.) Berkeley/Los Angeles: University of California Press.

Aoki, Haruo. 1979. *Nez Perce Texts*. (= *University of California Publications in Linguistics*, 90.) Berkeley/Los Angeles: University of California Press.

Aoki, Haruo, and Deward E. Walker, Jr. 1988. *Nez Perce Oral Narratives*. (= *University of California Publications in Linguistics*, 104.) Berkeley/Los Angeles: University of California Press.

Cooreman, Ann. 1987. *Transitivity and Discourse Continuity in Chamorro Narratives*. Berlin/New York/Amsterdam: Mouton de Gruyter.

Givón, T. 1983a. *Topic Continuity in Discourse: A Quantitative Cross-language Study.* (= *Typological Studies in Language*, 3.) Amsterdam/Philadelphia: John Benjamins.

Givón, T. 1983b. "Topic Continuity and Word-Order Pragmatics in Ute." Givón 1983a. 141-214.

Payne, Doris L. 1987. "Information Structuring in Papago Narrative Discourse." *Language* 63.783-804.

Phinney, Archie. 1934. *Nez Percé Texts.* (= *Columbia University Contributions to Anthropology*, 25.) New York: Columbia University Press.

Rude, Noel. 1985. *Studies in Nez Perce Grammar and Discourse.* PhD dissertation, University of Oregon.

Rude, Noel. 1986a. "Topicality, Transitivity, and the Direct Object in Nez Perce." *International Journal of American Linguistics* 52.124-153.

Rude, Noel. 1986b. "Discourse-Pragmatic Context for Genitive Promotion in Nez Perce." *Studies in Language* 10.109-136.

Rude, Noel. 1988. "Ergative, Passive, and Antipassive in Nez Perce: A Discourse Perspective." *Passive and Voice* ed. by Masayoshi Shibatani, 547-560. Amsterdam/ Philadelphia: John Benjamins.

Sundberg, Karen. 1987. "Word Order in Klamath." *Kansas Working Papers in Linguistics* 12.89-118.

Verb-Subject Order in Polish[1]

Barbara Jacennik & Matthew S. Dryer
University of Toronto *State University of New York at Buffalo*

1. Introduction

In recent years, studies of flexible word order in various languages have increasingly used information from text counts as a basis for both discovering and documenting discourse factors that govern or correlate with different word orders (cf. Givón, ed. 1983; Sun and Givón 1985, Givón 1988, 1989; Myhill 1984, 1985, 1986; Payne 1987). In this paper we continue this tradition in an examination of the factors that govern the order of subject and verb in Polish. Some of the results of this recent work are at odds with earlier views. The "standard" view, associated originally with the Prague School (cf. Firbas 1966, 1974), is that, at least in Slavic languages though widely assumed to be more or less universal, given or thematic information tends to occur earlier than new or rhematic information. An increasing number of studies (e.g., Givón 1988; Payne 1987), however, show that in at least some languages, the opposite principle seems to be at work. In such languages, nominals with previous reference in the text, particularly the immediately preceding text, more often **follow** the verb. It is important, therefore, to apply a methodology similar to Givón's to a Slavic language, to try to resolve this apparent contradiction. Givón (1988: 250, 1989: 224) cites results from Rybarkiewicz (1984) which suggest that Polish does conform to his principle by which nominals with more recent previous reference tend to follow the verb.[2] The question then is how to reconcile the Givón-Rybarkiewicz claims with the claims of the Prague School.

We examine below a variety of factors that correlate with the order of subject and verb in Polish. Among other things, we show that it is over-simplistic to simply contrast SV order with VS order: clauses in which the subject follows the verb but is itself followed by other material exhibit very different discourse properties from clauses in which the subject occurs at the end of the clause. We argue that neither the traditional theme-rheme view nor Givón's view can alone adequately account for the properties of postverbal subjects in Polish. We also show that the order of subject and verb varies with the position of other material in the clause: the subject tends to occur on the opposite side of the verb from other material, particularly nominals (objects, oblique noun phrases, and prepositional phrases). What this suggests is that the order of subject and verb is determined, not only by the discourse properties of the subject, but also by the discourse properties of other elements in the clause.

2. Data base

The text that forms the basis for the conclusions of this paper is Pajewski (1978), a book popularizing the history of the Polish-Turkish wars. This text was chosen for its simple and cohesive style as well as for its concreteness. Although there is a certain amount of variation among authors in terms of the SV/VS variation in Polish, this text seems to be relatively typical.[3] Only clauses with overt subjects and finite verbs were examined. Relative clauses, questions, and quotations were ignored.

Both orders of subject and verb are common in the text; out of 429 clauses, 260 (or 61%) are SV and 169 (or 39%) are VS. Table 1 gives a breakdown of these orders by clause type.

Examples (1) to (7) illustrate each of the seven types of main clauses listed in Table 1.

Lexical subject, verb other than *być*, object not clause or quotation:

(1) SV
Bitwa *trwała do zmroku.*
battle.NOM continued till dusk.GEN
'The battle continued till dusk.' (p. 95)

Table 1. Distribution of SV vs. VS by clause type

	SV	VS
In main clause:		
Lexical subject, verb other than *być* 'be', object not clause or quotation	182	131
Lexical subject, verb other than *być* 'be', nominal clause or quotation as object	26	0
Lexical subject, *być* plus Pred structure	18	22
Pronominal subject	4	11
In subordinate clause:		
In nominal clause	20	2
In adverbial clause	10	3
Total	260	169

(2) VS

Lewe skrzydło nieprzyjacielskie zajmowali ***Tatarzy.***
left wing.ACC enemy.ADJ occupied Tartars.NOM
'The left wing of the enemy occupied Tartars.' (p. 94)

Lexical subject, nominal clause or quotation as object:

(3) SV

Sobieski *obliczał, że w jego tylko dobrach*
Sobieski.NOM counted that in his only estate.LOC

zabito i uprowadzono ***30 tysięcy*** *ludzi.*
killed.NONFIN and taken.away.NONFIN 30 thousand people.GEN
'Sobieski counted that in his estate alone 30 thousand people were killed or taken into captivity.' (p.146)

Lexical subject, *być* plus Pred structure:

(4) SV

Rzeczpospolita *była bezsilna.*
republic.NOM was powerless
'The republic was powerless.' (p.163)

(5) VS
Duże były też ***straty*** ***materialne.***
large were also losses.NOM material
'There were also large material losses.' (p.146)

Pronominal subject:

(6) SV
On *to w roku 1683 poprowadził armię*
he.NOM EMPH in year.LOC led army.ACC

padyszacha pod Wiedeń.
padishah.GEN to Vienna.ACC
'In 1683 he led the Padishah's army to Vienna.' (p. 134)

(7) VS
Cieszyła się ***ona*** *dużym rozgłosem i powodzeniem.*
enjoyed REFL she.NOM large renown.INSTR and success.INSTR
'She enjoyed large renown and success.' (p.245)

A number of generalizations can be drawn from Table 1. First, when the object is a clause or quotation, the subject invariably precedes the verb in the text examined. Second, VS order is less common in subordinate clauses ($p < .01$).[4] Whether this difference is because there is a stronger syntactic preference for SV in subordinate clauses or because the discourse conditions under which VS occurs arise less often in subordinate clauses is not clear; a larger number of subordinate clauses than occur in this sample would have to be investigated to answer this question. VS seems to be particularly common when the predicate is *być* 'be', though this difference is not large and falls just short of statistical significance. Finally, although the number of pronominal subjects in this text is small, VS order is significantly more common when the subject is pronominal ($p < .025$).[5]

In what follows, we will restrict attention to the first type of clause in Table 1, those in which the subject is lexical, the verb is one other than *być* 'be', and the object is not a clause or quotation. We will further distinguish two types of VS clauses, those in which the subject occurs at the end of the clause, and those in which the subject is non-final, being followed by an object or adverbial expression. We will refer to the former as VS, the latter as VSX. That is, VS and VSX share the property that the subject follows the verb, but differ in that VSX clauses have material following the subject, as in (8).[6]

(8) *29 maja 1453 r. zdobyli* ***Turcy*** *Konstantynopol.*
29 May 1453 conquered Turks.NOM Constantinople.ACC
'On May 29, 1453, the Turks conquered Constantinople.' (p.22)

We will show that the discourse conditions in which these two types of postverbal subjects occur are very different. Of the 131 clauses with postverbal subjects listed in Table 1, 106 are VS (in this special sense in which the subject is final) and 25 are VSX. The relative frequency of the three types of clauses was therefore SV=58%, VS=34%, and VSX=8%. These three types of clauses were further examined for a number of different parameters. Fifty-two clauses of each sort were examined for these parameters. This means that additional instances of VSX were collected beyond those listed in Table 1.

3. Discourse properties of the subject

3.1 Previous reference

The first parameter we examined involves whether the subject introduces a new referent into the text or refers to something that has already been mentioned. We distinguish two ways in which a nominal might be referred to previously in a text. A direct previous reference involves a nominal in an earlier clause with the same denotation as the nominal in question; it need not be an identical lexical item (although it might be), as long as the denotation is the same. An indirect previous reference is related to the nominal indirectly by one of the following relationships: (1) group-member, member-group, e.g. *armia — żolnierze* 'army — soldiers'; (2) part-whole, whole-part, e.g. *Kraków — Polska* 'Cracow — Poland'; (3) separate parts of the same entity, i.e. part-part, e.g. *lewe skrzydło* 'left wing — center'; (4) entity-derivative, derivative-entity, e.g. *prezydent — prezydencki* 'president — presidential'; (5) set-member, member-set, e.g. *sztućce — widelec* 'cutlery — fork'; (6) participants, agents, "function holders" of a process, activity, institution, or organization, e.g. *szkoła — uczeń* 'school — student', *Turcja — Turcy* 'Turkey — Turks'; (7) typical concomitants, e.g. *głód — pragnienie* 'hunger — thirst', *zima — chłód* 'winter — cold'; (8) generalization-instantiation, e.g. *klęska — trzęsienie ziemi* 'disaster — earthquake'; and (9) anaphoric expression, e.g. *ten fakt* 'this fact', *ta okoliczność* 'this

Table 2. Previous reference of subject by clause type

	SV		VSX		VS	
	No.	%	No.	%	No.	%
Previous reference in preceding 20 clauses	40	78%	50	96%	24	46%
Previous direct reference in preceding 20 clauses	20	38%	35	67%	7	13%
Previous reference in the immediately preceding clause	17	33%	21	41%	8	15%

coincidence', *rezultaty* 'the results'. In the case of this last category, anaphoric expression, the previous reference might be a whole sentence.

Table 2 gives relevant data on previous reference for each of the three orders. The data for previous reference is calculated in three different ways. The first line is based on previous reference in the preceding 20 clauses, where the expression **previous reference** includes both direct and indirect previous references, as discussed above. The second line is based on previous direct reference in the preceding 20 clauses, where the expression **previous direct reference** refers to the stricter sense of previous reference in which the denotations of the two nominals are identical; these clauses are a subset of those included on the first line. The third line is based on previous reference in the immediately preceding clause; these clauses are also a subset of those included on the first line. Each of the percentage figures in Table 2 represents the percentage among the 52 clauses with the given order; for example, the figure "78%" on the first line indicates that 78% (40 out of 52) of SV clauses have a previous reference in the preceding 20 clauses.

It can be seen from Table 2 that VS clauses and VSX clauses are completely different with respect to preceding reference. Only 13% of subjects of VS clauses have equivalent (direct) antecedents in the preceding 20 clauses, and less than half involve previous reference even in the broad sense that includes both direct and indirect antecedents. On the other hand, VSX clauses almost always have a subject with previous reference in the preceding 20 clauses, even more often than SV clauses do. Clearly, we must distinguish VS from VSX. We cannot simply say that postverbal subjects tend to involve new participants in the discourse; this is not true for postverbal subjects which are followed by further material. The data for previ-

Table 3. Referential distance of subject by clause type

	SV	VSX	VS
Mean referential distance	6.83	3.69	13.04
Mean referential distance for subjects with previous reference in preceding 20 clauses	2.88	3.04	6.59

ous reference in the immediately preceding clause is similar; such is most common with VSX clauses and least common with VS.[7]

3.2. Referential distance

Similar results can be obtained by using Givón's measure of referential distance, i.e. counting the number of clauses back to the previous reference (with 20 used as the maximum, even in cases when there is no previous reference).[8] Table 3 shows that while VS clauses exhibit the highest mean referential distance (13.04), VSX exhibit the lowest (3.69), while SV is intermediate between the two (6.83).[9]

These differences are largely due to clauses in which the subject had no previous reference in the preceding 20 clauses. This is shown by the last line of Table 3: while the mean referential distance for clauses in which there **is** a previous reference (in the broad sense) in the preceding 20 clauses is still higher for VS clauses, there is little difference between SV and VSX, with SV now showing a slightly lower mean referential distance. What this means is that the difference in mean referential distance between SV clauses and VSX clauses (line 1 of Table 3) is due entirely to the fact that the subject in VSX clauses almost always has a previous reference in the preceding 20 clauses. In other words, the SV and VSX clauses differ only in terms of previous reference vs. no previous reference, rather than in terms of the actual distance to the preceding referent.

3.3 Grammatical function of previous reference in preceding clause

When we examine the grammatical function of a nominal in the immediately previous clause which has the same reference as the subject of the current clause, we again find a difference between the three kinds of clauses. Table 4 shows that if we restrict attention to subjects with a previ-

Table 4. Grammatical function of previous reference in preceding clause

	SV		VSX		VS	
	No.	%	No.	%	No.	%
Previous reference in preceding clause is oblique/predicate	1	6%	11	52%	0	0%
Previous reference in preceding clause is subject, object, or entire clause	16	94%	10	48%	8	100%
Total	17	100%	21	100%	8	100%

ous reference in the immediately preceding clause, it is more common to employ VSX order as opposed to either SV or VS if the nominal in the preceding clause is an oblique or a part of a predicate expression in that clause, rather than being the subject, the object, or the entire clause ($p < 0.05$). The percentage figures in Table 4 represent the percentage among just those clauses in which the subject has a previous reference in the immediately preceding clause.

The examples in (9) and (10) illustrate this difference between VSX clauses and the other two orders. Example (9) illustrates a VSX clause where the subject is an oblique in the immediately preceding clause. This situation arises significantly more often among VSX clauses than among SV or VS clauses. Example (10) illustrates an SV clause where the previous reference to the subject (the previous reference here involving a link of the indirect sort, that of father to son) is also the subject in the immediately preceding clause.

(9) *Z Chocimia można było szachować*
from Chocim.LOC can.NONFIN was hold.in.check.INF

Stefana i przeciwdziałać jego wrogim przedsięwzięciom.
Stefan.ACC and counteract.INF his hostile undertakings.DAT

Duże również znaczenie miała ***ta twierdza*** *jako*
large also significance.ACC had this fortress.NOM as

osłona kraju przed najazdami tatarskimi.
shield.NOM country.GEN against raids.INSTR Tartar.ADJ

'From Chocim one could hold Stefan in check and counteract his hostile undertakings. This fortress had also a large significance as the country's defense against Tartar raids.' (p.49)

(10) *Śmierć* *znalazł* *w* *wezbranych* *nurtach* *rzeki* *gdzieś*
death.ACC found in rising waters.LOC river somewhere

koło *Aleppo.* ***Syn*** ***jego*** ***Ertogrul,*** ***sławiony*** ***w***
near Aleppo.GEN son.NOM his Ertogrul.NOM praised in

starych ***kronikach*** ***jako*** ***potężny*** ***władca,*** *zdobył*
old chronicles.LOC as powerful ruler.NOM achieved

na *czele* *swych* *koczowników* *prawie* *niezależne*
at head.LOC his nomads.GEN almost independent

stanowisko.
position.ACC
'He found his death in the rising waters of the river somewhere near Aleppo. His son Ertogrul, praised in the old chronicles as a powerful ruler, achieved as the chief of his nomads an almost independent position.' (p.7)

It is not obvious why VSX clauses are different from the other two clause types in this respect. However, what obliques and predicate expressions appear to have in common is that they tend not to be topical. What this means is that subjects of VSX clauses are apparently **less** topical in the **preceding** clause than are subjects of SV or VS clauses. As discussed below, this bears a striking similarity to a claim Siewierska (1987) makes about Polish clauses with postverbal subject pronouns.

3.4 Subsequent reference

The studies in Givón, ed. (1983) have shown that it is important to examine not only previous reference in texts, but also subsequent references. Table 5 gives data for the three kinds of clauses on whether there is a reference in the subsequent text. The first line of Table 5 indicates the number of cases in which there is a reference in the immediately following clause; the second line indicates the number of cases in which there is a reference in one of the three following clauses. The percentage figures indicate percentages among the 52 clauses with the given order; for example, the first line indicates that 60% (or 31 out of 52) of SV clauses have a subject whose reference is the same as some nominal in the immediately following clause.

The three clause types differ less with respect to this parameter. None of the differences in Table 5 between the three clause types is statistically significant.[10]

Table 5. Reference in subsequent clauses

	SV		VSX		VS	
	No.	%	No.	%	No.	%
Reference in next clause	31	60%	21	40%	29	56%
Reference in one of next three clauses	34	65%	38	73%	36	69%

Table 6. Length of subject

	SV		VSX		VS	
	No.	%	No.	%	No.	%
Subject is complex (contains genitive, prepositional, appositive, or coordinated phrases)	20	38%	1	2%	21	40%
Subject is more than one word but not complex	12	23%	2	4%	18	35%
Subject is one word	20	38%	49	94%	13	25%
Total	52	100%	52	100%	52	100%
Average number of words in subject	3.0		1.2		3.2	

4. Grammatical/semantic properties of subject

4.1 Length of subject

Of the factors examined so far, all except those isolated in Table 1 involve the preceding or following discourse context. It is worth examining other parameters, however, that involve grammatical or semantic properties of the clause in question. Table 6 shows that VSX order differs from the other two orders in that the subject in such clauses tends to be short ($p < .001$).

Example (11) illustrates VS order with a complex subject, while (12) illustrates a typical VSX clause with a one-word subject, *muzulmanie* 'Muslims'.

(11) *Od jego imienia pochodzi* ***powszechnie używana***
from his name.GEN derives commonly used

nazwa imperium osmańskiego lub ottomańskiego
name.NOM empire.GEN Osman.ADJ or Ottoman.ADJ
'From his name derives the commonly used name of the Osman or Ottoman empire.' (p. 7)

(12) *Dość wcześnie weszli* ***muzułmanie*** *w kontakt*
relatively early entered Muslims.NOM in contact.ACC

z Turkami, przybyłymi z wielkich
with Turks.INSTR coming from great

stepów azjatyckich.
steppes.GEN Asian
'Muslims entered in contact with Turks, coming from the great Asian steppes, relatively early.' (p. 6)

The high frequency of one-word subjects in VSX clauses may be viewed in either of two ways. On the one hand, the length of a noun phrase correlates with its predictability; the fact that subjects in VSX clauses are shorter than subjects in SV and VS clauses fits in with the fact that such nominals more often have previous reference in the preceding text and thus are more predictable. Alternatively, the tendency for longer subjects to avoid internal position in VSX order may be an instance of the general tendency in language for more complex constituents to avoid positions internal to clauses (cf. Dryer 1980).

4.2 Humanness of subject

A second factor correlated with clause type is whether it is human or not, illustrated in Table 7. This table shows that subjects of VSX clauses are

Table 7. Humanness of subject

	SV		VSX		VS	
	No.	%	No.	%	No.	%
Human	30	58%	46	88%	27	52%
Nonhuman	22	42%	6	12%	25	48%
Total	52	100%	52	100%	52	100%

Table 8. Proper vs. common nouns

	SV		VSX		VS	
	No.	%	No.	%	No.	%
Proper names	18	35%	36	69%	6	12%
Common names	34	65%	16	31%	46	88%
Total	52	100%	52	100%	52	100%

human significantly more often than are subjects of SV or VS clauses ($p < .001$). Again, this difference coincides with the high predictability of subjects in VSX clauses. Human nominals tend to reappear more often in a text and are therefore more predictable.

4.3 Proper vs. common nouns

A third property of subjects that correlates with clause type is whether the noun is a proper noun or a common noun. Table 8 shows that subjects in VSX clauses are proper names more often than are subjects in each of the two other types of clauses ($p < .001$). This again fits in with the predictability of subjects in VSX clauses.

4.4 Length of subject vs. proper/common nouns

Although the high percentage of proper names in VSX clauses seems to support the predictability explanation of the tendency for subjects in VSX clauses to be one word, a comparison conducted within each lexical category renders some support to the second explanation, namely that there is a tendency for longer consituents to avoid sentence internal position. The relevant figures are represented in Table 9.

Table 9 shows that there is a strong tendency for proper name subjects to be one word: 87% of the proper name subjects are one word, but only 31% of common name ones are. However, if we focus on each category separately, clear differences between the VSX clauses and the two other orders emerge. Within the proper names category, the subjects in VSX clauses are one word significantly more often than in the two other orders combined ($p < .05$)[11]. Within the common names category, the subjects in VSX clauses are also one word significantly more often than the two other

Table 9. Length of subject vs. proper/common nouns

	SV		VSX		VS	
	No.	%	No.	%	No.	%
Proper name						
One word	13	72%	35	97%	4	67%
More than one word	5	28%	1	3%	2	33%
Total	18	100%	36	100%	6	100%
Common name						
One word	7	21%	14	88%	9	20%
More than one word	27	79%	2	12%	37	80%
Total	34	100%	16	100%	46	100%

orders combined ($p < .001$). Hence, the facts represented in Tables 7 to 9 can be taken to support the hypothesis that both factors, the predictability of the subject nouns and the tendency for the complex constituents to avoid sentence internal position, contribute separately to the observed frequency of one-word subjects in VSX clauses.

5. Properties of constituents other than the subject

5.1 Initial/final nonsubject nonverbal material

Focusing on the discourse, syntactic, and semantic properties of subjects in the three kinds of clauses can obscure the role of the properties of other constituents in the clause. The three clause types differ with respect to the frequency with which material **other** than the subject and verb occurs at the beginning of the clause or at the end of the clause, as illustrated in Table 10. As in previous tables, the percentage figures indicate the percentage of clauses with the property stated among clauses of the given order; for example, the figure 42% on the first line indicates that 42% (or 22 out of 52) of SV clauses have some nonsubject nonverbal initial material.

The first line of Table 10 shows that initial material occurs with greater frequency in VSX and VS clauses than in SV clauses ($p < .001$). What this means is that true verb-initial order is infrequent: either the subject or something else tends to precede the verb. Conversely, the second line of Table 10 shows that all clauses with SV order contain postverbal material.

Table 10. Nonsubject material

	SV		VSX		VS	
	No.	%	No.	%	No.	%
Some nonsubject nonverbal initial material	22	42%	48	92%	47	90%
Some nonsubject nonverbal final material	52	100%	52	100%	0	0%

The other two cells on the second line of Table 10 are both determined by definition: there can be no VS clauses with final nonsubjects or VSX clauses without a final nonsubject. But since neither VS nor VSX clauses can be verb-final, and since all of the clauses with SV order contain postverbal material, we see that verb-final order is not attested in this set of 156 clauses. Hence both verb-initial and verb-final order appear to be uncommon, indicating an apparent tendency to avoid placing the verb at the beginning or end of the clause. Among clauses containing only a subject and a verb in our sample, only VS order is attested; our sample contains 5 clauses of this sort.[12] This suggests that the tendency to avoid placing the verb at the end of the sentence may be stronger than the tendency to avoid placing the verb at the beginning of the sentence.

The tendency to avoid placing the verb at the beginning or end of the clause influences the order of subject and verb. In a clause containing a subject and another nonverbal element, the verb will tend to occur medially, with the subject occurring on the opposite side of the verb from the other element. In other words, there is a tendency towards SVX or XVS order. While in some cases the choice between SVX and XVS may reflect the discourse properties of the subject, it is likely that it will often reflect the discourse properties of the nonsubject. In other words, if the discourse properties of an element other than the subject or verb is such that it precedes the verb in a given clause, the subject will tend to follow the verb. Conversely, if the properties of such an element are such that it follows the verb in a given clause, the subject will tend to precede the verb. Hence, the fact that there is a tendency to place a subject on the opposite side of the verb from other material means that to some extent the position of the subject may depend on the discourse properties of that other material rather than on the discourse properties of the subject itself. As a result, any account of the position of the subject that appeals only to the discourse properties of the subject is likely to be inadequate.

5.2 Grammatical function of clause-initial material

The three clause orders also differ with respect to the grammatical or semantic function of preverbal material other than the subject and verb. Table 11 shows that in VSX and VS clauses, preverbal material is more often nominal, while in SV clauses this is generally not the case. The percentage figures indicate percentage among clauses containing preverbal nonsubject material.[13]

In the majority of SV clauses with preverbal material, the preverbal material is a temporal adverbial or a conjunction. In the majority of VS and VSX clauses, the preverbal material is nominal. VSX clauses differ from VS clauses in that preverbal temporal adverbials are more common in the former ($p < .001$). The basic generalization that can be drawn for the two more common clause types, SV and VS, is that a nonsubject nominal in a clause tends to occur on the opposite side of the verb from the subject: such nominals tend **not** to occur preverbally in SV clauses, but **are** common preverbally in VS. We discussed a similar generalization in the preceding section, but we can now say that this generalization applies particularly strongly with **nominal** elements rather than temporal adverbials, other adverbs, and conjunctions. The examples in (13) to (15) illustrate some of the more common types of SV and VS clauses in Table 11.

Table 11. Clause-initial material other than subject and verb

No. of clauses where	SV		VSX		VS	
initial material includes	No.	%	No.	%	No.	%
Object	0	0%	12	25%	7	15%
Oblique	2	9%	17	35%	28	60%
Nominal predicate	0	0%	0	0%	2	4%
Temporal adverbial and none of the above	13	59%	18	38%	4	9%
Other adverb and none of the above	1	5%	1	2%	4	9%
Conjunction and none of the above	6	27%	0	0%	2	4%
Total	22	100%	48	100%	47	100%

(13) SV with preverbal temporal adverbial and postverbal object

W drugiej połowie XI stulecia sułtani seldżuccy
in second half.LOC 11th century.GEN sultans.NOM Seljuk.ADJ
TEMPORAL SUBJECT

władali już wielkim państwem, które obejmowało
ruled already large state.INSTR which encompassed
VERB OBJECT

Persję, Mezopotamię, Syrię i dużą część
Persia.ACC Mesopotamia.ACC Syria.ACC and large part.ACC

Azji Mniejszej.
Asia.GEN Minor
'In the second half of the 11th century, the Seljuk sultans already ruled over a large state, encompassing Persia, Mesopotamia, Syria, and a large part of Asia Minor.' (p. 6)

(14) VS with preverbal object

Tym pokojowym tendencjom przeciwdziałał energicznie
this peaceful tendencies.DAT counteracted actively
OBJECT VERB

legat papieski, kardynał Julian Cezarini.
envoy.NOM papal cardinal.NOM Julian Cezarini.NOM
SUBJECT
'The papal envoy Cardinal Julian Cezarini actively counteracted these peaceful tendencies.' (p.13)

(15) VS with preverbal oblique

Od południa, od Bałkanów i Dunaju,
from south.GEN from Balkans.GEN and Danube.GEN
OBLIQUE

wzmagał się napór Turków.
increased REFL pressure.NOM Turks.GEN
VERB SUBJECT
'From the south, from the Balkans and Danube, the Turkish pressure increased.' (p.10)

It should be noted that the above generalizations do not take into account the VSX clauses. The situation with this less frequent type of clause is a little bit more complex as the majority of these clauses contain two nonsubject nominals. One of these nominals follows the subject, the other tends to occur preverbally. Examples (16) and (17) illustrate two VSX clauses with preverbal material.

(16) VSX with preverbal object

Większą	*część*	*swej*	*jazdy*	*wysłał*	*Sobieski*
bigger	part.ACC	his	cavalry.GEN	sent	Sobieski.NOM
		OBJECT		VERB	SUBJECT

w	*stronę*	*Lwowa,*	*rozkazując*	*jej*	*rozpędzać*
in	direction.ACC	Lwow.GEN	ordering	her	disperse.INF
	OBLIQUE				

czambuły	*tatarskie.*
forays.ACC	Tartars.ADJ

'Sobieski sent the bigger part of his cavalry towards Lwow with the order to disperse the Tartar forays.' (p.140)

(17) VSX with preverbal oblique

Na	*Bałkanach*	*zawładnęli*	*Turcy*	*Moreą*
in	Balkans.LOC	conquered	Turks.NOM	Morea.INSTR
	OBLIQUE	VERB	SUBJECT	

(Peloponez)	*oraz*	*znaczną*	*częścią*	*Albanii,*	*podbili*
Peloponez	and	substantial	part.INSTR	Albania.GEN	subdued
	OBJECT				

Bośnię	*i*	*Hercegowinę.*
Bosnia.ACC	and	Hercegovina.ACC

'In the Balkans, the Turks conquered Morea (Peloponez) and a substantial part of Albania, and subdued Bosnia and Hercegovina.' (p. 22)

5.3 Grammatical function of clause-final material

The three types of clauses do not differ significantly in terms of the grammatical or semantic function of final postverbal nonsubjects. By definition, VS clauses do not contain such material. The data for SV and VSX clauses is given in Table 12.

With both SV and VSX clauses, the final material generally includes a nominal, either an object or an oblique. SV clauses differ somewhat from VSX clauses in that the final material is less often an object with VSX

Table 12 Clause-final Material other than Subject and Verb

No. of clauses where final material includes	SV No.	SV %	VSX No.	VSX %
Object	21	40%	13	25%
Oblique	24	46%	36	69%
Nominal predicate	2	4%	0	0%
Temporal adverbial (with none of the above)	3	6%	3	6%
Other adverb (with none of the above)	2	4%	0	0%
Total	52	100%	52	100%

clauses than with SV clauses, but this difference falls short of statistical significance.[14]

5.4 Discourse properties of postverbal nonsubjects

Most of the clauses examined that are SV or VSX contain a postverbal nonsubject nominal. But the two kinds of clauses differ strikingly with respect to whether that postverbal nonsubject nominal has a previous reference in the immediately preceding clause, as shown in Table 13. The percentage figures indicate the percentage of clauses of the given sort among clauses containing postverbal nonsubject nominals.[15]

Table 13 shows that 10 out of the 47 postverbal nonsubject nominals in SV clauses do have a previous reference in the preceding clause, while none out of 49 postverbal nonsubject nominals in VSX clauses do. Example (18) illustrates one of the SV clauses where the postverbal nonsubject nominal (*kraju* 'the country') was referred to in the preceding clause.

Table 13. Previous reference to postverbal nonsubject

	SV No.	SV %	VSX No.	VSX %
Previous reference to postverbal nonsubject nominal in preceding clause	10	21%	0	0%
No previous reference to postverbal nonsubject nominal in preceding clause	37	79%	49	100%
Total with postverbal nonsubject nominal	47	100%	49	100%

(18) *Nowa wyprawa wojenna, niepopularna na Węgrzech,*
new expedition.NOM military unpopular in Hungary.LOC

miała najgorętszych przeciwników w Polsce.
had most.ardent opponents.ACC in Poland.LOC

Zjazd piotrkowski w sierpniu 1444 r., wobec
congress.NOM Piotrków.ADJ in August.LOC 1444 y. in.view.of

trudnej sytuacji wewnętrznej, wzywał króla
difficult situation.GEN domestic summoned king.ACC

do kraju.
to country.GEN

'The new military expedition, unpopular in Hungary, had its most ardent opponents in Poland. In August 1444, in view of the difficult domestic situation, the Piotrków congress summoned the king to come back to the country.' (p. 14)

It is not clear how to explain this pattern. One possible interpretation of this is that VSX clauses are used to background subjects relative to another (postverbal nonsubject) nominal which is thus highlighted. The possibility that the special function of VSX clauses is to background the subject is also supported by the tendency for the subjects in VSX to be less often present in the next clause as compared with the subjects of SV clauses (cf. footnote 10).

6. Properties of verb

6.1 Semantic class of verb

A final class of factors determining the order of subject and verb is the properties of the verb. The clearest generalization is that VS order is common with **presentative** verbs, i.e. verbs which denote the commencement of a process, event, state or institution, or the occurrence or lasting of an event or period, or the coming into being or into appearance of an entity, or the existence of an entity at a specific place or time. This order is also common with what we call **participant removal verbs**, i.e. ones which signal the removal of a participant, such as *milczeć* 'was silent', *zginąć* 'died violently', *polec* 'died in a battle', and *umrzeć* 'died'. Table 14 gives the frequency of these two kinds of verbs among the three types of clauses.

Table 14. Semantic class of verb

	SV		VSX		VS	
	No.	%	No.	%	No.	%
Presentative verb	4	8%	2	4%	18	35%
Participant-removal verb	0	0%	0	0%	6	12%
Total	52	100%	52	100%	52	100%

Nearly half (24 out of 52, or 46%) of the verbs in VS clauses belong to one of these two classes. Example (19) illustrates a VS clause with a presentative verb.

(19) *Lecz oto* ***nadbiegli*** *dalsi napastnicy.*
but EMPH came.running further attackers.NOM
'But then more attackers came running.' (p.271)

Example (20) illustrates an SV clause with a presentative verb *przybył* 'arrived'.[16]

(20) *Natomiast oddział najemników, werbowany*
on.the.other.hand detachment.NOM hirelings.GEN recruited

przez Piotra Wapowskiego, ***przybył*** *na Węgry już*
by Piotr Wapowski.ACC arrived in Hungary.ACC already

po klęsce warneńskiej.
after defeat.LOC Varna.ADJ
'On the other hand, the detachment of hirelings recruited by Piotr Wapowski didn't arrive in Hungary until after the defeat at Varna.' (p. 14)

Presentative verbs are clearly a major factor determining the use of VS order. But this association between presentative verbs and VS order is not found with VSX clauses. Again this shows clearly a functional difference between VS and VSX clauses. It also shows that presentational position is specifically clause-final, rather than just postverbal position.[17]

It should be stressed that we cannot infer from Table 14 that subjects of presentative verbs generally follow the verb in Polish. The data in all our tables (except Table 1) is based on 52 clauses of each of the three types. As noted above, the frequency of these three types in the original text examined was 260 SV, 106 VS, and 25 VSX. If we take these ratios as typical, and if we take the percentages in Table 10 as typical, this would lead us to expect to find in the original text 21 instances of presentative SV clauses, 1 instance of a presentative VSX clause, and 33 instances of presentative VS clauses. While the majority of presentative clauses in this extrapolated data are VS, the difference is not a large one: 33 presentative VS clauses vs. 22 presentative SV/VSX clauses. At best this allows us to estimate the relative frequency of VS vs. SV/VSX among presentatives as only 60%. Hence we cannot say that subjects of presentative verbs generally follow the verb in Polish.

6.2 Presentativeness and predictability

We showed in Section 3.1 and 3.2 that VS and VSX clauses differ with respect to the referential properties of the subject in that subjects of VSX clauses more often have a previous reference in the preceding text. One question that might arise is whether this difference might be due entirely to the fact observed in the preceding section, namely that VS clauses involve presentative or participant-removal verbs more often than VSX clauses do: it might be that presentative verbs take subjects that do not have a previous reference more often than other verbs. It is therefore useful to see whether the differences discussed in Sections 3.1 and 3.2 with respect to previous reference still obtain if we exclude from our calculations clauses with presentative or participant-removal verbs. We show in this section that removing clauses with such verbs does not alter our conclusions.

The figures in Tables 15 and 16 are calculated in the same way as those in Tables 2 and 3 earlier in the paper, except that we have excluded clauses with presentative or participant-removal verbs.

Table 15. Previous reference of subject by clause type (clauses with presentative or participant-removal verbs excluded)

	SV		VSX		VS	
	No.	%	No.	%	No.	%
Previous reference in preceding 20 clauses	39	81%	48	96%	12	50%
Previous direct reference in preceding 20 clauses	19	40%	34	68%	3	13%
Previous reference in the immediately preceding clause	15	31%	20	40%	4	17%
Total	48	100%	50	100%	27	100%

Table 16. Referential distance of subject by (clause type clauses with presentative or participant-removal verbs excluded)

	SV	VSX	VS
Mean referential distance	6.06	3.74	12.68
Mean referential distance for subjects with previous reference in preceding 20 clauses	2.85	3.06	5.30

The figures in Tables 15 and 16 are quite similar to those in Tables 2 and 3. They show that even after removing clauses with presentative or participant-removal verbs, VS and VSX are still clearly distinct in that subjects of VS clauses are much less predictable than subjects of VSX clauses.[18] For example, the second line of Table 15 shows that while 68% of VSX clauses have subjects with a direct previous reference in the preceding 20 clauses, only 13% of VS clauses do. Similarly, Table 16 shows that while the mean referential distance for subjects of VSX clauses is 3.74, the mean referential distance for subjects of VS clauses is 12.68. As in Tables 2 and 3, SV clauses are intermediate between VS and VSX clauses with respect to the various measures. In short, the overall differences between VS and VSX clauses with respect to previous reference are not due to the fact that VS clauses more often involve presentational or participant-removal verbs.

6.3 Transitivity of verb

The semantic property of presentativeness correlates with the transitivity of the verb, since presentative verbs are generally intransitive. Table 17 gives data specifically for the association between the three clause types and the transitivity of the clause.

Table 17. Transitivity of clause

	SV		VSX		VS	
	No.	%	No.	%	No.	%
Intransitive	22	42%	22	42%	38	73%
Transitive	30	58%	30	58%	14	27%
Total	52	100%	52	100%	52	100%

Table 18. Clauses with verbs that are not presentative or participant-removal

	SV		VSX		VS	
	No.	%	No.	%	No.	%
Intransitive	18	38%	20	40%	16	57%
Transitive	30	63%	30	60%	12	43%
Total	48	100%	50	100%	28	100%

As would be expected, VS clauses are intransitive more often than SV and VSX clauses ($p < .01$). But as we might expect from the pattern for presentative verbs in Table 14, there is no transitivity difference between SV and VSX clauses. On the other hand, this difference between VS clauses on the one hand, and SV and VSX clauses on the other, is largely attributable to the frequency of presentative and participant-removal verbs in VS clauses. Since all of the presentative and participant-removal verbs in Table 14 are intransitive, we can compute that the three types of clauses do not differ significantly with respect to the frequency of intransitive verbs that do not belong to one of these two classes, as shown in Table 18.

Although VS clauses still exhibit the largest proportion for intransitive verbs in Table 18, the differences between VS clauses and the other two clause types is much smaller than in Table 17 and is not statistically significant. Hence the difference between VS clauses and the other two clause types in Table 17 with respect to the transitivity of the verb is largely attributable to the frequency of presentative and participant-removal verbs in VS clauses.

6.4 Aspect of verb

A final relevant property of the verb is aspect. As in other Slavic languages, Polish makes a grammatical distinction between perfective and imperfective verbs. A breakdown for these two kinds of verbs for the three clause types is given in Table 19.

The verb in VSX clauses is perfective significantly more often than with either SV clauses ($p < .001$) or VS clauses ($p < .05$). The fact that the frequency of imperfective verbs is highest for SV clauses is in harmony with observations others have made regarding the relationship between aspect and word order in other languages, such as Hopper's (1979) observation of

Table 19. Aspect of verb

	SV		VSX		VS	
	No.	%	No.	%	No.	%
Perfective verb	29	56%	45	87%	35	67%
Imperfective verb	20	38%	5	9%	14	27%
Verb lacking contrast	3	6%	2	4%	3	6%
Total	52	100%	52	100%	52	100%

a correlation between durative aspect and SV order in Old English. On the other hand, the difference between SV and VS clauses is not statistically significant in our data, and the fact that VSX clauses exhibit perfective aspect significantly more often than VS clauses in Polish involves a difference that goes beyond the kind of difference Hopper observed for Old English.

7. Discussion

7.1 Summary of results

We have shown in this paper that the original question of what governs the order of subject and verb in Polish is an overly simple question, since there are two types of clauses with postverbal subjects, VS and VSX, which exhibit very different properties. Most importantly, while subjects of VS clauses tend to be less predictable than subjects of other clauses, including SV clauses, subjects of VSX clauses tend to be more predictable than other clauses, again including SV clauses. We have shown that subjects of VSX clauses differ from subjects of VS clauses in a number of other respects: they are more often human; they are more often short; and when they have a previous reference in the preceding clause, they tend to be less topical in that clause. We have also shown that VSX clauses differ from VS clauses in other respects: VSX clauses more often have initial temporal adverbials; and VS clauses more often have presentative or participant-removal verbs.

In some ways, the differences between VS and VSX clauses that we have discussed might seem surprising: why should a final X element make such a difference? We have shown the answer to be that the critical variable is not the order of subject and verb, but rather the contrast between clause-final position and earlier positions in the clause. The properties of VS clauses that we have discussed reflect the significance of final position in the clause; subjects of VS clauses occur in this position while subjects of VSX clauses do not. The properties of VSX clauses reflect the fact that the medial position in a clause is usually reserved for short predictable constituents.

7.2 VSX and postverbal pronouns

It is worth drawing attention to a number of ways in which the properties of VSX clauses we have discussed here resemble properties which Siewierska (1987) attributes to clauses with postverbal subject pronouns, as in (21).

(21) *Powrócił on przed niedawnym czasem z*
came.back he before not.too.long time.INSTR from

niewoli tureckiej i znów dzierżył buławę
captivity.GEN Turkish and again held baton.ACC

polną koronną.
field.ADJ Crown.ADJ
'He came back not too long ago from Turkish captivity and held again the Crown Field baton.' (p. 114)

First, we have shown that subjects of VSX clauses very often consist of a single word; clearly subject pronouns also have this property. Second, we have observed that subjects of VSX clauses are highly continuous in the sense of more often having previous reference in preceding clauses; again this is clearly true of postverbal subject pronouns as well. Third, Siewierska observes (p. 151) that postverbal subject pronouns are not separated from the verb by anything other than a clitic; only two of the 52 VSX clauses in our sample have anything between the verb and the subject. Fourth, Siewierska notes that postverbal subject pronouns very often have antecedents in the previous clause which are nontopical in that clause. Siewierska describes postverbal subject pronouns as indicating a switch of topic; the fact that they occur as subjects in the current clause suggests that they are now topics, even if they were not such in the preceding clause. We have shown a somewhat analogous result for subjects of VSX clauses: if they have an antecedent in the preceding clause, that antecedent is an oblique or part of a predicate expression significantly more often than is the case with antecedents of subjects of SV or VS clauses. In both cases — the postverbal subject pronouns that Siewierska examined and the subjects of VSX clauses that we examined — an antecedent in the preceding clause was often non-topical. Finally, and perhaps most significantly, while Siewierska does not explicitly distinguish what we have called VSX and VS clauses, various points suggest that the clauses she discusses with postverbal subject pronouns are VSX. For one thing, the three examples she cites with postverbal subject pronouns are all VSX. She furthermore mentions an infrequent class of clauses containing what she calls "final subject pronouns", in which the subject pronoun occurs at the end of the clause. These pronouns, unlike the pronouns that are the focus of her paper, are stressed and display characteristics more typical of preverbal pronouns. This suggests that VSX clauses and clauses with postverbal subject pronouns are probably instances of the same general phenomenon.

7.3 Theme-rheme order vs. highly predictable postverbal nominal

Let us turn now to the question with which we began this paper. Is it possible to reconcile the traditional claim of theme-rheme order as the unmarked order in Slavic languages with Givón's claim that postverbal nominals universally tend to be more predictable in the sense of having closer previous references in the preceding text? Although there are various possible interpretations of the theme-rheme distinction, the traditional claim would nevertheless seem to predict that postverbal subjects should have a higher mean referential distance than preverbal subjects, while Givón's claim predicts that postverbal subjects should have a lower mean referential distance. But because VSX clauses in Polish exhibit very different properties from VS clauses, it is clear that either claim would be mistaken as a **general** claim about postverbal subjects. We have seen that subjects in VSX clauses tend to be more predictable, while subjects in VS clauses tend to be less predictable. In other words, the properties of VS clauses conform to the traditional claim, while the properties of VSX clauses conform to Givón's prediction.

There seems to be little way to reconcile the properties of VSX clauses with the traditional claim: these clauses tend to have subjects which are more predictable and hence presumably more thematic than subjects of SV clauses. It should be noted, however, that VSX clauses are noticeably less frequent than VS clauses. Over samples from six authors, the average frequency of the three clause types (see footnote 3) is SV 65.7%, VSX 5.8%, and VS 28.5%. In other words VS is about five times more common than VSX. Hence, the category that includes the majority of postverbal subjects conforms to the traditional claim. Furthermore, we observed above that VSX clauses resemble clauses with postverbal subject pronouns. But Siewierska (1987) observes that the latter type of clause is most frequent in expository written Polish, as opposed to novels and (probably) spoken Polish. Since our study has been based entirely on nonfictional written Polish, this suggests that VSX may be even less frequent in other genres of Polish than in the texts we examined.

While the properties of VSX clauses provide support for Givón's claim, there are a couple of reasons why they provide only limited support for this claim. First, while it is the case that subjects of VSX clauses are more "continuous" in the sense that they exhibit a lower mean referential distance than the other two clause types (cf. Tables 2 and 3), they are **less** continuous in the sense that they exhibit an apparent tendency to be referred to less often in the immediately subsequent clause (cf. Table 5), though this tendency fell short of statistical significance; but in so far as there is a trend, it is in the opposite direction from what Givón's claim predicts. Second, since SV order is much more common than VSX order, there is no basis for saying that nominals with low referential distance tend to follow the verb.

Turning to VS clauses, we have seen that the properties of these clauses support the traditional claims regarding theme-rheme order. Is there any way to reconcile the properties of these VS clauses with Givón's claim? Givón (1988: 266-271) admits that what he calls existential-presentative clauses in many languages offer an apparent counterexample to his claim, but offers a possible historical explanation of why these clauses behave the way they do. Since we have seen that almost half of the VS clauses in our data employ presentative or participant-removal verbs, the question arises whether the properties of VS clauses in Polish can be explained away in the same way. The answer is apparently that they cannot.

Givón's argument is based on presentative clauses containing a verb 'be' or 'have' preceding the subject, as in the English there-construction, in which an indefinite subject follows a verb 'be':

(22) *There's a man at the front door.*

Givón argues that the verb in such constructions has lost its verbal properties, and that the verb (or, in the case of English, *there* plus the verb) has been grammaticized as a marker of referential indefinite subject constructions. Whatever the merits of this as an explanation for the properties of constructions like the one in (22), it cannot explain the Polish facts since the clauses we are describing as presentative are ones like (23), in which the verb is not 'be' or 'have', but a "normal" verb carrying all the typical tense and agreement markers as well as lexical stress, and one whose semantics involves a participant coming onto the scene.

(23) *Lecz oto* ***nadbiegli*** *dalsi napastnicy.*
but EMPH came.running further attackers.NOM
'But then more attackers came running.' (p.271)

Nor is there any obvious way in which Givón's explanation could be extended to account for presentative cases like these.

8. Conclusion

Although we have demonstrated that a variety of different factors correlate with the choice between the three types of clauses, SV, VS, and VSX, a lot remains to be done before we have a clear understanding of Polish word order. First, our study is based on the writings of a single author. Study of different individuals, of other forms of written Polish, and especially of spoken Polish, is clearly required. Second, while we have demonstrated a number of significant differences between the three types of clauses, we have not attempted to address in any way the difficult problem of predicting which of the three types will be used in a given context. Third, although we have shown that many of these factors correlate with the choice of clause order, some of these correlations may be epiphenomenal: since many of these factors correlate with each other, some of the correlations between factors and clause order may be artifacts of two separate correlations, the first being a correlation between a real factor and clause order, the second being a correlation between a real factor and an epiphenomenal factor.[19]

A final way in which this study falls short of being a complete account of Polish word order is that it is limited to a study of textual factors that correlate with the different orders. However, it is likely that these textual factors are, at best, indications of cognitive factors that really underlie the different orders (cf. Givón 1989: 216; Tomlin 1987). Only a methodology like experimental psycholinguistics, which directly examines such cognitive factors, would be able to demonstrate what really underlies the word order alternations.

Notes

1. The work of this paper began while both authors were associated with the University of Alberta.
2. Rybarkiewicz' results are presented in terms of Givón's measure of **referential distance**, the mean distance in clauses back to a previous reference in the text. Givón reports that in Rybarkiewicz's data, postverbal subjects have a mean referential distance of 3.1, while preverbal subjects have a mean referential distance of 6.5. Rybarkiewicz's paper is an unpublished paper cited by Givón (1988, 1989) which we have not seen.
3. The following table illustrates the relative frequency of the three types of clauses to be discussed in this paper, SV, VSX, and VS, in the excerpts from our primary source, Pajewski (1978), and five other written sources. One hundred clauses with lexical subjects were examined from each of the five sources. In each case, the 100 clauses consisted of 5 blocks of 20 consecutive clauses, each block taken from different parts of the source. Still to be investigated are the sources of the observed variation in the frequency of the three clause types and the question of to what extent the conclusions of this paper can be generalized to other authors or to spoken language.

Table A. Comparison of primary source with five other authors' percentages of three clause types among clauses with lexical subjects

	SV	VSX	VS
Primary source (as percentage)	58	8	34
Source 1 (popular history)	71	3	26
Source 2 (popular history)	76	0	24
Source 3 (adolescent novel)	74	2	24
Source 4 (biography)	63	1	36
Source 5 (biography)	52	21	27
Mean	65.7%	5.8%	28.5%

4. Throughout this paper, the citations of levels of statistical significance are based on the Chi-Square test with Yate's correction. Where we say that a given difference is not statistically significant (not sig) later in the paper, we mean that it is

not significant at the .05 level using the Yate's correction. Where we cite a difference between one clause type and the other two clause types, in most cases, we have computed the difference between the one clause type and each of the other two clause types separately, so that all our tables are 2x2. In those rare cases where we have computed the difference between one clause type and the two others combined, it is so indicated.

The Chi-square test showing that VS order is less common in subordinate clauses is based on Table B, which collapses the data in Table 1.

Table B

	SV	VS
In main clause	230	164
In subordinate clause	30	5

5. Siewierska (1987: 149) found that postverbal subject pronouns are more common than preverbal subject pronouns in a set of expository and biographical texts. However, she found the reverse to be the case in a novel and short stories.

6. Some of these VS and VSX clauses have material preceding the verb and/or intervening between the verb and the subject. Similarly SV clauses may have material preceding the subject, following the verb, or intervening between the subject and verb.

7. The significance levels of the differences between the three types of clauses for the three categories in Table 2 are given in Table C.

Table C

	SV vs. VS	SV vs. VSX	VSX vs. VS
Previous reference in preceding 20 clauses	$p < .01$	$p < .01$	$p < .001$
Previous direct reference in preceding 20 clauses	$p < .01$	$p < .01$	$p < .001$
Previous reference in the immediately preceding clause	not sig.	not sig.	$p < .01$

8. The broad (direct and indirect) sense of previous reference was assumed in computing the levels for referential distance.

9. The significance levels of the differences between the three types of clauses for the three categories in Table 3 are given in Table D.

Table D

	SV vs. VS	SV vs. VSX	VSX vs. VS
Mean referential distance	$p < .001$	$p < .02$	$p < .001$
Mean referential distance for subjects with previous reference in preceding 20 clauses	$p < .05$	not sig.	not sig.

10. Although none of the between-clauses contrasts in Table 5 are significant when tested by Chi-square with Yate's correction, the SV vs. VSX contrast on the first line is significant when tested by simple Chi-square ($p < .05$). The fact that it just misses the significance level suggests that there may be some tendency for the subjects in SV clauses to be present in the next clause more often than is the case with the subjects in VSX clauses. On the other hand, we do not find this apparent trend when we consider reference in any of the next three clauses, as on the second line of Table 5.

11. The contrasts for Table 9 were calculated differently from for other tables. Since the frequencies in some of the cells in this table are very low, the contrasts here are between VSX and SV/VS combined, rather than between VSX and each of the two other orders separately.

12. Three of these five clauses contain just the verb and subject. The other two contain pronouns between the verb and subject, one an object pronoun, the other oblique.

13. The category oblique includes prepositional phrases and noun phrases functioning as neither subject nor object. The category of clauses that contain an object includes two VSX clauses that contain both an object and an oblique; these two clauses are not included with the clauses containing an oblique, in order that no clause be counted in more than one category.

14. If this difference is a real one (i.e. if it falls short of statistical significance only because of the small size of our sample), then the effect of this difference would be that SVO clauses are much more common than VSO clauses, especially since VSX clauses are much less common than SV clauses (the original sample outlined in Table 1 contains 182 SV clauses, but only 25 VSX clauses). We discuss the relationship between clause type and the transitivity of the verb below.

15. The difference in Table 13 between SV and VSX clauses with respect to whether there is a previous reference to the postverbal nonsubject nominal in the preceding clause is statistically significant ($p < .01$).

16. A possible explanation for the use of SV order in (20) is that the sentence presupposes that the detachment of hirelings arrived, and primarily asserts that the arri-

val took place after the defeat at Varna; this is unlike (19) where the fact that the attackers came running is the primary assertion.

17. This difference between VS on the one hand and SV and VSX on the other is statistically significant ($P < .01$).

18. The significance levels of the difference between the three types of clauses for the three categories in Table 15 are given in Table E. The significance levels of the differences between the three types of clauses for the three categories in Table 16 are given in Table F.

Table E

	SV vs. VS	SV vs. VSX	VSX vs. VS
Previous reference in preceding 20 clauses	$p < .001$	$p < .05$	$p < .001$
Previous direct reference in preceding 20 clauses	$p < .05$	$p < .01$	$p < .001$
Previous reference in the immediately preceding clause	not sig.	not sig.	$p < .05$

Table F

	SV vs. VS	SV vs. VSX	VSX vs. VS
Mean referential distance	$p < .01$	$p < .02$	$p < .001$
Mean referential distance for subjects with previous reference in preceding 20 clauses	$p < .05$	not sig.	$p < .05$

19. Myhill (1984, 1985, 1986) illustrates a methodology for teasing out these distinctions, but his method would require a larger sample than the one we have used here.

References

Dryer, Matthew S. 1980. "The Positional Tendencies of Sentential Noun Phrases in Universal Grammar." *Canadian Journal of Linguistics* 25.123-195.

Firbas, Jan. 1966. "On Defining the Theme in Functional Sentence Analysis." *Travaux Linguistiques de Prague* 1.267-280.

Firbas, Jan. 1974. "Some Aspects of the Czechoslovak Approach to Problems of Functional Sentence Perspective." *Papers on Functional Sentence Perspective* ed. by F. Daneš, 11-37. The Hague: Mouton.

Givón, T., ed. 1983. *Topic Continuity in Discourse: A Quantitative Cross-Language Study*. Amsterdam: John Benjamins.

Givón, T. 1988. "The Pragmatics of Word-Order: Predictability, Importance and Attention." *Studies in Syntactic Typology* ed. by M. Hammond, E. Moravcsik, and J. Wirth, 243-284. Amsterdam: John Benjamins.

Givón, T. 1989. *Mind, Code, and Context: Essays in Pragmatics*. Hillsdale, N. J.: Lawrence Erlbaum.

Hopper, Paul. 1979. "Aspect and Foregrounding in Discourse." *Discourse and Syntax* (= *Syntax and Semantics* 12), ed. by T. Givón, 213-241. New York: Academic Press.

Myhill, John. 1984. *A Study of Aspect, Word Order, and Voice*. University of Pennsylvania PhD dissertation.

Myhill, John. 1985. "Pragmatic and Categorial Correlates of VS Word Order." *Lingua* 66.177-200.

Myhill, John. 1986. "The Two VS Constructions in Rumanian." Linguistics 24:331-350.

Pajewski, Janusz. 1978. *Bunczuk i koncerz. Z dziejow wojen polsko-tureckich*. Warsaw: Wiedza Powszechna.

Payne, Doris. 1987. "Information Structuring in Papago Narrative Discourse." *Language* 63.783-804.

Rybarkiewicz, W. 1984. Word-Order Flexibility in Polish. University of Oregon, Eugene. Ms.

Siewierska, Anna. 1987. "Postverbal Subject Pronouns in Polish in the Light of Topic Continuity and the Topic/Focus Distinction." *Getting One's Words In Line: On Word Order and Functional Grammar* ed. by Jan Nuyts and Georges de Schutters, 147-161. Dordrecht: Foris.

Sun, Chao-Fen, and T. Givón. 1985. "On the So-Called SOV Word Order in Mandarin Chinese." *Language* 61.329-351.

Tomlin, Russell. 1987. "Linguistic Reflections on Cognitive Events." *Coherence and Grounding in Discourse* ed. by Russell Tomlin, 455-479. Amsterdam: John Benjamins.

The Pragmatics of Word Order Variation in Chamorro Narrative Text[1]

Ann Cooreman
Katholieke Universiteit Brabant, Tilburg, The Netherlands

1. Introduction

In recent years, a number of studies have investigated the function of word order inversion in languages where both SV and VS word order are allowed. Textual evidence from these languages (Ute [Givón 1983a], Spanish [Bentivoglio 1983], Biblical Hebrew [A. Fox 1983], and Tagalog [B. Fox 1985], among others) suggest that the variation in word order can be explained in terms of two pragmatic principles. First, in a given clause the position of the subject relative to the verb correlates with the degree of referential continuity of the subject referent. This degree of referential continuity essentially depends on the degree of recency with which a referent is mentioned in the context. Referents which have not been mentioned for some time have a low degree of referential continuity, whereas recent reference to some object or person in the text results in a high degree of referential continuity for that referent. In the four studies mentioned above, placing the subject before the verb correlates highly with referential discontinuity. In other words, SV word order marks a disruption in the referential continuity in the sense that the subject in this pattern commonly refers either to a new person or object, or to one which has not been mentioned recently. As such, subject preposing is used in these languages to mark subject referents which are somehow unexpected, or surprising at a particular moment in discourse. VS word order, on the other hand, seems to mark referential continuity since it correlates highly with maintaining the same referent as subject as found in the previous clause. I will refer to this first pragmatic principle as the principle of **referential continuity**.

Second, these same languages also provide evidence for a correlation between the type of word order and the position of the clause in the "thematic paragraph." The latter term stands for a narrative unit in which one or more participants are involved in one or a series of activities which form a unified whole and which move towards the same general goal. A paragraph boundary can be established when a new line of action starts, when a different participant is introduced with his own actions and goals, when the location of events changes drastically, and so on (for a short discussion of narrative units and episode structure see B. Fox 1987 and Tomlin 1987, among others). Often such changes co-occur in narrative texts. SV order in Ute, Spanish, Biblical Hebrew, and Tagalog is more commonly found when the thematic unity of the paragraph is disrupted, either at the beginning of a new paragraph, or when the paragraph theme is temporarily suspended, for example to give meta-comments, to elaborate, describe, or give information not directly pertaining to the "theme" of the paragraph (e.g. the Chamorro example in 5 below), but is later resumed. VS word order is more common in paragraph medial and final position, where clauses generally contribute to the thematic development. I will call this second pragmatic principle the principle of **thematic continuity**.

While referential continuity is a reflection of the organization of the text as it occurs in real time, i.e. sentence by sentence, thematic continuity operates on the basis of the hierarchical structure of the text. For referential continuity each clause in the narrative is taken into account and given the same value as a building block of the total text. For thematic continuity clauses are given differential weights, since some clauses contribute to the development of the theme in a paragraph, while others do not. Descriptions, elaborations, meta comments, etc. usually do not add to the development of the story line.

In Chamorro the basic word order is VSO. It is the word order pattern obtained during direct elicitation of sentences with neutral stress, and in addition, most intransitive clauses with (non-emphatic) pronominal and full subject reference reflect the VS pattern. Even so, in narrative texts SV is not uncommon. As Table 1 shows, both patterns seem to be equally common (76 VS clauses compared with 82 SV clauses). These numbers are, of course, slightly misleading since most transitive propositions do not contain full reference to the subject which is usually indicated through verb agreement or Ø-anaphora alone.[2] In the remainder of this paper I will explore the pragmatic function of the two different word order patterns for transitive propositions[3] in Chamorro spoken narratives. In particular, I will examine the data with reference to the two pragmatic principles outlined above and show that word order variation in Chamorro narratives is part of a complex phenomenon in which a number of variables seem to play a role. I will show that the choice between the unmarked VS and the marked SV order correlates most strongly with the principle of thematic continuity.

2. Data and methodology

The data base for this study (and some others reported in Cooreman 1987), consisted of 200 pages of transcribed spoken narratives collected on the island of Saipan (Northern Marianas). In order to assess the appropriateness of the principle of referential continuity in accounting for the word order variation found in the narratives, subject NPs were subjected to a quantitative method proposed by Givón (1979, 1980, 1983c). This method provides an operational characterization of referential continuity. This continuity at the level of the participants itself contributes to the global coherence of a text. The method provides an adequate, empirical way to measure the degree of continuity of any referent in discourse. The degree of continuity of a referent can be understood as an indicator of the relative importance of that referent in the narrative. Since importance is a rather abstract notion which cannot be measured directly, Givón proposed a quantitative method of measuring the extent to which each NP establishes textual coherence at the participant level. Two different measurements have been suggested. Each of the measurements reflects a different aspect of coherence: (a) referential distance measures anaphoric coherence ("look-back"), and (b) persistence measures cataphoric coherence ("look-ahead").

The parameter of referential distance measures the degree of continuity of a referent in terms of how many clauses intervene to the left between the last mention of that referent and the new reference in the clause under scrutiny. The measurement is applied to all subject NPs and the values for each token within a certain category (in this case, subjects in SV or VS order, respectively) are added up and averaged. The average values provide the basis of comparison between the categories. In theory, the referential value for a *new* referent in a discourse could be infinite. Since we cannot deal with infinity (one instance of infinity would turn the average into infinity as well), the maximum value for referential distance is arbitrarily set at 20 (but see Givón 1983b, footnote 6). This means that we stop looking for previous reference at 20 clauses to the left of a new reference to that same participant. There are reasons to believe that this maximum value of 20 is overestimated since the maximum value of the most discontinuous referent, i.e. one which reintroduces a referent after a very long gap in the narrative, never exceeded 15 clauses in my data. (Similar observations can be made for other languages; see some of the studies in Givón 1983c.)

The parameter of persistence involves the persistence of a referent as a participant in the following discourse, i.e. in how many contiguous clauses to the right of the clause in question will the same referent persist as an argument of a proposition, regardless of its semantic or syntactic role, and regardless of its morphosyntactic form (e.g. as a full definite NP with or without modifiers, as a pronoun, by means of verb agreement, or even through a Ø-anaphor). The minimum value is, of course, 0 for a totally discontinuous referent and there is no theoretical upper boundary for the value of persistence of any given referent.

In this study only the first of the two measurements has been applied to all subjects of both VS and SV clauses.[4] The second measure of persistence does not provide any conclusive results. The NPs in this study are restricted to pronouns and definite NPs only. There were no indefinite NPs since such referents are generally introduced in presentational clauses, introduced with *guaha*, 'exist/be'. (See (3) below.) Of the two types of explicit NPs which can occur in clauses as sentential subjects, the definite NPs comprise an overwhelming majority (i.e. 98%) and a number of interesting factors influencing their appearance will be discussed as well in the course of this article. Pronouns are not very likely to occur, since pronominal referents are usually known referents and Chamorro speakers tend not to refer to known elements explicitly; rather Ø-anaphora are used.

In order to assess the applicability of the principle of thematic continuity as a viable explanation for word order variation in Chamorro, all VS and SV clauses are categorized as to whether they maintained thematic continuity or not with respect to the previous context. Clauses which occur in the middle or at the end of a paragraph usually maintain thematic continuity, whereas clauses at the start of a new paragraph, by virtue of their position, provide a disruption. Examples of this second category also include those clauses which do not aid in the development of the story but do occur within the paragraph. These are clauses which contain comments by the narrator, descriptions, short interruptions, elaborations, etc. These disruptions provide a temporary *break* in the thematic paragraph, after which the story line can be picked up again.

All subject referents in the data were coded with respect to their values for referential distance and with respect to the status of the clause in which they appear as maintaining or disrupting thematic continuity. The numerical relationships between word order and the factors referential distance (as a measure of referential continuity) and paragraph position (as a measure of thematic continuity) were evaluated by means of a number of non-parametric statistical tests. These tests allow a precise, quantifiable evaluation of the ways in which certain discourse pragmatic principles influence the choice of word order.

3. Some sample VS and SV sentences

3.1 VS in initial position[5]

(1)

Pues	*un*	*dia,*	*guaha*	*un*	*taotao*	*lokkue'*	*na*	*ma-lo-loffan*
then	one	day	exist	one	man	also	COMPL	RED-walk

gi	*chalan*	*ya*	*ha-sangan*	*taiguini*	*na*	*taya'*	*ti*
LOC	road	and	E.3SG-say	like.this	COMPL	nothing	NEG

u-ma-tungo'	*u-ma-ke-tungo'*	*ya*	*taya'*	*ti*
IRR.3SG-PASS-know	IRR.3SG-PASS-try-know	and	nothing	NEG

u-ma-li'e	*u-ma-ke-li'e'.*	*Ha-hungok*	*si*	*rai*	*este*
IRR.3SG-PASS-see	IRR.3SG-PASS-try-see	E.3SG-hear	UNM	king	this

na	*kuentos.*	***Lalalo'***	***si***	***rai***	***ya***	***ilek-ña...***
LINK	speech	mad	UNM	king	and	say-3SG.POSS

'Then one day, there was a man passing by on the road and he was talking like this that there is nothing one does not know, one will not try to know and there is nothing one cannot see, one will not try to see. The king heard this speech. The king got mad and said...'

There seems to be a major break between the highlighted clause in this excerpt and the preceding text. The highlighted VS clause starts a new paragraph. There is no continuity with the action or the unnamed participant in the first part of the text example.

3.2 VS in paragraph medial position

(2) *Despues di k-um-uentos i bihu guaha um-i-'ipe i*
after LINK SG-speak the old.man exist EI-RED-cut the

manha siha ya ha-na-na'i i biha.
green.coconut PL and E.3SG-RED-give the old.lady

Ha-gimen i biha i manha siha, *despues*
E.3SG-drink the old.lady the green.coconut PL after

k-um-uentos. Guaha diferentes klase-n action siha yan
SG-talk exist different type-N action PL and

kuen-to-tos-ña.
talk/RED-3SG.POSS
'After the old man had talked, someone was cutting the green coconuts and was giving them to the old lady. The old lady drank the green coconuts and then she talked. There were different types of things she did and different ways she was speaking.'

This portion of the text is clearly about an old lady and the highlighted clause, 'The lady drank the green coconuts', is in the middle of the paragraph, being the third proposition. The subject 'the old lady' occurs in postverbal position.

3.3 SV in initial position

(3) *Guaha man-mañu-ñule' nenkanno', gimen yan guaha lokkue'*
exist PL-AP/RED-get food drink and exist also

i mañu-ñule' guatu tinifok, cheggai yan kulales
the AP/RED-get there basket shells and beads

halomtano' pot di para uma-na'-neste i
forest in.order.to LINK IRR IRR.3PL-CAUS-adorn the

taotao pat ayu i bisita ni man-halom giya Chulu.
people or that the visitor REL PL-enter LOC Chulu

Ya ti apmam i tinaotao pat i natibu siha
and NEG long the people or the native PL

ma-'atende i tres na ñafrago-n Españot ni
E.3PL-attend the three LINK outsider-N Spanish REL

man-halom giya Chulu ginen i batko-n Concepsion.
PL-enter LOC Chulu from the boat-N Concepsion

***I heffi as Taga'**, anai esta silensio i baruka,*
the hero UNM Taga' when already silent the noise

pues ayu nai si Taga' ha-faisen i tres na bisita
then that when UNM Taga' E.3SG-ask the three LINK visitor

nu ayu i ha-susedi guihi na puengi.
OBL that the E.3SG-experience there LINK night

'There were some who were getting food, drinks, and there were also those who were bringing baskets, shells, and beads from the forest in order to adorn the people or those visitors who had entered (the land) at Chulu. And before long the people or the natives attended to the three Spanish outsiders who had entered in Chulu from the boat named Concepsion. So the hero Taga', when the noise had subsided, that's when Taga' asked the three visitors about what he had experienced that night.'

The text in example (3) starts with a description of the natives' activities preparing a welcome for the visitors. With the highlighted phrases the focus of attention shifts back to Taga', the hero of the story (and the subject of many Chamorro myths and legends). The change of participants and also the discontinuity in the action brings about a change in theme. The following clauses remain focussed on Taga' and his wish to find out the meaning of his experience the previous night when he had a vision of the Virgin Mary.

3.4 SV in medial position

(4) *Matto i tiempo na g-um-ai interes si Joaquin*
come the time COMPL SG-have interest UNM Jack

as Rosa. Ya-ña si Rosa na palaoan. ***Parehu i***
OBL Rose Like-3SG.POSS UNM Rose LINK woman same the

dos achacha ma-atende i gima' Yu'us.
two both E.3PL-attend the house Jesus
'The time came that Jack was interested in Rose. He liked the girl Rosa. Both of them attended the same church.'

This paragraph is about two young teenagers, Jack and Rose, and their budding love for one another. The highlighted SV clause is part and parcel of the development of this theme in which more information is added about the situation of the two thematic participants.

3.5 SV at paragraph break

(5) *Gof na'-ma'ase' i patgon. K-um-a-ka'dideng gi kada*
very CAUS-pity the child SG-RED-hop LOC every

k-in-alamenta-n-ña. Unu ha' addeng-ña, unu ha'
NOM-move-N-3SG.POSS one only leg-3SG.POSS one only

kannai-ña, lamita ha' tiyan-ña, lamita ha'
arm-3SG.POSS half only belly-3SG.POSS half only

pachot-ña, gui'eng-ña yan ilu-n-ña. ***Mampos i***
mouth-3SG.POSS nose-3SG.POSS and head-N-3SG.POSS very the

nana ni-na'-ma'ase' ni lahi-ña. *Guiguiya ha'*
mother PASS-CAUS-pity OBL son-3SG.POSS RED/EMPH.3SG only

na maisa h-um-ugando si Juan. Taya' ni un patgon
LINK self SG-play UNM John Nothing OBL one child

malago' h-um-ugando yan si Juan.
want SG-play with UNM John
'The child was very pitiful. He was just hopping at every movement he made. He only had one leg, only one arm, only half a stomach, only half a mouth, nose and head. The mother was very sorry for her son. John played only by himself. Not one child wanted to play with John.'

In this paragraph the speaker focusses on the pitiful state of the child. The highlighted passive clause with the Patient/subject preceding the verb does not provide more information about the child, nor does it add to the description of his fate; rather, the speaker comments on the feelings of the mother concerning her son. The shift of attention from the child to the mother and back to the child causes a break in the thematic development of this particular paragraph.

4. Principle 1: Word order inversion as a correlate of referential continuity

Following the predictions made by Givón (1983b) — predictions which are borne out by evidence from Ute (Givón 1983a), Spanish (Bentivoglio 1983), and Biblical Hebrew (A. Fox 1983) — one might expect that subject referents in SV word order are more discontinuous than subjects in VS order, so that the measure for referential distance for subjects of SV clauses should be higher than for subject referents in VS clauses. Table 1 shows that the values for referential distance for subjects form a bimodal distribution: A large number of subject referents have a very low value for referential distance (i.e. 1 or 2) and in addition, a relatively large number of subject referents show the maximum value for referential distance, i.e. 20.

Due to the bimodal nature of the distribution, statistical significance was calculated on the basis of two non-parametric tests, i.e. the Mann-

Table 1. Distributional frequency of referential distance values for subjects in VS and SV patterns

Value	VS	SV
1	31	30
2	15	11
3	3	3
4	4	3
5	4	0
6	1	4
7	1	1
8	3	1
9	0	2
10	1	2
13	0	1
14	3	1
15	1	0
20	18	33

Table 2. Mean ranking for referential distance values for subject in SV and VS order (Mann-Whitney U — Wilcoxon Rank W Test)

	Number of Cases	Mean Rank
VS	85	83.0
SV	92	94.5

Z = 1.54, p = .06 (for directional prediction, corrected for ties)

Whitney U-test and the Wilcoxon Rank Sum W test. Table 2 shows that there is no significant correlation between word order and referential distance overall. (Statistical significance is reached when $p \leq .05$.)

Even though the data tend in the direction of higher referential continuity for subjects in VS order as opposed to subjects in SV order, the difference between the two falls just short of significance.

However, when thematic continuity is maintained, i.e. in clauses occurring in paragraph medial or paragraph final position, the values for referential distance for subjects in the SV pattern are significantly higher than for subjects in VS order, as shown in Table 3. This suggests that when thematic continuity is maintained, SV order marks subjects which **disrupt** referential continuity, while VS order marks subjects which are more likely to **maintain** referential continuity.

One might expect that referents at the beginning of a new paragraph or at the position of a break in the paragraph will have a higher value for referential distance, since new paragraphs are often induced by the introduction or reappearance of a different thematic participant. Referents in the middle

Table 3. Mean ranking for referential distance values for subject in SV and VS order in paragraph medial and final position (Mann-Whitney U — Wilcoxon Rank W Test)

	Number of Cases	Mean Rank
VS	66	44.1
SV	27	54.1

Z = 1.7, $p < .05$ (for directional prediction, corrected for ties)

or at the end of a paragraph are expected to show an overall lower value for referential distance since these participants — if they function as thematic participants as well — have already been introduced and are assumed to continue playing a major role (Givón 1983b). There is no evidence for this assumption in the Chamorro narrative data examined in this paper. That these assumptions are based on gross oversimplifications and are not quite in tune with the narrative facts has been shown in some detail for English narratives in Fox (1987). In English written narratives, and in Chamorro spoken narratives as well, paragraphs do not necessarily involve a change of thematic participant, and indeed often maintain reference to the same thematic participant found in the previous paragraph. Admittedly, I have not investigated in detail the frequency with which reference to thematic participants "switches" at paragraph boundaries; however, an impressionistic survey of the Chamorro story material supports the analysis made by Fox (1987).

5. Principle 2: Word order inversion as a correlate of thematic continuity

I have shown in the previous section that there is only a weak correlation between word order choice and referential continuity in Chamorro narratives. The correlation comes to light only when thematic continuity is maintained. There is no significant difference between the two word order types in paragraph initial/break position. Hence, we can safely conclude that referential continuity is only marginally responsible for the choice between VS and SV word order in Chamorro narratives.

We are still left with the question whether the choice between SV and VS in Chamorro narratives can be accounted for in a more systematic and comprehensive way. To test the dependence of the two nominal variables word order and paragraph position, a Chi Square was used.

Table 4 shows that there is a statistically significant difference in the frequency of occurrence of preposed subjects (SV) and postposed subjects (VS) between clauses at paragraph initial/break position and paragraph medial/final position. This difference highlights the strong correlation between SV and paragraph inital/break position on the one hand and VS and paragraph medial/final position on the other.

Table 4. Distributional frequency of SV and VS word order in paragraph initial/break position and paragraph medial/final position (Chi Square test)

	Initial/Break	Medial/Final
VS	19	66
SV	65	27

$\chi^2_{(DF=1)} = 39.42$ (continuity corrected) $p < .001$

The evidence from Chamorro narratives thus corroborates the second pragmatic principle which has been suggested as an explanation for the choice between SV and VS. Word order choice reflects the hierarchical organization of a narrative in Chamorro. VS word order, the basic order in Chamorro, is used in the unmarked context where thematic continuity is maintained. SV, which is a marked pattern, is used with a significantly higher frequency when this continuity is disrupted. Thus, Chamorro speakers — like their Spanish, Ute, Biblical Hebrew, and Tagalog counterparts — tend to use SV to mark thematic discontinuity.

6. Explicit reference and ambiguity resolution

As I have just shown, word order choice in Chamorro is most strongly influenced by the thematic organization of the narrative. Referential organization also plays a role, albeit weakly and only when thematic continuity is maintained.

However, the story about word order is a "tale without a tail" without a detailed look at the factors involved in the use of full NPs for referential identification in discourse. As mentioned previously, the large majority of subjects involved in the choice between SV and VS are definite expressions. Only definite NPs (and an occasional pronoun) can occur in both preverbal and postverbal position. Pronominal elements usually refer to known elements in the discourse and such items tend to occur as Ø-anaphora in Chamorro narratives.

Table 1 already suggested that the kinds of definite NPs do not form a homogeneous class. The value for referential distance for all the subject referents varies from 1 to 20, with about a third of all subject referents clustering at each end of the scale. (About 34% of the subjects which have a value of 1 for referential distance maintain referential continuity, while about 29% of the subjects which have a value of 20 for referential distance are referentially maximally discontinuous.) Subject referents at each end of the spectrum are thus pragmatically very different.

In order to avoid the proverbial "apples and oranges" dilemma, I have compared the different types of NPs with respect to referential distance, thematic continuity, and ambiguity resolution. (The factor of ambiguity resolution will be discussed momentarily.) This comparison also sidesteps glossing over potential confounds when dealing with a heterogeneous class of elements.

Definite NPs in narrative discourse are most commonly used when the speaker assumes the hearer may have some trouble identifying the referent of an NP. The larger the gap between the previous mention of the participant and the new reference, the more likely a speaker tends to use a full definite NP (Givón (ed.) 1983c in general, and Cooreman 1983 specifically for Chamorro). This accounts for the fact that referents with a value of 20 for referential distance need to be coded as full NPs.

However, highly continuous NPs can also be coded as definite full NPs. There are two pragmatic reasons why a referent which maintains maximum referential continuity is coded as a definite full NP. First, the immediately preceding context may allow for some ambiguity as to the identity of the subject in the new clause. There may be more than one referent in the discourse register which could potentially fit a particular semantico-syntactic role in a new clause. This potential ambiguity can be resolved through the use of a full NP.

In addition, explicit reference may be made to referentially continuous subjects when a new paragraph is started or when a paragraph is resumed after a break. This particular phenomenon has also been discussed for English written narratives by Fox (1987).

Before giving the results of the data analysis, I will illustrate how potential ambiguity may come about.

a. The thematic participant may be broadened in scope:

(6) *Pues mu-maolek-ñaihon i nana. Parehu i nana yan*
then SG-good-little the mother same the mother and

i tata ma-toktok guatu i lahe-n-ñiha.
the father E.3PL-hug there the son-N-3PL.POS
'Then the mother started to feel somewhat better. Both the mother and the father hugged their son right there.'

The referential distance of 'both the mother and the father' is 1 since the referent of the previous clause, i.e. 'mother,' is continued as part of the reference. However, the referential identity is expanded to include the father and this expansion needs to be indicated explicitly. This is done by means of a full definite NP.

b. The thematic participant may have been narrowed in scope:

(7) *Ma-planeha para uma-na'-guaha dankolo na*
E.3PL-plan IRR IRR.3PL-CAUS-have big LINK

bautispo para i patgon-ñiha. Pues man-hasso
baptismal.party for the child-3PL.POSS then AP-think

i lahe ya ilek-ña...
the man and say-3SG.POSS
'They planned to have a big baptismal party for their child. Then the man thought of something and said...'

In Chamorro intransitive clauses, dual number is not indicated on the verb by means of a plural agreement marker, but by the morpheme for singular agreement. In transitive clauses, either singular or plural agreement (as in the first clause in (7)) can be found. Failure to use a definite NP to indicate exact reference to the singular subject in the antipassive clause above may lead to the mistaken identification of the subject with the dual referent (i.e. the mother and the father) of the previous sentence. The coding of the subject referent with a definite NP rules out any potential ambiguity.

c. Topic-shift:

(8) *...guaha um-i-'ipe i manha siha ya*
have EI.-RED-cut the green.coconut PL and

ha-na-na'i i biha. Ha-gimen i biha i
E.3SG-RED-give the old.lady E.3SG-drink the old.lady the

manha ya...
green.coconut and...
'...someone was cutting the green coconuts and giving them to the old lady. The old lady drank the green coconuts and...'

The subject of the last clause is the direct object of the previous clause. There is a shift from the referent 'someone' to 'the old lady' as the subject of the new clause. Without explicit reference to the 'old lady' the hearer may infer that the subject referent remained the same from one sentence to the next, i.e. that someone not only cut the coconuts and gave them to the old lady, but also drank them. Admittedly, this interpretation is somewhat implausible given the sequence in which the actions are presented in the narrative; nevertheless, the potential ambiguity exists. Thus the shift in primary topic (i.e. subject) between the two clauses calls for the use of a definite NP to ensure unambiguous reference.

There are possibly other situations in which ambiguity may arise and thus necessitate coding the subject as a definite NP even though the referential distance value is only one. In addition, one cannot but acknowledge the fact that speakers sometimes use the definite NP coding device without apparent reason, as in (9).

(9) *Ha-hungok ta'lo si rai este bunitu na klase-n son.*
E.3SG-hear again UNM king this pretty LINK type-N sound

Taya' si rai nai ha-hungok este siha,...
nothing UNM king when E.3SG-hear this PL
'Again the king heard these pretty tunes. Never (before) had the king heard these...'

In example (9), the second clause contains a subject which is referentially continuous. There is no potential ambiguity as to the identity of the subject in the second clause since no other plausible candidate for the role of subject is available in the immediate environment. Yet, the speaker chooses to code this unambiguous referent as a definite NP.

Ambiguity resolution correlates in a highly significant way with low values of referential distance (i.e. 1 or 2 in 88% of all instances of potential ambiguity resolution). It thus plays an important role in the use of definite full NPs for referentially continuous participants in the discourse. This is shown in Table 5.

One question remains to be resolved at this point: How does ambiguity resolution feature in the total picture of word order variation in Chamorro oral narratives?

Even though there was no significant interaction between word order and ambiguity resolution overall, Table 6 shows that within the group of clauses occurring at paragraph initial/break position, there was a statisti-

Table 5. Mean ranking for referential distance values for potentially ambiguous and non-ambiguous subject referents (Mann-Whitney U — Wilcoxon Rank W Test)

	Number of Cases	Mean Rank
potentially ambiguous	33	46.5
unambiguous	144	98.7
$Z = 5.5$, $p < .001$ (for directional prediction, corrected for ties)		

Table 6. Distributional frequency of potentially ambiguous and non-ambiguous subject referents in SV and VS clauses in paragraph initial/break position (Chi Square Test)

	Potentially ambiguous	Unambiguous
VS	6	13
SV	6	59
$\chi^2_{(DF=1)} = 4.31$ (continuity corrected) $p < .001$		

cally significant difference in the frequency with which potentially ambiguous as opposed to non-ambiguous referents appeared in the two possible word orders. (There was no such correlation within the group of clauses at medial/final paragraph position.)

Taking into account that SV is used more frequently in paragraph initial/break position than VS, Table 6 shows that VS is used with relative greater frequency than SV to mark potentially ambiguous referents. While the distributional frequency of SV and VS clauses in relation to potentially ambiguous and non-ambiguous referents is significantly different in paragraph initial/break position, no such statistical significance is reached when the three variables are taken into consideration at once.

However, there is evidence for a **trend** towards the preferred use of VS word order over SV word order as a marker for potentially ambiguous referents. This trend is shown in Table 7.

Table 7. Distributional frequency of SV and VS clauses over paragraph position for all potentially ambiguous subject referents (Chi Square Test)

	initial/break	medial/final
VS	6	16
SV	6	5

$\chi^2_{(DF=1)} = 2.08$ (continuity corrected) $p = .08$

It is worth noting that the data reported in Table 6 and Table 7 provide further indirect support for the claim that the marked SV order is essentially a marker for thematic discontinuity in Chamorro spoken narratives.

We are still left with a vexing question, however. Based on the results from the previous section regarding thematic continuity and the distribution of the two word order patterns, we would expect to find SV word order to occur more frequently at paragraph initial or break position. However, when the speaker resolves a potential ambiguity in the identification of a subject referent by means of the use of a definite NP, we may observe that the choice for VS is significantly more frequent in this position (see Table 6).

In view of this observation, I would like to reword the results from Section 5 as follows : Speakers choose the marked word order SV in paragraph inital/break position when all things are equal. But what happens if things are not equal? What if, in addition to keeping track of the organizational structure of the discourse, the speaker also feels the need to identify the subject referent in such a way as to prevent potential misidentification by the hearer?

I would like to suggest that in such a case, the speaker's cognitive ability to handle a number of complexities all at once may get overtaxed. Explicitly marking a referent to ensure proper identification may be cognitively costly and may prevent the speaker from paying due attention to matters of structural organization. The marked SV word order subsequently does not get used since the speaker does not have sufficient resources to process both marked situations at the same time. The use of a definite NP is marked since most subject referents in on-line discourse are already known, understood, and easlily retrievable from the context (see footnote 2) and are, as a result, only minimally coded in the narrative discourse (i.e. through a Ø-anaphor, or through verb agreement). The use of SV word order is marked since it occurs with highest frequency in situations where thematic continuity is disrupted. Again, the maintainance of thematic continuity can be assumed to be the norm since more propositions maintain rather than disrupt this continuity.

Intuitively, at least, it seems more crucial that the hearer can properly identify all the participants involved in the narrative than that he is explicitly made aware of how a particular clause features in the thematic development of the narrative by means of a special "flag", such as a change in word order. It seems that the latter type of information is more easily deduced from the context than the proper identity of an argument when there is more than one contender for the position. It should then not be too surprising that the speaker pays more attention to the process of reference tracking.

7. Conclusions

In this paper I have tried to explain the word order variation observed in Chamorro oral narratives. Earlier claims that word order inversion signals discourse cohesion or the lack thereof are supported by the Chamorro data. Two types of pragmatic principles at work in the maintenance of discourse cohesion have been compared: referential continuity and thematic continuity.

In general, word order variation is essentially dependent on the use of definite expressions in Chamorro, so that the choice of word order patterns will interact strongly with the pragmatic and/or semantic reasons for employing a definite expression in the on-going narrative.

With regard to the narratives examined for the present study, we can make the following observations: Definite noun phrases are used in subject position for mainly three reasons: (i) to resolve potential ambiguity as to the identity of the subject referent in the new clause (mainly with referentially continuous participants); (ii) when the subject referent is referentially discontinuous, i.e. when its value for referential distance is relatively high; and (iii) when the thematic continuity is disrupted either because a new paragraph starts or because the main event line is resumed after a break in the thematic paragraph.

In all three instances both SV and VS word order patterns **can** be used. However, there is a strong correlation between the use of the unmarked, basic VS word order and the first two instances, when thematic continuity is preserved. This should not be too surprising since preservation of thematic continuity is also the norm in a narrative. More clauses maintain rather than disturb this continuity, since there are far fewer breaks and paragraph beginnings than there are clauses in a story.

SV word order reflects most strongly the organizational structure of the discourse. SV is used most frequently when the thematic development of the story line is discontinued or temporarily disrupted. Despite the fact that SV is a marked word order, the data reported here show that — at least for transitive propositions — its occurrence is as frequent as that of the basic VS pattern. The reason for this — as indicated in the introduction — is that participants which maintain continuity are usually not coded explicitly, but rather are indicated solely by verb agreement in transitive clauses or Ø- anaphora in intransitive clauses.

While in some languages strong evidence can be found for a correlation between word order inversion and the degree of referential continuity displayed by the participants in subject position, the choice between VS and SV order in Chamorro does not seem very sensitive to this pragmatic principle. There is only a weak, though significant correlation between the use of the marked SV word order and more referentially discontinuous participants in the story when thematic continuity is maintained (see Table 3).

The Chamorro data thus provide further evidence for the existence of a hierarchical structure in narrative texts and underscore the need to take this structural organization into account when looking for functional explanations of linguistic phenomena in discourse.

Notes

1. This paper was supported in part by a grant for the Improvement of Doctoral Dissertation Research from the National Science Foundation No. BNS-8208781, and by a four year research grant from the Belgian National Fund for Scientific Research. It is an extensive revised version of part of chapter 8 in Cooreman (1987). I am grateful to my colleagues at the University of Tilburg, especially to Gisela Redeker, who initiated me in some useful statistical analyses reported in this paper.

Special thanks go to Talmy Givón who was a real inspiration during the course of the initial research. This paper also would never have come into existence without the help of a number of Chamorro native speakers who provided the narratives, helped transcribe and analyze them, and in general guided me towards a better understanding of some aspects of their language and culture. To them I dedicate this chapter.

2. As Dubois (1987) has shown, full reference to Agents in active transitive clauses is uncommon in narratives, since these are likely to be known, understood, and easily retrievable from the context. This claim is also substantiated in Chamorro.

3. The restriction to transitive propositions in this paper is a purely pragmatic one. The present study took place in the framework of a larger project on transitivity in Chamorro narratives in which the data base consisted of constructions coding transitive propositions only; these were entered into a computer data file for easy access. However, I also looked at a smaller sample of intransitive clauses, and the reader can be assured that the inclusion of intransitive propositions would not change the outcome of the present analysis in any major way.

4. Focus constructions containing the ergative infix *-um-* on the surface look like clauses in which the subject has been inverted and placed in preverbal position (see Cooreman 1987, chapter 7). However, these clauses are not taken into consideration in this paper for two reasons. First, they are pragmatically more marked than the SV clauses examined in this study, since they involve marked emphasis on the subject and occur in marked situations. Second, it is quite likely that these focus constructions should be analyzed as underlying VS clauses in which the extracted, focussed subject functions as the predicate of the rest of the clause, containing the only new piece of information in the entire proposition. The remainder of the clause is — as I have argued elsewhere (Cooreman 1987, chapter 7) — presupposed. Example:

a. *Ha-sakke i patgon i kareta.*
E.3S-steal the child the car
'The child stole the car.'

b. *I patgon s-um-akke i kareta.*
the child EI-steal the car
'It was the child who stole the car.'

5. The following abbreviations have been used in the morpheme-by-morpheme transcription of the sample sentences: E.1S, etc. ergative agreement, first person, singular, etc., EI ergative infix, IRR irrealis complementizer, IRR.1SG, etc. first singular irrealis agreement, etc., N epenthetic *n*.

References

Bentivoglio, Paola. 1983. "Continuity and Discontinuity in Discourse: A Study on Latin-American Spoken Spanish." *Topic Continuity in Discourse: A Quantitative Cross-Language Study* (= *Typological Atudies in Language 3*) ed. by T. Givón, 255-311. Amsterdam: John Benjamins.

Cooreman, Ann. 1983. "Topic Continuity and the Voicing System of an Ergative Language: Chamorro." *Topic Continuity in Discourse: A Quantitative Cross-Language Study* (= *Typological Studies in Language 3*) ed. by T. Givón, 425-489. Amsterdam: John Benjamins.

Cooreman, Ann. 1987. *Transitivity and Discourse Continuity in Chamorro Narratives* (= *Empirical Approaches to Language Typology 4*). Berlin: Mouton de Gruyter.

Dubois, John W. 1987. "The Discourse Basis of Ergativity." *Language* 63.805-855.

Fox, Andrew. 1983. "Topic Continuity in Biblical Hebrew." *Topic Continuity in Discourse: A Quantitative Cross-Language Study* (= *Typological Studies in Language 3*) ed. by T. Givón, 215-254. Amsterdam: John Benjamins.

Fox, Barbara. 1985. "Word Order Inversion and Discourse Continuity in Tagalog. *Quantified Studies in Discourse* ed. by T. Givón, 138-159. Special issue of Text.

Fox, Barbara. 1987. "Anaphora in Popular Written English Narratives." *Coherence and Grounding in Discourse* (= *Typological Studies in Language 11*) ed. by Russell S. Tomlin, 157-174. Amsterdam: John Benjamins.

Givón, T. 1979. *On Understanding Grammar*. New York: Academic Press.

Givón, T. 1980. *Ute Reference Grammar*. Ignacio, Colorado: Ute Press.

Givón, T. 1983a. "Topic Continuity and Word Order Pragmatics in Ute." *Topic Continuity in Discourse: A Quantitative Cross-Language Study* (= *Typological Studies in Language 3*) ed. by T. Givón, 141-214. Amsterdam: John Benjamins.

Givón, T. 1983b. "Topic Continuity in Discourse: An Introduction." *Topic Continuity in Discourse: A Quantitative Cross-Language Study* (= *Typological Studies in Language 3*) ed. by T. Givón, 1-42. Amsterdam: John Benjamins.

Givón, T. (ed.) 1983c. *Topic Continuity in Discourse: A Quantitative Cross-Language Study (= Typological Studies in Language 3)*. Amsterdam: John Benjamins.

Tomlin, Russell S. 1987. *Linguistic Reflections of Cognitive Events. Coherence and Grounding in Discourse* (= *Typological Studies in Language 11*) ed. by Russell S. Tomlin, 455-479. Amsterdam: John Benjamins.

Word Order and Temporal Sequencing

John Myhill
University of Michigan

Cross-linguistic evidence suggests that among languages of a certain word order type there is a universal correlation between temporal sequencing and verb-subject (VS) word order.[1] The strongest hypothesis consistent with presently available data is the following: in all languages with over 60% VS word order overall, VS word order is statistically correlated with temporally sequenced clauses, while SV word order is associated with unsequenced clauses. In languages with less than 40% VS order, there does not seem to be any correlation between sequencing and word order; in languages with between 40% and 60% VS order, if there is a correlation, it will be relatively weak. Thus far, this correlation has only been investigated in languages which are strongly verb-object (VO), having this order more than 90% of the time; it is not clear what will be found in languages with a higher incidence of OV order.

A temporally sequenced clause is one which advances the time reference of a narrative. This is exemplified in (1):

(1) *I was reading in the library. This guy walked up to me and asked me if we had met somewhere. I looked at him carefully. He had a long nose...*

The temporally sequenced clauses here are those with the verbs *walked, asked*, and *looked*. The other clauses are unsequenced: *reading* is progressive, *met* is perfect/anterior, having taken place earlier, and *had* is stative. Habitual clauses (*I read in the library every day*) are another type of unsequenced clause. This concept of "temporally sequenced clause" is equivalent to what Labov (1972) calls a **narrative clause** and what Hopper

(1979) calls a **foregrounded clause**. I prefer to use the term "temporally sequenced" because the terms "narrative" and "foregrounded" have other possible referents.

Thus far, correlations between sequencing and VS order have been found in Early Biblical Hebrew (Givón 1977), the Mayan languages Tzotzil and Chorti, and 17th century Spanish (Myhill 1984). Data showing this are given in Tables 1-4.[2]

Table 1. Tzotzil (from Myhill 1984)

	Overall	Sequenced	Unsequenced	
N	899	244	655	
VS%	80%	92%	76%	$p<.005$

Table 2. Early Biblical Hebrew (from Givón 1977)

	Overall	Sequenced	Unsequenced
Genesis			
N	424	194	230
VS%	64%	87%	44%
Kings			
N	446	227	219
VS%	65%	77%	52%
Esther			
N	239	125	104
VS%	66%	73%	56%

Table 3. Chorti (from Myhill 1984)

	Overall	Sequenced	Unsequenced	
N	184	32	152	
VS%	51%	72%	47%	$p<.025$

Table 4. Spanish (from Myhill 1984)

	Overall	Sequenced	Unsequenced	
N	2000	316	1684	
VS%	44%	58%	41%	$p<.005$

Hopper 1979 also reports that VS order is associated with temporal sequencing in Old English, which has approximately the same frequency of VS order as Spanish. (But he but does not give quantitative data to demonstrate this.) In all of these cases, the frequency of VS order is higher with sequenced clauses than with unsequenced clauses. This is not to say that sequencing alone is what determines order of subject and verb in these languages. As can be seen, the relationship between sequencing and VS order is far from categorical, nor is there a perfect correlation between lack of sequencing and SV order. Other factors also play an important role in determining word order in these languages, for example, the discourse status of the subject and whether the clause is a main clause or a subordinate clause. Nevertheless, Tables 1-4 clearly show that all four languages display the same type of relationship between word order and sequencing.

Let us now consider some concrete examples of this pattern. Example (2), from Biblical Hebrew, shows 5 instances of VS order in temporally sequenced clauses:[3]

(2)

va-yo7mer	*7elohim:*	*'yəhi*	*7or'*	*va-yhi*	*7or;*	*va-yar7*
and-said(IMP)	God	is	light	and-was	light	and-saw(IMP)
V	S			V	S	V

7elohim	*7et*	*ha-7or*	*ki*	*tov*	*va-yavdel*	*7elohim*
God	ACC	the-light	that	good	and-divided(IMP)	God
S					V	S

beyn	*ha-7or*	*u-veyn*	*ha-ḥoshex,*	*va-yiqra7*
between	*the-light*	*and-between*	*the-darkness*	*and-called(IMP)*
				V

7elohim	*la-7or*	*yom...*
God	to-the-lightness	day
S		

'...and God said: "Let there be light", and there was light, and God saw the light, that it was good, and God divided between the light and the darkness, and God called the lightness Day...' (Genesis 1:3-5)

Example (3) has two more instances of temporally sequenced VS clauses. However, the final clause of (3) is anterior, since the snake's action of deceiving the woman has already been reported; thus SV order is used in the final clause:

(3)

va-yo7mer	*7elohim*	*la-7ishah*	*mah-zot*	*9asita*
and-said(IMP)	God	to-the-woman	what-this	you-did(PRF)
V	S			

va-to7mer	*ha-7ishah*	*ha-naḥash*	*hishi7ani*
and-said(IMP)	the-woman	the-serpent	deceived-me(PRF)
V	S	S	V

'...and God said to the woman "What have you done?" and the woman said "The serpent deceived me"...' (Genesis 3:13)

Similarly, in (4) the temporally sequenced action of the man talking is VS, while the action of the woman giving the fruit to the man is unsequenced and SV:

(4)

...va-yo7mer	*ha-7adam:*	*'ha-7ishah*	*asher*	*natatah*	*9imadi*
and-said	the-man	the-woman	who	you-gave	to-me
V		S			

hi7	*natnah*	*li*	*min*	*ha-9ec*	*va-7oxel...'*
she	gave	to-me	from	the-tree	and-I-ate
S	V				

'...and the man said: "The woman you gave me, she gave to me from the tree and I ate."' (Genesis 3:12)

Example (5) from Chorti illustrates the same pattern.

(5)

...i	*kondixto*	*lumui,*	*kai*	*u-tx'*	*u-iotot-o7p*	*otro*
and	when	left	began	3-do	their-house-PL	other

niahr	*i*	*e-txan*	*iaha7a*	*io7opa*	*tama*	*inte7e*	*lugar*
time	and	the-snake	that	came	to	a	place
		S		V			

u-7ka7pa7a	*santa*	*barba.*	*pero*	*e-lugar*	*aro7pna*	*al*
its-name	S.	B.	but	the-place	is-called	El

inkuentro.	*por ke7e*	*txe*	*ke7e*	*ia*	*u-tahu'*	*u7p'-o7p*
I.	because	say	that	there	3-met	each-other-pl
					V	

e-txan	*iaha7a*	*taka*	*otro*	*'nte7e*	*txan*	*tari*	*tama*
the-snake	that	with	other	a	snake	came	from
					S		

e-parte Ipala...
part I.
'...and when she (the snake) had passed, they began to build their houses again, and that snake came to a place called Santa Barbara, but that place is called El Encuentro ("The Meeting" in Spanish). Because they say that that snake met with another snake (who) had come by way of Ipala.' (Fought 1972:104)

In example (5), the snake has just destroyed a village. In the first two clauses the scene is still this village. In the third clause, the scene shifts to the snake coming to Santa Barbara. This action is not sequenced with the preceding clause. (Because of the scene shift, it is not clear whether the snake came to Santa Barbara first, or the people began to rebuild their houses first). The clause is therefore SV. However, when the snake meets another snake, this is clearly sequenced relative to the snake coming to Santa Barbara, and the clause is VS.

The association between VS order and sequencing appears to be restricted to languages with a relatively high incidence of VS order. In languages with more SV order, this tendency diappears (and may even be reversed). Thus consider data from Rumanian in Table 5.[4]

The data in Table 5 actually suggest that in terms of percentages, sequencing is more associated with **SV** order; however, a multivariate analysis taking other factors affecting word order into consideration found that temporal sequencing did not have a significant effect upon word order.

Even more striking are data from Biblical Hebrew, a language written over a period of several hundred years and showing varying frequencies of VS order across time. Table 6, from Givón (1977), shows that the three books with the highest overall incidence of VS order, Genesis, Kings, and Esther (which are, according to Givón, diachronically the earliest), are the only three books where VS order is more likely in sequenced clauses; in the books with a lower overall incidence of VS order, there is actually a tendency for sequencing to be associated with SV order.[5]

There is fairly little difference in the frequency of VS order in unsequenced clauses in the five books. There is, however, an enormous difference in the frequency of VS order in sequenced clauses. Thus, the change in frequency of VS order in Biblical Hebrew was basically a change in the order of **sequenced** clauses; unsequenced clauses hardly changed their frequency of VS order at all.

Table 5. Rumanian (from Myhill 1984)

	Overall	Sequenced	Unsequenced
N	554	113	441
VS%	31%	22%	33%
SV%	69%	78%	67%

Table 6. Biblical Hebrew (from Givón 1977)

	Overall	Sequenced	Unsequenced
Genesis			
N	424	194	230
VS%	64%	87%	44%
Kings			
N	446	227	219
VS%	65%	77%	52%
Esther			
N	239	125	104
VS%	66%	73%	56%
Ecclesiastes			
N	262	52	210
VS%	44%	21%	50%
Song of Solomon			
N	158	33	125
VS%	35%	18%	39%

We have seen evidence suggesting that the correlation between sequencing and VS order is limited to languages with a relatively high incidence of VS order. A multivariate analysis done on the data from Tzotzil, Chorti, Spanish, and Rumanian, considering simultaneously other factors affecting word order, found that the effect of sequencing is strongest in the most strongly VS languages, growing weaker in languages with less VS order, and finally disappearing in Rumanian, which has only 31% VS order. This is consistent with the data from Biblical Hebrew (on which I have not done a multivariate analysis because I have not had access to it), where we see that sequencing favored VS order when the language had a high overall frequency of VS order, but the correlation between VS order and sequencing disappeared as SV order become more common overall.

In Tzotzil, the language with the highest incidence of VS order of those investigated (80%), a distinction was made between **topicalization** SV constructions (translating as, e.g. *As for Bill, he hates beans*) and **focus** SV constructions (translating as, e.g. ***Bill*** (as opposed to anyone else) *hates beans*). These two types of SV constructions are clearly distinguished in Tzotzil by both intonation and the presence of special markers. Such topicalization and focusing of the subject do not, of course, produce a change in word order in English, which is SV in any case, but they do produce a change in Tzotzil, which is normally VS. Note that in focused SV constructions, everything besides the subject is presupposed. In topicalized SV constructions, on the other hand, the non-topicalized part of the sentence represents non-presuppositional information. Focused SV constructions are characteristic of the most strongly VS languages; put another way, those languages with the strictest VS order (e.g. Irish and Squamish) use SV order **only** for focused subjects, not for topicalized subjects. If the strongest correlation between VS order and sequencing is to be found in the most strongly VS languages, then we would expect sequencing to most strongly disfavor subject focusing, which is characteristic of the most strongly VS languages. We will see that this is indeed the case.

Multivariate analyses were done of the factors affecting the frequency of five different types of SV order, that is, SV focusing in Tzotzil, SV topicalization in Tzotzil, and SV order in Chorti, Spanish and Rumanian. The statistical analysis (VARBRUL-2 (see Sankoff and Labov 1979)) produces PROB[6] values between 0 and 1, with values larger than .5 favoring SV order and factors lower than .5 disfavoring SV order. The results are shown in Table 7.

Table 7. Relationship between frequency of SV order and effect of sequencing

	Frequency	Non-sequencing PROB
Tzotzil focusing	5%	.82
Tzotzil topicalization	15%	.66
Chorti SV	49%	.67
Spanish SV	56%	.57
Rumanian SV	69%	.47

Table 7 shows that the more common an SV construction is in the language overall, the less strongly it is associated specifically with unsequenced clauses. The least common type of SV construction, Tzotzil subject focusing, is almost exclusively found in unsequenced clauses, while the most common SV construction, in Rumanian, is found essentially equally in sequenced and unsequenced clauses. Thus the factors affecting word order variation are not constant from one language to another, but vary depending upon the relative overall frequency of VS and SV order.

The data presented here suggest that variation in frequency of VS order in the languages investigated mostly just amounts to variation in frequency of VS order in **sequenced** clauses. These languages show much less variation in frequency of VS order in **unsequenced** clauses. It is of course hardly surprising that the frequency of VS order in sequenced clauses increases as we look at languages with a higher overall frequency of VS order. What is more surprising (and interesting) is that the frequency of VS order in **unsequenced** clauses does **not** increase sharply as we look at languages with a higher overall frequency of VS order. For example, the data in Table 6 show that there was little or no correlation between overall VS frequency and unsequenced clause VS frequency in the different stages of Biblical Hebrew. The change from VS to SV order was really just a change in order in sequenced clauses; order in unsequenced clauses stayed pretty much the same.

Up to this point I have only talked about the order of the subject and the verb. It appears that in general in the languages under consideration, temporally sequenced clauses have the verb before **any** other constituent (not just the subject),[7] while unsequenced clauses have **some** constituent before the the verb; if the subject is not preverbal, then something else will be. This is exemplified in (6-7) from Biblical Hebrew and (8) from Tzotzil. In (6), when God creating man is first mentioned, the clause is sequenced and verb-initial. The two subsequent mentions of God creating man are not sequenced, since they specify the manner in which God created man:

(6)	*va-yivra7*	*7elohim*	*7et*	*ha-7adam,*	*bə-celem*	*7elohim*
	and-created(IMP)	God	ACC	the-man	in-image-of	God
	V	S			PP	

	bara7	*7otam,*	*zaxar*	*u-nqeyva*	*bara7*
	he-created(PERF)	them	male	and-female	he-created(PERF)
	V		COMP NP		V

7otam...
them
'...and God created Man, in the image of God He created them, (as) male and female He created them...' (Genesis 1:27)

In (6), the fronted preverbal constituents are a prepositional phrase and a nominal complement. In (7), a direct object is fronted in the unsequenced clause:

(7) *...va-yo7mer* *lo* *7ayekah,* *va-yo7mer* *7et*
and-he-said(IMP) to-him where-are-you and-he-said(IMP) ACC

qol-xa *shama9ti* *bagan...*
voice-your I-heard(PERF) in-the-garden
OBJ V
'...and He said to him "Where are you?" and he (the man) said "I heard Your voice in the garden..."' (Genesis 3:10)

In (8), from Tzotzil, a direct object is focused. Note that the clause with the focused object is unsequenced: the previous clause mentions that they ate at the house, and they could not have eaten until they were given something:

(8) *...te* *live7otikotik* *ta* *s-na* *li* *7otro* *jun* *7intyo* *7une,*
there ate(1PL) at his-house the other a Indian

bek'et *7iyak'...*
meat gave(3SG)
FOCUS V
'We ate there at the house of the other Indian, meat he gave us...' (Laughlin 1980:13)

Statistical evidence also shows that object focusing in Tzotzil resembles subject focusing in being almost categorically incompatible with sequencing (there was a single token each of a focused subject and a focused object in sequenced clauses). This is shown in Table 8.[8]

Table 8. Object focusing in Tzotzil

	Overall	Sequenced	Unsequenced	
N	899	348	563	
Focusing%	5%	0%	9%	$p < .005$

It has been noted (e.g. Givón 1983) that preverbal constituents often serve a contrastive function. This can be shown to relate to the correlation between lack of sequencing and non-verb-initial syntax. Consider, for example, the following passage from Biblical Hebrew:

(9)

va-yhi	*hevel*	*ro9eh*	*co7n*	*və-qayin*
and-became(IMP)	Abel	shepherd	of-flocks	and-Cain
V	S			S

hayah	*9oved*	*7adamah,*	*va-yhi*	*miqec*	*yamim*
became(PERF)	tiller	of-ground	and-was(IMP)	end	of-days
V				V	S

va-yave7	*qayin*	*mi-pri*	*ha-7adamah*	*minḥah*
and-brought(IMP)	Cain	from-fruit-of	the-ground	offering

lə-YHWH,	*və-hevel*	*hevi7*	*gam-hu7*	*mi*
to-Jehovah	and-Abel	brought(PERF)	also-he	from
	S	V		

-bxorot	*co7n-o*	*umeḥelvehen,*	*va-yisha9*
-the-firstlings-of	flocks-his	even-of-their-fat	and-favored(IMP)
			V

YHWH	*7el-hevel*	*və-7el-minḥat-o*	*və-7el-qayin*
Jehovah	to-Abel	and-to-offering-his	and-to-Cain
S			INDIRECT OBJ

v-7el-minḥat-o	*lo*	*sha9ah...*
and-to-offering-his	not	(he)favored(PERF)
		V

'...and Abel became a shepherd of flocks, and Cain became a tiller of the ground, and it was the end of the day, and Cain brought an offering to Jehovah of the fruit of the ground, and Abel also brought from the firstlings of his flocks, even from their fat, and Jehovah favored Abel and his offering and He did not favor Cain and his offering...' (Genesis 4:2-5)

It seems reasonable to suggest on the basis of these data that a clause can be integrated into a narrative in (at least) two possible ways. First, a clause can be seen as one of a series of events which basically tell what happened in a narrative in the order that it happened. The thematic link between these events is temporal, in that they are assumed to have occurred in the temporal order in which they are narrated. Clauses integrated into the text in this way will be verb-initial in a strongly VS language like the Biblical Hebrew of Genesis, so that a list of the clause-initial verbs in a narrative will give a skeletal outline of the temporal development of the narrative. The second possibility is for a clause to be seen as one of a series of clauses each of which says something about one of a set of thematically linked entities (e.g., in (9), Cain and Abel are thematically linked by being brothers). When a clause serves this latter purpose, initial position in Biblical Hebrew is occupied by the constituent referring to the member of the set of thematically linked entities. Consider how this applies to (9); the skeleton of the narrative structure of (9) can be paraphrased as (10):

(10) *Cain and Abel took jobs, and it was the end of the day, and they brought offerings to Jehovah, and Jehovah reacted to their offerings.*

Three of these four events are represented by separate clauses for Cain and Abel in (9). In each case, when the first of these events is reported, the time reference of the narrative is advanced, another of the actions in (10) is reported for the first time, and the verb comes first in the clause; these clauses are integrated into the narrative in terms of their temporal reference, as one of a group of clauses which advance the story line. On the other hand, the second of each of these matched clauses is integrated into the narrative by evoking a comparison between the brothers, and the constituent referring to the brother is put before the verb. In this case, temporal organization is irrelevant: thus, it is not clear and does not matter whether Abel became a shepherd first or Cain became a farmer first. On the other hand, it **does** matter that God reacted to their offerings **after** they were brought to him (in fact the story only makes sense that way). Thus temporal sequencing is essentially incompatible with contrast between characters so that the correlation between contrast and non-verb-initial order noted by Givón is the other side of the coin of the correlation between temporal sequencing and verb-initial order discussed in the present paper.

We can say that in languages with a relatively high frequency of VS order, the basic principle of discourse organization is that the most important new information in the clause comes first. If there is only one piece of new information in the clause, i.e., if some constituent is focused, that constituent comes first.[9] If some NP, PP, or adverb is used contrastively, that comes first. If the verb is temporally sequenced and tells the next in a series of events, then the verb comes first. This principle of "new information first" in strongly VS languages contrasts with the principle of "old information first" which has been argued for in strongly SV languages (Contreras 1978).

As stated in the introduction, this pattern of associating temporally sequenced clauses with VS order in strongly VS languages has only been investigated in strongly VO languages. However, the genetic diversity of the languages investigated which demonstrate this pattern makes it reasonable to suggest that this correlation may be a language universal. It remains to be seen whether similar patterns hold for languages with a greater frequency of OV order.[10]

Notes

1. I thank Doris Payne for her helpful comments on an earlier draft of this paper. The first studies discussing the relationship of VS order and temporal sequencing were Givón (1977) and Hopper (1979), which discussed this relationship in individual languages (Biblical Hebrew and Old English, respectively). The suggestion that this relationship is found in all and only languages with a high overall frequency of VS order was to my knowledge first made in Myhill (1984).

2. The Tzotzil data were taken from Laughlin (1977, 1980), the Chorti data were taken from Fought (1972), and the Spanish data were taken from Cervantes (1605). Multivariate analysis also showed all of the differences in Tzotzil, Chorti, and Spanish to be statistically significant. Givón (1977) does not report significance results for Biblical Hebrew. I have calculated the frequencies for Biblical Hebrew assuming that what I call "temporal sequencing" is equivalent to what Givón calls "continuity", which appears to be justified based upon Givón's discussion. However, I have counted copulas in the "continuity function" as not sequenced, as copulas are almost invariably not sequenced.

   Temporally sequenced clauses are statistically likely to be completive, and it might seem reasonable to suggest that it is completive aspect rather than sequencing which favors VS order. The only evidence I have bearing on this question is from Spanish, and this evidence suggests that it is sequencing rather than completive aspect which favors VS order. Spanish has a verb form, the preterite, which is used in past completive clauses; this form shows the highest frequency of VS order of any Spanish verb form, However, a multivariate statistical analysis of Spanish word order including both sequencing and verb form as independent variables showed that the preterite does not in itself have any effect on word order; rather, temporal sequencing is associated with both VS order and the use of the preterite, so that the correlation between the preterite and VS order is an artifact. This shows that it is sequencing and not completive aspect which favors VS order.

3. I thank Gene Schramm for his help in transliterating the Biblical Hebrew data.

4. The Rumanian data were taken from Eliade (1969a, 1969b) and Niculescu (1969).

5. Givón also gives data from another book, Lamentations, but, for reasons which are not explained, he excludes copulas from the data from Lamentations although he includes them in his data from the other books. Copulas are, in general, associated with SV order in Biblical Hebrew (and to my knowledge all strongly VO languages with a relatively high frequency of VS order). The following table gives Givón's data from Lamentations:

Word order in Lamentations

	Overall	Sequenced	Unsequenced
N	119	69	50
VS%	60%	49%	74%

Presumably, the VS percentage for "overall" and "unsequenced" here would be considerably lower if copulas were included (as they are in the data from the other Biblical Hebrew books), because in general the great majority of copulas are SV. On the other hand, since very few copulas are sequenced, the "sequenced" percentage here would be basically unchanged. Thus the overall VS percentage for Lamentations would be comparable to that of Ecclesiastes and Song of Solomon, and the VS percentage for sequenced and unsequenced clauses would be fairly close. The Lamentations data would then support the hypotheses that sequencing only favors VS order in languages with an overall high frequency of VS order, since these data would show a relatively low (less than 50%) frequency of overall VS order and no correlation between sequencing and VS order.

6. PROB is an abbreviation for "probability". This term here does not mean simply "percentage" but is used in the technical statistical sense to refer to the value assigned to the coefficient associated with a particular factor which produces the closest fit between the predicted and observed occurrences of each word order for all of the different combinations of factors.

7. I am not including conjunctions such as Hebrew *va-* in this statement.

8. I did not calculate the effect of sequencing on object topicalization in Tzotzil, as any kind of object topicalization in that language is extremely rare (about 2% of the data).

9. There is not universal agreement on how to use the term "new information", and some linguists might object to using it here to refer to focused constituents, which are frequently pronominal or definite NPs, in which case their referents must have already been mentioned in the discourse. I am here using the term "new information" as a convenient cover term, including (in addition to indefinite and contrastive NPs) any focused constituents, which are new in the sense that they represent the only information in their clause which cannot be presupposed from the immediately preceding discourse. I recognize of course that there are differences between these different types of "new information".

10. Hopper (1979) notes that temporal sequencing in Old English is associated with VS and OV orders and suggests that the real generalization is that temporally sequenced verbs tend to be **peripheral**. I do not know of any other studies of the relationship between sequencing and verb-**final** order and so this must remain speculation at this point.

References

Cervantes Saavedra, Miguel de. 1605. *El ingenioso hidalgo Don Quijote de la Mancha.*

Contreras, Heles. 1978. *El orden de palabras en español.* Madrid: Catedra.

Eliade, Mircea. 1969a. "Douăsprezece mii de capete de vita". *Tappe* 1969, 10-33.

Eliade, Mircea. 1969b. "Un om mare". *Tappe* 1969, 34-75.

Fought, John G. 1972. *Chorti (Mayan) Texts.* Philadelphia: University of Pennsylvania Press.

Givón, T. 1977. "The Drift from VSO to SVO in Biblical Hebrew: The pragmatics of tense-aspect". *Mechanisms of Syntactic Change*, ed. by Charles N. Li, 181-254. Austin: Univeristy of Texas Press.

Givón, T., ed. 1983. *Topic Continuity in Discourse: A Quantitative Cross-Language Study.* Amsterdam: John Benjamins.

Hopper, Paul J. 1979. "Aspect and Foregrounding in Discourse". *Syntax and Semantics vol. 12: Discourse and Syntax*, ed. by T. Givón, 213-41. New York: Academic Press.

Labov, William. 1972. "The Transformation of Experience in Narrative Syntax". *Language in the Inner City.* Philadelphia: University of Pennsylvania Press.

Laughlin, Robert. 1977. *Of Cabbages and Kings: Tales from Zinacantan.* Washington: Smithsonian Institution Press.

Laughlin, Robert. 1980. *Of Shoes and ships and Sealing Wax: Sundries from Zinacantan.* Washington: Smithsonian Institution Press.

Myhill, John. 1984. *A Study of Aspect, Word Order, and Voice.* University of Pennsylvania Ph.D. dissertation.

Niculescu, Mihai. 1969. "Cizmarul din Hydra". *Tappe* (ed.), 76-99.

Sankoff, David, and William Labov. 1979. "On the Uses of Variable Rules". *Language in Society* 8.189-222.

Tappe, Eric, ed. 1969. *Fantastic Tales.* London: Dillon's.

Word Order and Discourse Type
An Austronesian Example[1]

J. Stephen Quakenbush
Summer Institute of Linguistics

1. Introduction

Although several different methods have been employed to determine the basic word or constituent order of a language, it has been argued that textual frequency, the simplest method, yields a sufficiently clear indication in many cases.[2] It might be expected then, that a count of text data in a language commonly regarded as verb-initial would yield a majority of verb-first constructions. Austronesian languages, and Philippine languages in particular, are commonly characterized as verb-initial. Yet actual counts of texts in Agutaynen,[3] a Philippine language of Palawan province, show that in some types of texts, "subject-like nominals" precede the verb more often than not. If Agutaynen does indeed have a "basic" word order of V-first, how should we account for this preponderance of pre-verbal NPs? In this paper I will consider some of the recent research bearing on the issue of fronted NPs in variable word order languages, briefly discuss the notion of discourse type, and illustrate how pre-verbal NPs function in Agutaynen. I will argue that the notion of discourse type can be crucial in the analysis of constituent order.

1.1 Definition of pre-verbal NP

Before proceeding, it is necessary to define precisely the term "pre-verbal NP". I resorted to the term "subject-like nominal" above because the issue of what constitutes "subject" in Philippine languages is by no means clear-cut.[4] By this term I mean the nominal within a clause which obligatorily takes the case marker used to mark the sole argument of an intransitive clause. In Agutaynen, as in Tagalog, this marker is *ang*. In traditional Philippine analyses, *ang* is said to mark the "Topic" NP, or the NP that is "in focus". Alternatively, if an ergative analysis is accepted for such a Philippine language, *ang* would receive the label "absolutive marker".[5]

In Agutaynen, as in Tagalog, there are three case marking particles. Following tradition, I will refer to these as Topic, Non-Topic, and Oblique. (Alternatively, they could be called Absolutive, Ergative and Oblique.) Topic NPs are the most likely candidates for pre-verbal position in Agutaynen, and are the only constructions under consideration in this paper.[6] It is also possible, though rare, to front Oblique NPs and adverbial phrases. It is ungrammatical, however, to front a Non-Topic NP.

As is the case with many of the world's languages, many clauses in Philippine languages contain no verb. Schachter & Otanes (1972: 60) describe the two components of basic sentences in Tagalog as "predicate" and "topic", with the predicate being nominal, adjectival or verbal in form. In each case, the predicate is said to precede the topic. Thus, while it would be more precise to speak of "pre-predicate NPs", I will continue to use the more common expression "pre-verbal NP".

At least two types of pre-verbal *ang*-marked NPs can be distinguished in Agutaynen. These are illustrated in (1) through (4) below, with the pre-verbal NPs bracketed for ease of identification.[7]

Delimiting component

(1) *[Ang to-tok] ay masinggi tang kaloliot may lambong.*
TOP clothing INV red TOP pants and shirt
'[(As for) clothing], the pants and shirts are red.'

(2) *[Ang taw] ge-ley da lamang tang pama-bat.*
TOP people little already only TOP meet
'[(As for) people], (there are) now only a few who gather.‘

Fronted NP

(3) *[Ang tang gropo] ay pagpaita tang to-tok*
TOP one group INV shows DEF.NON-TOP clothing
tang mga kristiano.
GEN PL Christian
'[The one group] wears the clothing of the Christians.'

(4) *[Ang mga gamit] ay bangkaw may taming.*
TOP PL equipment INV spear and shield
'[The equipment] consists of spears and shields.'

In (1) and (2) the pre-verbal NPs serve as "delimiting components",[8] which are external to the main clause. They give "extra" information to orient the hearer to what is to follow, but they are not grammatically clause Topics, nor are they crucial for the semantic interpretation of the clauses with which they are associated. The grammatical Topics of (1) and (2) actually occur post-verbally.

In (3) and (4), on the other hand, the pre-verbal NPs are clause-internal. They serve grammatically as clause-level Topics, and are crucial to the proper interpretation of the meaning of their clauses. If the pre-verbal NP is deleted in (3), the resulting sentence becomes ambiguous out of context, with the possible meaning 'The Christians show the clothing'. It will be noted that in (4) the initial NP actually precedes a nominal predicate. If the initial NP is deleted here, we are left with a clause fragment that is uninterpretable out of context.

In (1), (3) and (4) the fronting of the pre-verbal NP is flagged by the Inversion marker *ay*. The occurrence of *ay* is optional, however, as can be seen from examples (2) and (5).

(5) *[Ang kristianos may moslim] pamagsoay.*
TOP Christian and Muslim fight
'[The Christians and Muslims] fight.'

Preliminary investigation indicates that speakers vary with regard to how frequently they use *ay* to indicate a pre-verbal NP. Since it can also signal a delimiting component or adverbial in initial position, in some texts there are more *ay*'s than pre-verbal NPs. In other texts there are about half as many *ay*'s as pre-verbal NPs.

It is possible to get both a delimiting component and a fronted NP in the same sentence, as in (6).

(6) *[Ang to-tok tang mga kristianos] [ang kolor*
TOP clothing GEN PL Christians TOP color

na] ay asol obin lagem.
3SG INV blue or black
'[(As for) the clothing of the Christians], [its color] is blue or black.'

What sort of explanation can we offer for the existence (and preponderance) of these pre-verbal NPs in Agutaynen? Before describing my database in greater detail, I will consider several recent works bearing on the issue.

2. Fronted NPs across languages

A good deal of recent linguistic research bears on the question of when NPs occur clause initially in flexible word order languages. Four streams can be distinguished according to the theoretical concepts utilized in investigating word order. I summarize them here as studies dealing with (1) continuity; (2) discourse units; (3) information packaging; and (4) discourse threads.

2.1 Continuity studies

In his well-known 1983 work, *Topic continuity in Discourse,* Givón and his associates demonstrated for a variety of languages the general principle that highly discontinuous (or contrastive, or "surprising") topics get flagged in special ways morpho-syntactically. To measure topic continuity, these researchers employed Givón's metrics of referential distance (look-back), potential interference (ambiguity), and persistence (decay). With regard to many flexible word order languages, it was shown that highly discontinuous topics tend to come in pre-verbal position. This pattern was convincingly demonstrated for such diverse languages as Spanish, Ute and Chamorro. The last language, which belongs to the Austronesian family, was characterized by Givón as a "fairly rigid verb-initial language that nevertheless allows highly contrastive/discontinuous NPs — primarily subject — to be moved pre-verbally (thus an SVO variant)" (1983: 29). He further generalized that in this respect Chamorro represented a situation that was "fairly characteristic of the V-first languages of the Austronesian family" (1983: 29).

Fox (1985) represented a further development and application of Givón's (1983) methods for measuring continuity. Analyzing *ay* inversion in Tagalog (which corresponds to pre-verbal NPs), she demonstrated again that high continuity yields low morphosyntactic complexity, and that low continuity yields high morphosyntactic complexity. With her broader measures for discourse continuity, Fox also showed that there was a strong correlation between *ay* inversion and the beginning of new episodes in a narrative.

2.2 Discourse units

In his 1987 collection, *Coherence and Grounding in Discourse*, Tomlin argued strongly against the recency/distance approach to topic continuity taken in Givón (1983), on the basis that it admitted too many potential counterexamples without any systematic explanation for them. Dealing with the use of noun phrases versus pronouns in spoken English participant reference, Tomlin pointed out that the following questions had to be asked: "How much distance is required to trigger a full NP?" and "How little distance is needed to guarantee the use of a pronoun?" A simple recency/distance approach cannot answer these questions, Tomlin says, but an "attention-driven episodic/paragraph model" can: "Individuals will use full nouns on first mention after an episode boundary ... and ... pronouns to sustain reference during an episode" (1987: 475).

In the same collection, Fox's article on "Anaphora in popular written English narratives" also demonstrated the shortcomings of a strictly linear approach, concluding that "if we are to understand the use of various linguistic devices in naturally-produced texts, we must accept as a major factor in such use the structure of those texts" (Fox 1987: 172). By structure, Fox is referring to the smaller internal units of a narrative corresponding to episodes or paragraphs.

2.3 Information packaging

D. Payne (1987; see also Payne, this volume) offers a different perspective in her work on Papago. Payne argues that although no basic order of grammatical relations can clearly be established for Papago narrative, there is a strong order condition on **types** of information presented. She posits two conditions for Papago under which information precedes the verb: (a) when it is "non-identifiable (indefinite) information" for which "the hearer is instructed to open a new active discourse file..., making it available for further deployment"; and (b) when the information is "pragmatically marked (including all information question-words)". The first condition indicates that a given piece of information is "important enough for the speaker to instruct the hearer to mentally 'tag' the entity as something to be available for further deployment" in the narrative (1987: 798). "Pragmatically marked" information includes information that is marked for contrastive focus, packaged in questions and answers, or constitutes a major topic change.

Mithun (1987; see also this volume) uses different terminology than Payne (1987), but her conclusions regarding pragmatically conditioned word order are similar. From her analysis of Cayuga (Iroquoian), Ngandi (Australian), and Coos (Oregon) she documents a general tendency to put the most "newsworthy" item first in the clause. An item is newsworthy if it: (1) represents significant new information; (2) introduces a new topic; or (3) points out a significant contrast (1987: 304).

2.4 Discourse threads

A fourth perspective in the literature that could bear on Agutaynen preverbal NPs is found in Hopper (1979). A major assertion of this article is that "the foreground/background distinction is a universal of some kind, one that may be realized formally in a number of different ways, depending on the language concerned" (1979: 217). Although Hopper's major emphasis is the role that elaborate tense-aspect systems play in some languages, he also noted that word order, particles, or some other device may be used in other languages to achieve the same purpose of marking out "a main route" through the narrative, diverting those parts which are not strictly relevant to that route (1979: 239). With regard to word order, he demonstrated that in Malay, foreground clauses tend to be verb-initial, while background clauses typically have a subject in pre-verbal position.

This verb-initial pattern for foreground material was also documented by Longacre (1979). Longacre found that in Biblical Hebrew the "event line" of a narrative was characterized by VSO clauses (along with a peculiar narrative tense), while "supportive material" was marked by SVO clauses (without the special narrative tense).

Myhill (this volume) uses the term "temporally sequenced clause" as an equivalent for Hopper's and Longacre's "foregrounded clause".

2.5 Summary

To summarize, there are a variety of factors which have been argued to condition pre-verbal NPs in "verb-initial" languages. On the basis of both

Givón (1983) and Fox (1985), we are led to hypothesize that pre-verbal NPs in Agutaynen correspond to highly discontinuous discourse topics. In view of Tomlin (1987), a reasonable hypothesis would be that they mark the beginning of larger units of discourse. Following Mithun (1987), we might be led to hypothesize that pre-verbal NPs in Agutaynen correspond to "newsworthy" information. And lastly, in light of Hopper (1979), we might expect to find that Agutaynen pre-verbal NPs signal background or supportive information, or in Myhill's terms, "non-temporally sequenced clauses".

It is crucial to point out here that all of the above studies were primarily carried out on the basis of one particular discourse type — the narrative. It remains an open question how applicable these procedures and findings are to other kinds of texts. In order to answer this question, we must first ask what kinds of texts are there in the world of discourse? I turn now to a brief discussion of this issue.

3. Discourse typology

Longacre (1983) distinguishes four basic notional types of discourse, which may take differing and slightly more varied surface forms.[9] The four notional, or "deep" types, consist of: narrative, procedural, behavioral and expository. As shown in Diagram 1, these four types are distinguished by plus or minus values on two parameters: contingent temporal succession and agent orientation. Narrative and procedural discourse types share temporal sequencing, in which "some (often most) of the events or doings are contingent on previous events or doings" (Longacre 1983: 3). Narrative and behavioral texts share a common orientation toward agents, "with at least a partial identity of agent reference running through the discourse" (1983: 3). Expository discourse is neither temporally sequenced nor agent oriented.

These four basic types can be subdivided further on the basis of two additional parameters: Projection (e.g., whether an event has already taken

	+Agent-Orientation	−Agent-Orientation
+Contingent Succession	NARRATIVE	PROCEDURAL
−Contingent Succession	BEHAVIORAL	EXPOSITORY

Diagram 1. Longacre's notional discourse types

place) and Tension (e.g., whether there is a struggle or polarization of some sort involved).

Although much of Longacre's work and many of his examples of discourse phenomena come from narrative texts, he argues that the mainline/supportive distinction common to narrative is a crucial distinction for all types. All types have something like a "plot", or organizing scheme, even though the nature of these has not been very clearly defined as of yet.

All of the researchers cited in Section 2 above have tacitly, if not explicitly, acknowledged the importance of discourse types in the selection of their database. Each has concentrated on the analysis of a specific type of text that is spoken (or written) by an individual speaker (or writer), and is organized on a contingent, chronological basis. In so doing they have reached conclusions that have been open to comparison across languages. If they had not recognized the great importance of discourse types from the start, they would have invalidated their own research. Emphasizing just such a danger, Longacre writes,

> So determinative of detail is the general design of a discourse type that the linguist who ignores discourse typology can only come to grief... For example, if in the study of word order typologies we include data from a language where different types of discourse (e.g., narrative versus expository) have differing word orders, then comparisons between two or more languages can be vitiated by the failure to control this difference. (1983: 1)

In this quote lies one of the main points of this paper — that basic constituent order, insofar as it is reflected by textual frequency, varies in some languages according to discourse type.[10] In order to demonstrate this principle more fully, I now turn to a discussion of pre-verbal NPs in Agutaynen narrative and expository discourse.

4. Pre-verbal NPs in Agutaynen

Pre-verbal NPs in Agutaynen (as defined in Section 1) pattern differently according to discourse type. For the following figures, a database of over 1000 clauses was categorized according to the four discourse types explained in Section 3, yielding 11 expository (388 clauses), 8 narrative (448 clauses), and 7 procedural texts (226 clauses).[11]

In the expository texts, pre-verbal NPs outnumber post-verbal NPs without exception, as summarized in Table 1.[12] If textual frequency is taken

Table 1. Pre-verbal versus post-verbal NPs in Agutaynen expository texts (ang NPs only)

	Clauses with Pre-verbal NPs		Clauses with Post-verbal NPs		Total clauses in text
Text 1	7	19%	4	11%	36
2	5	13%	2	5%	39
3	14	56%	1	4%	25
4	7	47%	3	20%	15
5	11	39%	5	18%	28
6	5	31%	3	19%	16
7	3	27%	0	0%	11
8	4	18%	2	9%	22
9	15	27%	7	12%	56
10	14	20%	9	13%	69
11	9	13%	7	10%	71
TOTAL	94		43		388
AVERAGE		28%		11%	

as the sole determiner of basic word order, the researcher might conclude from these texts that Agutaynen is not a verb-initial language at all, but rather has SVO order.

In direct contrast to the expository texts, narrative texts show post-verbal NPs outnumbering pre-verbal NPs — again, without exception. (See Table 2.) If narratives are taken to be more "basic" than expository, then Agutaynen could easily be classified as a verb-initial language.

When we compare the average percentage of pre- versus post-verbal NPs in expository and narrative texts, we get a mirror image,[13] best seen by comparing the averages for each discourse type, as in Table 3.

Care must be taken in interpreting the procedural texts, since the total number of clauses represented is much smaller. Still, it is interesting to note how the percentages of pre- and post-verbal NPs in procedural texts parallel those in narratives. Tables 4 and 5 summarize the procedural texts and compare them with narratives, respectively.

This parallel patterning of narrative and procedural texts can be explained in terms of the parameter which the two discourse types share by definition — contingent temporal succesion. Thus, the Agutaynen data further corroborate Myhill's (this volume) finding that VS order correlates with temporal sequencing in many verb-initial languages.

Table 2. Pre-verbal versus post-verbal NPs in Agutaynen narrative texts (ang NPs only)

	Clauses with Pre-verbal NPs		Clauses with Post-verbal NPs		Total clauses in text
Text 1	3	5%	12	21%	56
2	5	7%	31	41%	76
3	6	16%	9	24%	37
4	3	4%	14	17%	82
5	3	9%	10	29%	35
6	11	12%	12	13%	92
7	1	3%	3	9%	34
8	3	8%	5	14%	36
TOTAL	35		96		448
AVERAGE		8%		21%	

Table 3. Pre-verbal and post-verbal NPs in expository and narrative texts (*ang NPs only*)

	Clauses with with Pre-verbal NPs	Clauses with Post-verbal NPs
Expository	28%	11%
Narrative	8%	21%
chi-square (DF=1) = 11.5, $p < .001$		

Table 4. Pre-verbal versus post-verbal NPs in Agutaynen procedural texts (ang NPs only)

	Clauses with Pre-verbal NPs		Clauses with Post-verbal NPs		Total clauses in text
Text 1	0	0%	5	29%	17
2	0	0%	5	20%	25
3	2	4%	11	25%	44
4	3	13%	0	0%	23
5	1	2%	4	9%	42
6	5	10%	9	18%	49
7	1	12%	8	31%	26
TOTAL	12		42		226
AVERAGE		6%		19%	

Table 5. Pre-verbal and post-verbal NPs in narrative and procedural texts (ang NPs only)

	Clauses with with Pre-verbal NPs	Clauses with Post-verbal NPs
Narrative	8%	21%
Procedural	6%	19%
no significant difference		

4.1 Pre-verbal NPs in Agutaynen narrative discourse

What functions do pre-verbal NPs fulfill in Agutaynen narrative discourse? Surprisingly, in contrast with Cooreman's (this volume) findings regarding Chamorro, pre-verbal NPs in Agutaynen do not generally signal a new thematic paragraph or episode. Of the 35 tokens of pre-verbal NP in the data, none were found that clearly performed this function within a discourse. Six of the 8 narrative texts, however, did begin with a sentence containing a pre-verbal NP (N=4), or pre-verbal pronoun (N=2).

The remaining pre-verbal NPs were of two main types: those that were pragmatically marked (N=11), and those that occurred in clauses giving background or non-mainline information (N=20). The majority of the pragmatically marked NPs were those that indicated some sort of contrastive focus.[14] Some of these served to set up parallel constructions (N=6); others conveyed information that in some way went counter to the normal expectation of the hearer (N=4). One example functioned to shift the topic from an animate to inanimate entity.

Over half of the pre-verbal NPs (N=20) in the narrative data occurred in clauses that gave background or collateral information — clauses that were not temporally sequenced. Frequently these consisted of information concerning the time, location or physical characteristics of the events of participants. It appeared that the time and location clauses were almost formulaic, nearly always occurring in SV order.

In summary, pre-verbal NPs in Agutaynen narrative discourse appear to function in three ways: (1) to signal the very beginning of a discourse (but not thematic paragraphs or episodes within the discourse); (2) to highlight pragmatically marked information (mostly signalling contrastive focus); (3) to set apart background or non-temporally sequenced information.

4.2 Pre-verbal NPs in Agutaynen expository discourse

It is more difficult to clearly distinguish how pre-verbal NPs function in expository discourse. Indeed, some of the functions seem to be in opposition to each other. For example, 20 of the 94 pre-verbal NPs occuring in the expository data could be classified as "newsworthy" NPs, in that they refer to crucial concepts or participants. In contrast, 29 could be called "collateral" NPs, in that they do not directly employ major concepts or participants, but rather offer additional information about them. Many of these clauses describe physical characteristics, size or time factors (N=17). Others (N=12) define or explain terms introduced in prior clauses.

As with the narratives, pre-verbal NPs frequently mark the very beginning of an expository text. Nine of the 11 expository texts began with a pre-verbal NP, one began with a delimiting component (see Section 1), and one began with a time adverbial (but had a written title marked by *ang* supplied by the author).

Another function which pre-verbal NPs performed in both the narrative and expository texts is to mark contrastive focus. Nineteen of the 94 pre-verbal NPs in the expository data served this purpose.

Two apparent functions of pre-verbal NPs in the expository text data were not found in the narrative data. The first function could be considered an additional type of pragmatic marking: the summary statement. In four instances, pre-verbal NPs were used in a logical summary or concluding statement prefaced by the connector *animan* 'therefore'. The second function notably absent in the narrative data was to signal new thematic paragraphs (N=9). Even in the expository texts, however, this function was not primary, but rather inevitably interacted with other functions, such as the introduction of newsworthy topics.

Six pre-verbal NPs in the expository texts serve no obvious function. These may either reflect individual style, or may simply represent "discourse infelicities" similar to "performance errors", due to the speaker's inability to always be perfectly organized in his or her performance.

As an extreme example of frequent pre-verbal NPs, consider expository text number 3 ("What is a *sinolog*", included as Appendix 2). In this text of 25 clauses, 20 begin with some sort of pre-verbal element. Each of these clauses contributes some crucial piece of new information about some aspect of the *sinolog* dance. In this manner, the pre-verbal NPs appear to mark the main route through the text.

The *sinolog* text is an especially interesting example because there are two good possible reasons for fronting in most clauses. Besides giving new descriptive information in nearly each successive clause, the overall text exhibits an extremely parallel (hence, contrastive) structure. Clauses (3-8), describing the dancers dressed as Christians, stand in direct contrast to clauses (9-14), describing the dancers dressed as Muslims. Clauses (1-17) are all organized around this contrast between the Christians and Muslims. Only two clauses in this entire section do not begin with some pre-verbal element (14-15), and these both convey apparent "afterthoughts".

To summarize, pre-verbal NPs perform a variety of functions in Agutaynen expository discourse. As in narrative they (1) signal the very beginning of a discourse; and (2) highlight pragmatically marked information (as with crucial topics or participants, as well as with items in contrastive focus). An additional type of pragmatic markedness in the expository discourse was that of the logical conclusion or summary statement. Unlike what was found in the narrative data, pre-verbal NPs in expository were also seen to (3) signal new thematic paragraphs. It was noted, however, that even in expository discourse, this is not a primary function.

4.3 Pre-verbal NPs in Agutaynen procedural discourse

Summary statements about where pre-verbal NPs occur in procedural discourse are not very helpful at this point, due to the limited data (12 occurrences in 226 clauses). It can be said, however, that each of the functions listed for narrative and expository discourse types, and no obviously distinct functions, were observed.

4.4 Pre-verbal NPs across discourse types

In the Agutaynen narrative texts we found pre-verbal NPs encoding two main types of information: (1) that which was pragmatically marked; and more frequently (2) that which was not temporally sequenced. Given that narrative discourse prototypically and essentially exhibits temporal sequencing, any information in a narrative that is not temporally sequenced can also be considered "marked". It is tempting, therefore, to posit that pre-verbal NPs in Agutaynen narrative function simply to identify information that is is somehow "marked". A consideration of the expository texts, however, where pre-verbal NPs are actually more common than post-verbal NPs, shows that this is probably not the most revealing generalization.

A principle which could account for the use of pre-verbal NPs in both narrative and expository can be summarized as follows: information which primarily identifies or describes an entity is more likely to involve the use of a pre-verbal NP. This principle accounts for pre-verbal NPs under several circumstances: (1) discourse initially, where we must identify or establish what the discourse is about; (2) in instances of contrastive focus, where an entity is being identified in contrast to other possible entities; (3) in non-temporally sequenced clauses in narratives, where background information is given which more fully describes or explains referents and their actions.

Expository discourse represents a mirror image of narrative discourse, in that the type of descriptive or explanatory information which constitutes the background of narrative constitutes the very heart of expository. Accordingly, the patterning of pre-verbal NPs in Agutaynen narrative versus expository texts graphically reflects this mirror image: expository has more pre- than post-verbal NPs, narrative has more post- than pre-verbal NPs. In either case, pre-verbal NPs appear to be most crucially associated with information which primarily identifies and describes entities, as opposed to information which primarily reports the actions of previously identified participants.

5. Observations

In this section I will offer a few observations based on the preceding findings: first, on the applicability of topic continuity studies to expository discourse in general; and second, on the categorization of texts according to discourse type.

5.1 Expository texts and continuity studies

During the course of the present research it became evident that topic continuity studies such as those in Givón (1983) were by and large inapplicable to Agutaynen expository discourse.[15] This was so for two reasons: (1) the brevity of the texts; and (2) the constant switching of referents within the texts. Due to the brevity of the texts it was impossible to attain revealing figures for referential distance and persistence. The most distant topic of all might be only a few clauses away; the most persistent of all might last for only a few clauses. The procedure for calculating these two measures for narrative involves disqualifying a given number of discourse initial and final clauses. One cannot afford to do this if the entire text is only 11 clauses. The result is that meaningful comparisons of these measures among shorter texts is impossible.

A more serious difficulty with the topic continuity approach to expository discourse involves the way this type of discourse is structured. While there is generally a “global topic” or “theme” to expository, the “local topic” can switch almost constantly. Such frequent switching of “local topic” renders invisible to quantitative measures the continuity which is actually there.

This masking of continuity is highlighted by the *sinolog* text (Appendix 2). Because it switches referents nearly every clause, the *sinolog* text shows almost zero (local) topic continuity. And yet there is (global) topic continuity in the text. For example, clauses (3-8) are all about the Christian dancers (global topic), but each clause describes some different aspect of their dress (local topic). Clauses (9-14) function precisely the same way with regard to the Muslim dancers. On a broader scale, the entire text can be said to be about the maximally global topic of the *sinolog* dance. Thus, at least some expository texts are structured in such a way as to render useless studies of topic continuity as exemplified in Givón (1983).

5.2 Categorization of discourse types

Another concern which this research brings to the fore is that of categorizing texts according to discourse type. In many cases assigning a text to a particular type is not problematic. But some texts present such a blend or medley of discourse types that it is impossible to assign them to one or another. In Longacre’s (1983) terminology the first case constitutes a skewing of notional and surface discourse features, while the second case constitutes embedding. Both phenomena are extremely common.

One text in the Agutaynen data had to be disqualified for this study because it could not clearly be assigned to any one discourse type. Although it purported to be a description of harvesting (according to its initial and final clauses), in actuality it consisted of several discourse types in sequence: a procedure for clearing the field, a list of tools necessary for harvest, a one-clause comment on the possibility of a good or bad harvest, and a rather lengthy exhortation to work hard in the harvest, complete with motivating principles and possible dire outcomes if the plea is not heeded.

No part of the text actually described how harvesting is done. In this case, one gets the feeling that there is not so much embedding as chaining of one loosely related discourse after another.

It should also be noted here that the issue of how many discourse types there are has not been finally settled, and that some texts which have been classified as expository in this study may actually be examples of another distinct, "descriptive" type. Longacre warns that "descriptive discourse, in which we simply are describing something which we see" may be "essentially different from expository" (1983: 10). The *sinolog* text, in particular, appears to be arranged on such a visual basis — simply detailing the things we would see if we were to watch the *sinolog* being performed, first describing one set of dancers, then the other.

In contrast, a more prototypical expository discourse, such as a text on "Why we respect the elders", would be organized according to culturally determined rules of "logical argumentation". Such argument- or proof-oriented texts could possibly yield a different patterning of pre-verbal NPs than is the case with the descriptive texts considered here. It is perhaps significant that the text on "Cockfighting" is one of the most argument-oriented texts (not only describing the care and use of fighting cocks but also concluding with the suggestion that cockfighting be institutionalized on Agutaya), and also shows the least preference for pre- versus post-verbal NPs (pre- 13%, post- 10%).[16]

6. Conclusion

In the introduction to this paper we posed the question, "If Agutaynen does indeed have a 'basic' word order of V-first, how should we account for this preponderance of pre-verbal NPs?" We are now prepared to answer that question.

First of all, we must decide how basic constituent order is to be determined. Hawkins (1983: 13) discussed three criteria — textual frequency, frequency within the grammatical pattern, and grammatical markedness — and determined that textual frequency was often a sufficiently sensitive criterion on its own.

If we use textual frequency as our primary basis for determining basic constituent order in Agutaynen, then we must choose our texts carefully. As demonstrated in this paper, different text types will present differing basic orders. If we look only at narrative texts, we can easily establish that Agutaynen is a verb-initial language, and that pre-verbal NPs frequently indicate contrastive focus or non-temporally sequenced clauses. If, on the other hand, we look at expository texts, we are presented with an interesting mirror image, where pre-verbal NPs are in the majority, and it is no longer revealing to consider them all "marked" cases. It seems, rather, that pre-verbal NPs in Agutaynen, whatever the discourse type, are crucially associated with information which identifies or describes an entity.

The vast majority of discourse analysis up to the present has been done on narrative texts, and it is likely due to this fact that the verb-initial status of Austronesian languages in general has remained entirely un-controversial. While it may be necessary and even preferable to focus on narrative or some other specific type in initial discourse analysis, we must be aware that generalizations based on one discourse type may not adequately reflect properties of the language as a whole. The Agutaynen case clearly illustrates that there is something to be gained from a careful investigation of varying discourse types.

Appendix 1

Agutaynen Texts

Expository Texts	Source	Mode	Clauses
(1) "When someone dies on Agutaya"	A	W	36
(2) "Young men on Agutaya"	A	W	39
(3) "What is a sinolog (dance)?"	A	W	25
(4) "What is a komposo (dance)?"	A	W	15
(5) "Courtship on Agutaya"	A	W	28
(6) "The botod (house christening)"	A	W	16
(7) "Fiesta time"	A	W	11
(8) "A good leader"	B	S	22
(9) "Rice planting"	C	W	56
(10) "When someone dies"	D	S	69
(11) "Cockfighting"	E	S	71

Narative Texts			
(1) "The day I got embarrassed"	A	W	56
(2) "A frightening experience"	D	W	76
(3) "My worst boat trip"	A	W	37
(4) "What happened in Negros"	D	W	82
(5) "A difficult time"	D	W	35
(6) "The time I saw a ghost"	F	W	92
(7) "The fish that got away"	G	S	34
(8) "The time I fell overboard"	G	S	36
Procedural Texts			
(1) "How to gather coconut-wine"	A	W	17
(2) "Cultivating and harvesting"	A	W	25
(3) "Midwifery"	H	S	44
(4) "Betelnut"	I	W	23
(5) "Trapping"	J	S	42
(6) "Making mats"	J	S	49
(7) "Making *siakoy* (pastries)"	J	S	26

Mode: W = Written; S = Spoken

Sources: Age, Sex, Highest formal education
A = 20s, male, postsecondary
B = 60s, male, elementary
C = 50s, female, elementary
D = 20s, male, postsecondary
E = 50s, male, secondary
F = 60s, male, secondary
G = 40s, male, postsecondary
H = 40s, female, elementary
I = 20s, male, secondary
J = 40s, male, secondary

Appendix 2

An Agutaynen expository text written by Jerry Caab

(with all fronted elements in bold italics, including delimiting components and pre-verbal pronouns)

Onopa *tang sinolog?*
what TOP sinolog
'What is a sinolog?'

(1) ***Ang sinolog*** *ay tayaw ta mamola=ng lali*
TOP sinolog INV dance NON-TOP young=LNK male
mga mepet ang lali obin mga soltiros ang
PL old LNK male or PL young.man REL
*ga=liliag ang mag=*tayaw.
IMPERF.AF=want LNK IRR.AF=dance
'The sinolog is a dance for boys, old men or young men who want to dance.'

(2) ***Na*** *ay doroa=ng gropo*
this INV two=LNK group
'This (dance) has two groups.'

(3) ***Ang tang gropo*** *ay pag=paita tang to-tok*
TOP one group INV IMPERF.AF=show DEF.NON-TOP clothing
tang mga kristiano.
DEF.GEN PL Christian
'One group sports the dress of the Christians.'

(4) ***Ang mga gamit*** *ay bangkaw may taming.*
TOP PL equipment INV spear and shield
'(Their) equipment is spears and shields.'

(5) ***Na,*** *ag=poni=an pa ta mga papil.*
this IMPERF=streamer=GF also NON-TOP PL paper
'These are decorated with paper streamers.'

(6) ***Ang karakelan ang kolor tang po=poni***
TOP majority TOP color DEF.GEN IMPERF.INSTR=streamer

ay asol.
INV blue
'Mostly what is used for streamers is blue.'

(7) ***Ang to-tok tang mga kristianos, ang kolor na***
TOP clothing DEF.GEN PL Christians TOP color 3SG.POSS

ay asol obin lagem, belag lamang ta masinggi.
INV blue or black not only NON-TOP red
'The clothing of the Christians is blue or black, just not red.'

(8) ***Ang mga lambong*** *ay asol ka obin kolit.*
TOP PL shirt INV blue also or white
'The shirts are blue or white.'

(9) ***Ang dobali=ng gropo*** *ay gropo tang mga*
TOP opposite=LNK group INV group DEF.GEN PL

moslim (moros).
Muslim Moors
'The other group is the group of the Muslims.'

(10) ***Na, ang gamit*** *ay ged may taming.*
this TOP equipment INV bolo and shield
'This (group), (their) equipment is bolo-knife and shield.'

(11) ***Na,*** *ag=poni=an ka.*
this IMPERF=streamer=GF also
'This (equipment) is also decorated with streamers.'

(12) ***Ang karakelan ang po=poni*** *ay masinggi.*
TOP majority TOP IMPERF.INSTR=streamer INV red
'Mostly what is used for streamers is red.'

(13) ***Ang to-tok*** *ay masinggi tang kaloliot may lambong.*
TOP clothing INV red TOP pants and shirt
'The clothing (consists of) red pants and shirts.'

(14) *Teta poidi ka tang kolit ang lambong.*
sometimes can also TOP white LNK shirt
'Sometimes white shirts can also (be used).'

(15) *Pamag=pedeng pa sia.*
IMPERF.AF.PL=headgear also that
'Those (dancers) also wear headgear.'

(16) ***Ang gropo tang moslim, pedeng na*** *masinggi.*
TOP group DEF.GEN muslim headgear 3SG.POSS red
'The Muslim group, their headgear is red.'

(17) ***Ong kristianos*** *asol.*
OBL Christians blue
'(On) the Christians blue.'

(18) *Mga mag=tayaw da ngani,* ***ang ag=to-tog=on***
When IRR.AF=dance already indeed TOP IMPERF=play=GF

ay tambor.
INV drum
'When they start dancing, what is played is the drum.'

(19) ***Na,*** *ag=paita na* ***ang kristianos may moslim***
this IMPERF.GF=show COMP TOP Christians and muslim

(moros) pamag=soay, mga tayaw=en da.
(Moors) IMPERF.AF.PL=fight when dance=IRR.GF already
'This (dance) shows that the Christians and Muslims are fighting, once it is being danced.'

(20) ***Na, tanira*** *pamagin=iteg mintras ta=tayaw.*
this 3PL.TOP IMPERF.AF.PL=shout while IMPERF.AF=dance
'(In) this (dance), they shout while they dance.'

(21) Mga tapos da agpaita na ***ang kristianos***
when finish already IMPERF.GF=show COMP TOP Christians

ay pirdi.
INV lose
'When it is over it shows that the Christians lose.'

Notes

1. This paper was conceived during a Non-narrative Discourse Workshop led by Doris and Tom Payne held at the Nasuli center of the Summer Institute of Linguistics — Philippines. I am grateful to the Paynes and to Rudy Barlaan for their comments and encouragement during that time. I have benefited from subsequent discussions with Doris Payne and with Charles Peck. Credit for many of the paper's insights must go to these colleagues. I would be more than willing to share with them the blame for any shortcomings as well.

2. See Hawkins (1983) and Mithun (1987, and this volume) for a discussion of various methods used to determine basic constituent order.

3. Agutaynen is a Meso-Philippine language belonging to the Kalamian subgroup of northern Palawan province spoken by roughly 10,000 speakers. The researcher has conducted fieldwork in an Agutaynen community since 1984 through the Summer Institute of Linguistics and the Philippine Department of Education, Culture and Sports. To date there are no published grammatical descriptions of Agutaynen, but Quakenbush (1986) gives detailed sociolinguistic information on this multilingual speech community.

4. For a discussion of subject properties in Philippine languages, see especially Schachter (1976).

5. Agutaynen *ang* has the phonological variant *tang*, which can occur clause medially after a vowel. In contrast to Tagalog, which generally allows only one *ang* per clause, Agutaynen uses *tang* to mark all definite NPs, even if they are grammatically Genitives or Non-Topics. To complicate matters, the homophonous form *ang* (Tagalog *na*) functions as a ligature between a noun and its modifier, or to introduce relative or complement clauses.

6. The position of pronouns, which may pattern somewhat differently than full NPs, remains to be investigated. Post-verbal pronouns are phonologically bound, while pre-verbal pronouns take distinct, phonologically free forms.

7. A practical Agutaynen orthography is used for the examples in this paper. The letter "e" represents a high central unrounded vowel. The symbol "-" represents glottal stop, and "=" represents morpheme breaks, where indicated.

8. This term is from Dooley (1982: 309-311).

9. See Peck (1984) for a larger, more etic inventory of discourse types, as well as an overview of types posited by different linguists. This work is in revision, to appear as *How to Analyze a Language*.

10. Doris Payne (personal communication) disagrees with this assessment, arguing that constituent order varies according to discourse **function** rather than discourse **type**, and that some functions may be more common in one discourse type than another. In speaking of discourse **function**, Payne takes a "micro" perspective; in referring to discourse **type**, I am taking a "macro" perspective. I see no great conflict here, particularly if discourse types are defined in terms of speaker goals or purposes, as I believe Longacre does to an extent when he assigns labels to his structurally defined "notional" types.

11. These texts were selected from a larger database of oral and written texts collected over a 2-year period in the Agutaynen speech community. All expository texts in the database were included for this study, and for comparison's sake, a roughly equivalent number of personal narratives. The procedural texts, comprising a much smaller percentage of the total, are considered only briefly here. A title for

each text is included in Appendix A, where they are also grouped according to speaker. I am particularly grateful to the two Agutaynen speakers with whom I have worked most closely, Jerry B. Caab and Pedrito Z. Labrador.

12. Here and elsewhere, if delimiting components and pre-verbal pronouns were included in the counts, the patterns would be even more pronounced.

13. Robert Longacre (personal communication) reports that Trique exhibits a similar pattern of more pre-verbal NPs in expository than in narrative.

14. I am using "contrastive focus" here as a cover term for several types of focus described in Dik (1981), namely selective, expanding, restricting, replacing, and parallel focus. This functional use of the term "focus" should not be confused with the traditional Philippinist use of the term to describe "Actor-Focus", "Goal-Focus", etc.

15. These observations specifically pertain only to Givón's (1983) measures of "referential" or "topic" continuity, which constitute only part of Givón's larger concept of "discourse continuity". In narrative, referential continuity is easy to measure and operationalize. In expository, it is not.

16. This text was spoken by a middle-aged man who had completed elementary school. As a former elected official, he was experienced in public oratory.

References

Cooreman, Anne. 1983. "Topic Continuity and the Voicing System of an Ergative Language: Chamorro." Givón, ed., 425-489.

Dik, Simon, et al. 1981. "On the Typology of Focus Phenomena." *Perspectives on Functional Syntax* ed. by Teun Hoekstra, et al., 41-74. Dordrecht: Foris.

Dooley, Robert A. 1982. "Options in the Pragmatic Structuring of Guarani Sentences." *Language* 58.307-331.

Fox, Barbara. 1985. "Word-Order Inversion and Discourse Continuity in Tagalog." *Text* 5(1-2).39-54.

Fox, Barbara. 1987. "Anaphora in Popular Written English Narratives." Tomlin, ed., 157-174.

Givón, T., ed. 1983. *Topic Continuity in Discourse: A Quantitative Cross-Language Study*. Amsterdam/Philadelphia: John Benjamins.

Hawkins, John. 1983. *Word Order Universals*. New York: Academic Press.

Hopper, Paul J. 1979. "Aspect and Foregrounding in Discourse." *Discourse and Syntax* (=*Syntax and Semantics 12*) ed. by T. Givón, 213-42. New York: Academic Press.

Longacre, Robert F. 1979. "The Discourse Structure of the Flood Narrative." *Journal of the American Academy of Religion* 47.1 Supplement (March 1979) B 89-133.

Longacre, Robert F. 1983. *The Grammar of Discourse*. New York/London: Plenum.

Mithun, Marianne. 1987. "Is Basic Word Order Universal?" Tomlin, ed., 281-328.

Payne, Doris L. 1987. "Information Structuring in Papago Narrative Discourse." *Language* 63.783-804.
Peck, Charles. 1984. *A Survey of Grammatical Structures*. Dallas: Summer Institute of Linguistics.
Quakenbush, J. Stephen. 1986. *Language Use and Proficiency in a Multilingual Setting: A Sociolinguistic Survey of Agutaynen Speakers in Palawan Province*. Georgetown University Ph.D. dissertation, Washington, DC. (Published in 1989 under same title =*Special Monograph Issue 28*, Manila: Linguistic Society of the Philippines.)
Schachter, Paul. 1976. "The Subject in Philippine Languages: Topic, Actor, Actor-Topic, or None of the Above?" *Subject and Topic* ed. by Charles N. Li, 491-518. New York: Academic Press.
Schachter, Paul & Fe T. Otanes. 1972. *Tagalog Reference Grammar*. Berkeley: University of California Press.
Tomlin, Russell S., ed. 1987. *Coherence and Grounding in Discourse* (=*Typological Studies in Language 11*.) Amsterdam/Philadelphia: John Benjamins.

Addendum

Since completing this study, two articles have been brought to my attention: Longacre (1982) and Hopper (1987). Longacre (1982) demonstrates that Biblical Hebrew narratives are primarily VSO in structure, whereas expository texts in that language are primarily SVO. Longacre attributes this alternation to the "topic-comment" structure of expository discourse, and argues that "it is to be expected that VSO languages will necessarily vary to something on the order of S(VO) in expository discourse" since "topic-to-the-left" is "presumably a linguistic and cultural universal" (1982: 484). The Agutaynen data are consistent with Longacre's position.

Hopper (1987) explains VN/NV alternation in Malay (narrative) by appealing to two different kinds of discourse orientation — one toward the verb, the other toward the noun. He summarizes with the following statement: "Verb-initial clauses narrate, noun-initial clauses describe" (1987: 471). My own findings are consistent with this summation, but go a step further. As stated above, pre-verbal NPs in Agutaynen appear to be most crucially associated with information which primarily describes or identifies. Specifically, the function of identifying can account for the use of pre-verbal NPs in temporally sequenced clauses where the participant is pragmatically marked to receive contrastive focus.

That the conclusions of the present study were reached in ignorance of the specific findings of Longacre (1982) and Hopper (1987) strongly confirms the prior work of these linguists. The Agutaynen study clearly documents a type of word order variation predicted by Longacre, and substantiates a principle formulated by Hopper, showing more fully how NV order can function across narrative and expository discourse types.

Additional references

Hopper, Paul J. 1987. "Stability and Change in VN/NV Alternating Languages: A Study in Pragmatics and Linguistic Typology." *The Pragmatic Perspective* (=*Pragmatics & Beyond Companion Series* 5) ed. by Jef Verschueren & Marcella Bertuccelli-Papi, 455-476. Amsterdam: John Benjamins.

Longacre, Robert F. 1982. "Discourse Typology in Relation to Language Typology." *Text Processing* ed. by Sture Allen, 457-486. Stockholm: Almqvist & Wiksell International.

On Interpreting Text-Distributional Correlations
Some Methodological Issues*

T. Givón
University of Oregon

1. Background

In a well-known classic, Li and Thompson (1975) had suggested that the pre-verbal position of NPs in Mandarin — both subjects and objects — signalled definiteness, and the post-verbal position signalled indefiniteness. Their conclusions were given in the following two tendencies, the first synchronic, the second diachronic:

(1) "...*Tendency A*: Nouns preceding the verb tend to be definite, while those following the verb tend to be indefinite..." (Li and Thompson 1975: 170)

"...*Tendency B*: Mandarin is presently undergoing a word order shift from SVO to SOV..." (*ibid*, 185)

In a subsequent quantified text-based study of the pragmatics of word-order in Mandarin Chinese (Sun and Givón 1985), the opposite conclusions emerged, first concerning the synchronic correlation between word-order (form) and definiteness (function):

(2) a. It could not possibly be the case that OV/VO word-order contrast in Mandarin Chinese is used to code the functional contrast of **definite** vs. **indefinite**, respectively.

b. Rather, there is an almost **categorial** correlation between the OV word-order in Mandarin and the feature of **contrastiveness**.

c. It is most unlikely that Mandarin Chinese shows any discernible diachronic drift from predominantly VO to predominantly OV syntax.

The numerical results on which conclusions (2a-c) were based are reproduced, in a slightly compressed form, in Tables 1 and 2 below.

Table 1. Distribution of word-order in written Mandarin (after Sun and Givón, 1985)

category	WORD ORDER					
	VO		OV		TOTAL	
	N	%	N	%	N	%
REF-INDEFINITE	276	99.0	3	1.0	279	100.0
NON-REF INDEF.	45	93.1	3	6.9	48	100.0
DEFINITE	870	92.2	73	7.8	943	100.0
TOTAL:	1191	93.8	79	6.2	1270	100.0

Table 2. Distribution of word-order in spoken Mandarin (after Sun and Givón, 1985)

category	WORD ORDER					
	VO		OV		TOTAL	
	N	%	N	%	N	%
REF-INDEFINITE	109	99.0	1	0.0	110	100.0
NON-REF INDEF.	41	87.2	6	12.8	47	100.0
DEFINITE	289	90.3	31	9.7	320	100.0
TOTAL:	439	92.0	38	8.0	477	100.0

In a commentary on our (1985) paper a while later, Johanna Nichols (unpubl.) challenged our conclusions, specifically their synchronic portions (2a) and (2b). In the course of her thought provoking challenge to our empirical findings, Nichols also raised a number of important methodological and theoretical issues that are worth further discussion. They concern the methodology of studying the distribution of grammar in text, a mainstay of many recent studies on the pragmatics of word-order.

In evaluating Nichols' arguments here, I will follow the natural progression: From the empirical, through the methodological, to the theoretical. The distributional facts themselves are not at issue, but rather two themes that crop up periodically when one attempts to interpret text-distribution correlation between grammar and discourse-pragmatic function. The first theme is methodological, the second theoretical:

(a) The correlations are most often **skewed**; they are much stronger — or predictable — in the direction from function to structure, but considerably weaker in the opposite direction, from structure to function.

(b) Distributional correlations by themselves are often less than meaningful. Once they are obtained, the burden remains on the investigator to **explain** them.

2. Form-function distributional correlations in text

2.1. The Mandarin facts

In her paper, Nichols observed that a Chi-square analysis shows that there is indeed a **certain type** of correlation between definiteness and OV syntax in Mandarin Chinese. The correlation is, indeed, quite visible to the naked eye looking at the distribution tables in Sun and Givón (1985). It is, to be precise, a skewed, **one-way conditional** correlation. That is, the predictability from the function **definite** to the form **OV** is exceedingly low, roughly at the level of **8 percent**. This is the essence of our empirical claim (2a). On the other hand, the opposite predictability, from the form OV to the function definite,[1] is indeed high, somewhere around **90 percent**. This turns out, eventually, to impel us toward making our empirical claim (2b).

Here is how we discussed that second — high — correlation in our study:

> Thus in Spoken Mandarin (Table 2), out of the total of 38 tokens of OV order, 31 (82%) involve definite objects... The same can be seen for the written language (Table 1): out of 79 tokens of OV order, 73 (92%) involve definite objects..." (Sun and Givón 1985: 344)

One may summarize the facts of this one-way conditional association between the function definite and the form OV roughly as follows:

(3) a. **From function to form**: if DEF then OV = 8%
b. **From form to function**: if OV then DEF = 90%

This skewed distribution may be also given as the following Ven diagram:

(4)

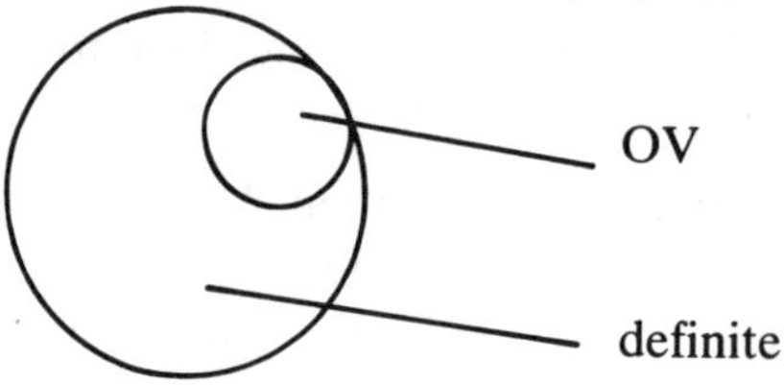

In other words, almost all members of the form-class **OV** are also members of the function-class **definite**. But the vast majority of definites are *not* members of the form-class OV, but rather of the form-class **VO**. How come then the Chi-square test, as reported by Nichols (unpubl.), shows a significant statistical association between the function definite and the form OV?

The answer is simple. The Chi-square test for correlations is blind to skewed directionality. All it can tell you is what it told Nichols: that there is a strong **association** between the function definite and the form OV. Having ourselves observed the correlation without the use of Chi-square, we were impelled in the original study to ask: but what does such a skewed correlation could mean?

2.2. Explaining the skewed correlation between OV and definite in Mandarin

In Sun and Givón (1985: 345-348) we went ahead and suggested an explanation for that skewed correlation. Our explanation — or **hypothesis** — may be summarized as follows:

(5) a. The observed skewed correlation means that there is an **indirect** correlation between OV order and definite in Mandarin; in other words, some other discourse-functional feature **mediates** the correlation.
b. That other functional feature is the so-called **Y-movement** (also known as contrastive topicalization). That function correlates at the almost categorial level — roughly 95% — with OV order in Mandarin.

c. It is well known that Y-movement generally applies only to **topical** NPs, thus typically involving either definite or non-referential NPs, but rejecting referential-indefinites;
d. Topical NPs — in normative human-oriented narrative — are overwhelmingly definite (with a small residue of non-referential NPs, as our samples indeed show);
e. Thus, the high — 90% — practically categorial — uni-directional correlation (predictability) **OV** > **definite** is simply due to the equally high correlation (predictability) **topical** > **definite**.

The contrastive Y-movement construction shares systematic restrictions with other topicalizing constructions, such as L-dislocation and cleft-focus. These restrictions are easy to demonstrate, involving a shared aversion for REF-indefinite NPs. As illustration, consider:

(6) **Y-movement**:
a. **NON-REF**: (I don't like tomatoes.) **Potatoes** I like.
b. **REF-DEF**: (I didn't see Mary.) **John** I saw right away.
c. **REF-INDEF**: *(I didn't see a horse.) **A cow** I saw.

(7) **L-dislocation**:
a. **NON-REF**: As for **potatoes**, I seldom eat any
b. **REF-DEF**: As for **Mary**, I saw her yesterday.
c. **REF-INDEF**: *As for **one man**, I saw him yesterday.

(8) **Cleft**:
a. **NON-REF**: It's **potatoes** I like, not tomatoes.
b. **REF-DEF**: It's **Mary** I saw, not John.
c. **REF-INDEF**: *It's **one man** I saw, not one woman.

While not a conclusive proof, these facts are compatible with our hypothesis; they buttress our interpretation of the OV word-order in Mandarin as a contrastive, topicalizing device. Our initial distribution tables show the OV category to consist of a majority of definite-referring NPs, a significant minority of non-referring NPs, an insignificant trace of REF-indefinite NPs (see fn. 1).

2.3. Falsificatory testing of a hypothesis

In support of our explanatory hypothesis we marshalled the following arguments:

First, we showed (Sun and Givón 1985, Tables 6,7,8,9, pp. 340-343) that two discourse-based measures that tend to correlate consistently with Y-movement and other contrastive devices (see Givón, ed. 1983) — relatively low referential distance (RD) and relatively high potential interference (PI) — indeed characterize the OV construction in Mandarin.

Second, we showed (1985, Table 12, p. 345) that the OV construction in Mandarin compares rather well, in both its general text distribution and in the two discourse-measured properties (referential distance, potential interference), with the Y-movement construction of a run-of-the-mill, *bona fide* VO language, Biblical Hebrew (A. Fox, 1983). The data in Table 3 below recapitulate these two arguments.

Table 3. Text frequency, referential distance (RD) and potential interference (PI) of pre- and post-verbal objects in Mandarin Chinese and Biblical Hebrew (after Sun and Givón, 1985)

	WRITTEN MANDARIN		SPOKEN MANDARIN		BIBLICAL HEBREW	
MEASURE	VO	OV	VO	OV	VO	OV
% in text	94	6	92	8	97	3
average RD	10.0	3.0	4.0	2.0	12.1	2.5
average PI	1.09	1.47	1.14	1.80	1.69	2.00

Third, we took the entire sample of OV constructions from our spoken Mandarin text (Sun and Givón 1985: 346-347) and attempted to show that in each case some species of contrastiveness was involved. Have we done enough to prove our point? Let us turn to put this question in its wider methodological context. To be sure, we did not "prove" our hypothesis. Indeed, in science there is never conclusive verification of hypotheses, only failure to falsify them. And such failure is by nature only temporary, lasting until one — or one's peers — devised the next falsificatory test. To put this in Karl Popper's inimitable words:[2]

> ...The game of science is, in principle, without end. He who decides one day that scientific statements do not call for any further [falsificatrory; TG] test, and that they can be regarded as finally verified, retires from the game... (Popper 1959: 53)

In subsequent correspondence over these issues, Nichols (in personal communication) complained about the fact that what we have offered is "only" a hypothesis:

> ... Your claim that OV order responds to contrast is only a hypothesis. The survey in S&G (1985) cannot possibly test this hypothesis, since you did not independently code for contrast. Your paper makes it clear that this is only a hypothesis... I have no quarrel with your hypotheses, and no grounds for proposing any of my own... (Nichols, ipc, pp. 2-3)

Such an argument, we feel, disregards the standard methodological practice of normal empirical science, where one subjects one's hypothesis to as many falsificatory tests as one could think up, given constraints of time, means and common sense, trying to prove false. Given more time, means and ingenuity, one — or one's peers — is bound to keep trying.[3]

3. Wider context of the Mandarin data

3.1 The cognitive basis for the pragmatics of word-order

There is a wider context within which both empirical conclusions reported in Sun and Givón (1985) were embedded. And as elsewhere in science,[4] knowing the context is important for understanding the chain of reasoning that ties together, however tentatively, fact, method and explanation. Let me briefly outline what is at issue here.

In a wide array of studies on the pragmatics of word-order flexibility, performed on a wide range of unrelated and typologically diverse languages, we had observed a rather consistent pattern of the discourse contexts in which the **pre-posing** of nominal constituents (i.e. subjects and objects) tends to occur. The correlation between the discourse contexts and NP-pre-posing, discussed extensively in Givón (1987), may be summarized as follows:

(9) a. A constituent is fronted in the context of either **low informational predictability** or **high thematic importance**;
b. The use of the same structural device — preposing — to signal both predictability and importance is not an accident. Rather, what unifies the two contexts is the psychological dimension: Pre-posing a constituent is a cognitively-transparent device for **attracting attention** to them.

It is easy to see now why the Mandarin Chinese distribution of OV and VO syntax was of great interest to us: A definite NP is by definition more predictable from the preceding ("anaphoric") discourse. An indefinite NP is by definition less predictable, appearing as it is for the first time in the discourse. In all the previous text-based studies where the DEF/INDEF contrast was investigated, a strong tendency had been found for definite NPs to be **post**-posed, and for indefinites to be **pre**-posed. If it now turned out that Li and Thompson (1975) were right in their claim about Mandarin Chinese, that language would have constituted a major, disturbing counter-example to our seemingly universal applicability of principle (10a), above. Our findings (2a) thus made our initial worry, at the very least, a moot point.

Further, in the same text-based studies summarized in Givón (1987) it was also noted that a very strong correlation existed between **pre**-posing of NPs and **contrastiveness**.[5] The text-distributional data on the Mandarin OV construction reported in Sun and Givón (1985), and our explanation of those data (however tentative one may wish to consider it), again turn out to be consistent with all the other cross-linguistic evidence.

3.2 The systematic bias in form-function correlations

There is another general theoretical context within which our findings concerning Mandarin fit rather snugly. There is a traditional tendency in function-oriented linguistics to assume that the idealized **one form, one function** correlation always holds. This may be seen in the following quote from Dwight Bolinger (1977):

> ...the natural condition of language is to preserve one form for one meaning, and one meaning for one form... (Bolinger 1977: x)

Put in other words, Bolinger assumes that the conditional association between form and meaning is **equally strong** in either direction. But as Haiman (1985: 21-22) points out, Bolinger's assumption is somewhat over-extended: In human language **polysemy** is quite common, but its converse — **homophony** — is rare. What is more, the iconicity (or fidelity) of the linguistic code, particularly the grammatical code, is subject to corrosive diachronic pressures from both ends of the semiotic equation: First, the code (form) is constantly eroded by **phonological attrition**, leading to increased ambiguity (polysemy). Second, the message (function) is constantly reshaped by **creative elaboration**, so that the scope of a form is extended to different though similar functions — again yielding increased ambiguity. Both diachronic processes thus create the same pressure, toward **one-to-many** correlation — thus low predictability — from form to function, but **one-to-one** correlation — i.e. high predictability — from function to form.

This systematic bias in the linguistic code may be understood in terms of the different processing tasks confronting the speaker and hearer. The speaker, who proceeds from function to form, uses **automated** procedures for quick on-line coding decisions. A one-to-one association — high predictability — from function to form. In contrast, the hearer who has to decode form into function can tolerate a certain level of ambiguity, resolving it by recourse to **context**. Lower predictability in going from form to function is thus understandable.

Now here is the seeming rub: The general considerations outlined here go exactly in the opposite direction than the skewed correlations we seem to have found in Mandarin, where the predictability from form to function (OV to DEF) is much *stronger* than that from function to form. However, we already noted that the predictability from function to form in Mandarin is *not* from-DEF-to-OV, but rather **from-CONTRAST-to-OV**. And *that* predictability is just about categorial. And so, the difference between the speaker's and hearer's processing — coding vs. de-coding — boils down to a difference of roughly 10% in this case: A 100% predictability from contrast to OV, a 90% predictability from OV to contrast. Tentatively, one may thus conclude that code fidelity at the level of 80-90% is the norm that hearers can cope with. In other words, the recourse to disambiguation via conscious scanning of context is an option exercised at the level of 10-20% in communication.

4. Another case of skewed form-function distributional

In the preceding sub-sections I suggested that the skewed correlation between OV and DEF in Mandarin is due to its **indirect** nature — it is mediated by another feature. That other feature — contrastiveness — happens to correlates almost categorially with definiteness. One may as well note that skewed text-distributional form-function correlation of the same type are rather common. Let us consider another — clearer — case, where one form seems to code several sub-functions.

In a recent study, B. Fox (1985) investigated the correlation — in Tagalog, a V-first language — between **NP pre-posing** and a cluster of discourse functions all coming under the general heading of **(dis)continuity**, referential as well as thematic. The text-based measures used by Fox to assess thematic or referential continuity were the following, expressed in terms of the directly-preceding (anaphoric) discourse context of the clause:

(10) a. paragraph initial (discontinuous)
vs.
paragraph non-initial (continuous)

b. following a period (discontinuous)
vs.
following a comma or zero punctuation (continuous)

c. temporal discontinuity
vs.
temporal continuous

d. not following same-referent (DS, discontinuous)
vs.
following same-referent (SS, continuous)

For each one of these measures taken independently, the Chi-square test showed a statistically significant correlation between pre-posed NP syntax and discontinuity in discourse. However, the correlation is much more dramatic when expressed as a predictability **from function to form** than it is as a predictability **from form to function**. To illustrate this, consider the rerendition of Fox's (1985, Table 1), given in table 4 below, expressing the results of measure (10a) above.

Table 4. Pre-posing and position in the paragraph: Percent distributions of structure in function (from Fox, 1985, Table 1)

	position in the paragraph					
	initial		non-initial		total	
syntax	N	%	N	%	N	%
pre-verbal NP	61	27%	165	73%	226	100%
post-verbal NP	50	13%	338	87%	388	100%

The differences in Table 4 above — a 27-73 ratio vs. 13-87 ratio — seem rather undramatic. The categorial tendency in both is overwhelmingly in the same direction: The bulk of both pre-posed and post-posed NPs still appear at the paragraph **medial** position. Nonetheless, Fox's (1985) Chi-square test yielded a highly significant correlation between the presence vs. absence of NP pre-posing (form) and the discourse context (function) in Table 4.: Chi-square 18.24, significant at the respectable level of $p < 0.01$.

The very same data given in Table 4 can be re-computed, as correlations **from function to form**. And when this is done, with the Chi-square test yielding the very same values, the correlation looks much more dramatic, as may be seen in Table 5 below. While neither is categorial, the ratios for the two functions now go in the opposite direction — 55-45 vs. 32-68.

Table 5. Re-computed correlations: Percent distributions of function in structure (recomputed from Fox, 1985, Table 1)

	syntax					
	pre-verbal NP		post-verbal NP		total	
position in the paragraph	N	%	N	%	N	%
paragraph initial	61	55%	50	45%	111	100%
paragraph non-initial	165	32%	338	68%	503	100%

With minor variation, similar results can be seen with each one of the four individual measures employed by Fox (1985). In each case, the correlation — or predictability — from function to structure looks much more dramatic than the predictability from structure to function. But why should this be the case? The theoretical answer to this question has already been given above: One-to-many association between form and functions — i.e. an ambiguous, lower predictability for the hearer/de-coder — is the more common case in language.

More specific reasons also exist. The various studies of word-order pragmatics summarized in Givón (1987) show that the very same syntactic device — pre-posing — is consistently used in one language after another to code the degree of discontinuity — or unpredictability — in the discourse regardless of the source of that unpredictability: Referential, temporal, locational, actional, thematic. What we have here is a **complex** notion of discourse function: Each one of the sub-types of discourse discontinuity measured by Fox may, by itself, precipitate NP pre-posing. Conversely, the thematically continuous paragraph-medial position precipitates NP-postposing at a level of predictability approaching 70%, as can be seen in Table 5.

Once again, the predictability is much stronger **from function to form** than **from form to function**. But in this case the reason may be different. The four measures performed by Fox (1985) are not really four separate discourse functions. Rather, they are four heuristics measuring different sources that together contribute to one epiphenomenon — **thematic coherence**.

The clincher of this explanation comes when B. Fox (1985: 46-47 and Table 5.) shows the effect of feature clustering, i.e. of piling up gradually all four sub-variables of discourse dis-continuity. When all four are present, the predictability from structure to function — which for theoretical reasons we never expect to be fully categorial — improves immensely. And the fewer of the four features are present, the less dramatic that predictability is.

4. The crux of the matter: Hypotheses about the text vs. hypotheses about the mind

In her criticism of our Mandarin conclusions, Nichols (unpubl.) proceeded to raise an important theoretical issue, one that is worth discussing here. From her perspective, Sun and Givón (1985) was an example of the evils of so-called **essentialism** in linguistics. Presumably, essentialism characterizes one's attempt to find a categorial correlation between form and function. Nichols contrasts this with Labov's **text distributionalism**:

> ...Standard structuralist dogma imposes **essentialist** thinking, while what is usually needed for non-formalist grammatical analysis is **population** thinking. When **Jacobsonian structuralists** say that a form codes a meaning, they generally mean that the meaning is a necessary and sufficient condition for use of the form...But in population-oriented terms, the meaning would be seen as a factor (usually one of several or many)...Neither necessity nor sufficiency is important in population thinking. What matters is whether the putative effect of a factor on a distribution is significant... (Nichols, unpubl., p. 5)

In Nichols' view, one must make a choice between these two methodological extremes. One might suggest, however, that there are cogent reasons why *both* extremes are absolutely essential in order to do empirical linguistics the right way. However, the domains of applicability — or utility — of the two are rather different.[6]

We owe to Bill Labov (e.g. Labov 1975) our resurgent understanding of why one cannot simply assume categorial, invariant, one-to-one form-function correlations. One must test them empirically, distributionally, with some reasonable statistics, in some actual piece of text, one that was produced by someone who was actually communicating (as against merely indulging in the intuitive production of linguistic examples). This is where our empirical honesty is at stake, where it rises or falls.

But text distributions by themselves are not the **end** of the investigation, they are only its empirical **means**. Our hypotheses, what we endeavor to construct as explanations, must not be **about the text**. Rather, to be theoretically valid they must be **about the mind** that produced or perceived the text. And this is where a dose of good old essentialism (if one is forced to continue using the term, which I do not find particularly endearing) comes into play. The mind — of both the text produced and text perceiver — must make **coding decisions** — **generalizations** — about which functions pair with what code units. And such decisions — especially in speech perception — cannot be made below a certain threshold of "approximate categoriality". There is such an enormous body of psychological literature on this subject, which is not at all specific to language, that I will simply take it here as a given. My own tentative cutting point has been that somewhere about or above the level of 80% correlation, the perceiving mind begins to bet on a 100% categorial distribution and ignore the margins.[7] In other words, in processing codes the mind requires some minimal threshold-level of **code fidelity**. And it is just as absurd to go with Nichols' extremism and assume that the level of core-coherence could ever be as low as 8%, as it is to go with Chomsky's and assume that it must always be 100%.[8]

In our concern for explaining the workings of the text-processing, communicating mind, some measure of essentialism is — forgive the pun — essential. The speech perceiver's mind cannot detect — by Chi-square or other inductive means — weak correlations, such as between the function DEF and the form OV in Mandarin. But the speaker's mind has no trouble at all coding from the function CONTRAST to OV, with a dramatic categorial correlation. This is the essence — again forgive the inevitable pun — of the essentialism that Sun and I practiced in our study of Mandarin. And it is indeed a rather sensible, methodologically sound, theoretically transparent practice. And it is fairly clear that some reflection of such essentialism — in making explanatory hypotheses — is indispensible, if our work is to progress, as I think it must, from the study of the artifact (text) to the study of the mind that produces and interprets the text.[9]

Notes

* I am indebted to Dwight Bolinger, Dorie Payne and Sandy Thompson for many helpful suggestions, and to Johanna Nichols for prompting my renewed interest in the subject.

1. Actually, as we claimed, not "definite" but rather "topical", since the category **NON-REF indefinite** in our sample behave very much like **REF-definite**. We have also noted (Sun and Givón 1985: 344), that "...in Spoken Mandarin...referential indefinites account for only a single token (2.6%) of the entire OV sample...[and in the written language] referential indefinite objects account for only three tokens (3.7%) [of the OV sample]..."

2. See Popper (1959) for an extensive discussion of this.

3. Obviously we could have devised more falsificatory tests. In principle, if Popper (1959) is to be taken seriously, the testing hypotheses by the falsificatory method is endless.

4. See exhaustive discussion about the contextual interaction between data and hypotheses in Hanson (1959).

5. One may argue, as I have done in Givón (ed., 1983), that contrastiveness is one sub-species of **low informational predictability** (viz. principle (10a)). In other words, it represents a context where the speaker assumes — or actively sets up — certain expectations on the part of the hearer, then proceeds to release information that is contrary to those expectation.

6. From a methodological perspective, one argues here against **reductionism**, i.e. the idea that a scientific methodology must perforce be "pure". For a similar plea against extreme reductionism in methodology, and for the empirical utility of methodological pluralism, see Feyerabend (1970). What Feyerabend points out, in his context, closely parallels my argument below: Both extreme inductivism (Nichols' text distributionalism) and extreme deductivism (Nichols' essentialism) misrepresent the reality of empirical science.

7. Cf. Givón (1977; 1979, ch. 5; 1985).

8. The study Sun and I had proposed to falsify, Li and Thompson (1975), may illustrate how even the very best of us must not forget to use the tools — means — of Labov's text distributionalism, or else remain exposed to extreme "essentialism". Equally well, some otherwise rather admirable Labovian studies, such Estival (1985) for example, illustrate just as vividly how barren the mere facts of text distribution could remain, unless coupled to a liberal measure of essentialist hypothesizing about the communicator's mind. Estival demonstrated a strong correlation between the use of passive clauses and the use of passive syntax in immediately-preceding clauses:

    > ...Syntactic priming also plays a role at least in discourse production...Weiner and Labov (1983) found that the passive alternant is more likely to be chosen by the speaker if there is a passive in the immediate discourse preceding the sentence... (Estival 1985: 7)

    The study contented itself with labeling this correlation "syntactic priming", without attempting to explain the distributional facts observed in the text.

9. At the methodological end, once again, two sensible quotations come to mind, both from an astute nature philosopher, Stephen J. Gould:

    > ...The solution to great arguments is usually close to the golden mean..." (1977: 18)

    > ...I doubt that such a controversy could have arisen unless both positions were valid (though incomplete)... (1977: 59).

References

Bolinger, Dwight. 1977. *The Form of Language*. London: Longmans.

Estival, D. 1985. "Syntactic Priming of the Passive in English." T. Givón (ed., 1985), 7-22.

Feyerabend, P. 1970. "How to Be a Good Empiricist: A Plea for Tolerance in Matters Epistemological," ed. by B. Brody *Readings in the Philosophy of Science*, 319-342. Englewood Cliffs, NJ: Prentice-Hall.

Fox, Andrew. 1983. "Topic continuity in Early Biblical Hebrew." T. Givón (ed., 1983), 215-254.

Fox, Barbara. 1985. "Word Order Inversion and Discourse Continuity in Tagalog." T. Givón (ed., 1985), 39-54.

Givón, T. 1977. "The Drift from VSO to SVO in Biblical Hebrew: The Pragmatics of Tense-Aspect." C. Li (ed.) *Mechanisms for Syntactic Change*, 184-254. Austin: University of Texas Press.

Givón, T. 1979. *On Understanding Grammar*. NY: Academic Press.

Givón, T. ed., 1983. *Topic Continuity in Discourse: Quantified Text Studies* (= *Typological Studies in Language 3*). Amsterdam: J. Benjamins.

Givón, T. 1985. "Structure, Function and Language Acquisition." D. Slobin (ed.) *The Crosslinguistic Study of Language Acquisition*, 1005-1027. vol. II, Hillsdale, NJ: Erlbaum.

Givón, T., ed., 1985. *Quantified Studies in Discourse*. (= a special issue of *Text*, 5.1/2).

Givón, T. 1987. "The Pragmatics of Word-Order: Predictability, Importance and Attention." Michael Hammond *et al.* (eds.) *Studies in Syntactic Typology* (= *Typological Studies in Language 17*), 243-284. Amsterdam: J. Benjamins.

Gould, Stephen J. 1977. *Ontogeny and Phylogeny*. Cambridge: Harvard University Press/The Belknap Press.

Haiman, John. 1985. *Natural Syntax*. Cambridge: Cambridge University Press.

Hanson, R.N. 1959. *Patterns of Discovery*. Cambridge: Cambridge University Press.

Labov, William. 1975. "Empirical Foundations of Linguistic Theory." R. Austerlitz (ed.) *The Scope of American Linguistics*, 77-133. Lisse: The Peter de Ridder Press.

Li, Charles & Sandra Thompson. 1975. "The Semantic Function of Word Order in Chinese." C. Li (ed.) *Word Order and Word Order Change*, 163-195. Austin: University of Texas Press.

Nichols, Johanna. (unpublished) "On SOV Word Order in Mandarin." UC at Berkeley (ms).

Popper, Karl. 1959. *The Logic of Scientific Discovery* (revised edition, 1968). NY: Harper & Row.

Sun, C.-F. & T. Givón 1985. "On the So-Called SOV Word-Order in Mandarin Chinese: A Quantified Text Study and its Implication." *Language*. 61.329-351.

In the TYPOLOGICAL STUDIES IN LANGUAGE (TSL) series the following volumes have been published thus far and will be published during 1992:

1. HOPPER, Paul (ed.): *TENSE-ASPECT: BETWEEN SEMANTICS & PRAGMATICS.* Amsterdam/Philadelphia, 1982.
2. HAIMAN, John & Pam MUNRO (eds): *PROCEEDINGS OF A SYMPOSIUM ON SWITCH REFERENCE, Winnipeg, May 1981.* Amsterdam/Philadelphia, 1983.
3. GIVÓN, T. (ed.): *TOPIC CONTINUITY IN DISCOURSE: A QUANTITATIVE CROSS-LANGUAGE STUDY.* Amsterdam/Philadelphia, 1983.
4. CHISHOLM, William, Louis T. MILIC & John GREPPIN (eds): *INTERROGATIVITY: A COLLOQUIUM ON THE GRAMMAR, TYPOLOGY AND PRAGMATICS OF QUESTIONS IN SEVEN DIVERSE LANGUAGES, Cleveland, Ohio, October 5th 1981 - May 3rd 1982.* Amsterdam/Philadelphia, 1984.
5. RUTHERFORD, William E. (ed.): *LANGUAGE UNIVERSALS AND SECOND LANGUAGE ACQUISITION.* Amsterdam/Philadelphia, 1984. 2nd edition 1987.
6 HAIMAN, John (ed.): *ICONICITY IN SYNTAX. Proceedings of a Symposium on Iconicity in Syntax, Stanford, June 24-6, 1983.* Amsterdam/Philadelphia, 1985.
7. CRAIG, Colette (ed.): *NOUN CLASSES AND CATEGORIZATION. Proceedings of a Symposium on Categorization and Noun Classification, Eugene, Ore. October 1983.* Amsterdam/Philadelphia, 1986.
8. SLOBIN, Dan I. & Karl ZIMMER (eds): *STUDIES IN TURKISH LINGUISTICS.* Amsterdam/Philadelphia, 1986.
9. BYBEE, Joan L.: *Morphology. A Study of the Relation between Meaning and Form.* Amsterdam/Philadelphia, 1985.
10. RANSOM, Evelyn: *Complementation: its Meanings and Forms.* Amsterdam/Philadelphia, 1986.
11. TOMLIN, Russ (ed.): *COHERENCE AND GROUNDING IN DISCOURSE.* Outcome of a Symposium on -, Eugene, Ore, June 1984. Amsterdam/Philadelphia, 1987.
12. NEDJALKOV, Vladimir P. (ed.): *TYPOLOGY OF RESULTATIVE CONSTRUCTIONS.* Translated from the original Russian edition publ. by "Nauka", Leningrad, 1983, English translation edited by Bernard Comrie. Amsterdam/Philadelphia, 1988.
14. HINDS, John, Senko MAYNARD & Shoichi IWASAKI (eds): *PERSPECTIVES ON TOPICALIZATION: The Case of Japanese 'WA'.* Amsterdam/Philadelphia, 1987.
15. AUSTIN, Peter (ed.): *COMPLEX SENTENCE CONSTRUCTIONS IN AUSTRALIAN LANGUAGES.* Amsterdam/Philadelphia, 1987.
16. SHIBATANI, Masayoshi (ed.): *PASSIVE AND VOICE.* Amsterdam/Philadelphia, 1988.
17. HAMMOND, Michael, Edith A. MORAVCSIK & Jessica R. WIRTH (eds): *STUDIES IN SYNTACTIC TYPOLOGY.* Amsterdam/Philadelphia, 1988.
18. HAIMAN, John & Sandra A. THOMPSON (eds): *CLAUSE COMBINING IN GRAMMAR AND DISCOURSE.* Amsterdam/Philadelphia, 1988.
19. TRAUGOTT, Elizabeth C. & Bernd HEINE (eds): *APPROACHES TO GRAMMATICALIZATION. 2 volumes.* Amsterdam/Philadelphia, 1991.
20. CROFT, William, Keith DENNING & Suzanne KEMMER (eds): *STUDIES IN TYPOLOGY AND DIACHRONY. Papers presented to Joseph H. Greenberg on his 75th birthday.* Amsterdam/Philadelphia, 1990.
21. DOWNING, Pamela, Susan D. LIMA & Michael NOONAN (eds): *THE LINGUISTICS OF LITERACY.* Amsterdam/Philadelphia, 1992.
22. PAYNE, Doris (ed.): *PRAGMATICS OF WORD ORDER FLEXIBILITY.* Amsterdam/Philadelphia, 1992.